Lecture Notes in Business Information Processing 121

Jorge E. Hernández   Pascale Zarate
Fátima Dargam   Boris Delibašić
Shaofeng Liu   Rita Ribeiro (Eds.)

Decision Support Systems – Collaborative Models and Approaches in Real Environments

Euro Working Group Workshops, EWG-DSS 2011
London, UK, June 23-24, 2011
and Paris, France, November 30 - December 1, 2011
Revised Selected and Extended Papers

Volume Editors

Jorge E. Hernández
University of Liverpool, UK
E-mail: j.e.hernandez@liverpool.ac.uk

Pascale Zarate
Tolouse University, France
E-mail: zarate@irit.fr

Fátima Dargam
SimTech Simulation Technology, Graz, Austria
E-mail: f.dargam@simtechnology.com

Boris Delibašić
University of Belgrade, Serbia
E-mail: boris.delibasic@fon.bg.ac.rs

Shaofeng Liu
University of Plymouth, UK
E-mail: shaofeng.liu@plymouth.ac.uk

Rita Ribeiro
UNINOVA – CA3, Lisbon, Portugal
E-mail: rar@uninova.pt

ISSN 1865-1348 e-ISSN 1865-1356
ISBN 978-3-642-32190-0 e-ISBN 978-3-642-32191-7
DOI 10.1007/978-3-642-32191-7
Springer Heidelberg Dordrecht London New York

Library of Congress Control Number: 2012942864

ACM Computing Classification (1998): J.1, I.6

Typesetting: Camera-ready by author, data conversion by Scientific Publishing Services, Chennai, India

Printed on acid-free paper

Springer is part of Springer Science+Business Media (www.springer.com)

Preface

This book contains extended and revised versions of a set of selected papers from the EWG-DSS workshops held in London and Paris, in June and in November 2011, respectively. These workshops were organized by the Euro Working Group on Decision Support Systems (EWG-DSS) and partially sponsored by the Association of European Operational Research Societies (EURO), in cooperation with the Management School University of Liverpool (ULMS) in the UK; the University of Toulouse, the Institute of Research in Informatics of Toulouse (IRIT) in France; the UNINOVA - CA3 - Computational Intelligence Research Group in Portugal; the School of Management, University of Plymouth in the UK; the company SimTech Simulation Technology in Austria; the Institute of Logic and Theory of Science (ILTC), Brazil; the University of Belgrade in Serbia; the School of Business, Economics and Informatics at Birkbeck, University of London in the UK; the Paris-Dauphine University in France; the Laboratoire d'Analyse et Modélisation de Systèmes pour l'Aide à la DEcision (LAMSADE) in France and the Decision Analysis Special Interest Group of the British OR Society (DASIG).

The purposes of the London and Paris 2011 EWG-DSS workshops were to bring together academics, researchers, practitioners, and enterprises interested in implementing collaborative perspectives for different kinds of environments. The workshops themes were "Decision Support Systems" and "Collaborative Decision Making," respectively. Hence, the scientific areas of interest for selected contributions from these two outstanding workshops were: (a) distributed group support systems; (b) collaborative decision making; (c) supply chain management; (d) information technologies; and (e) simulation. In addition, since effective collaboration leads to collaborative advantages and also to a better partnership performance, the proper understanding and visualization is to be supported by considering different perspectives of collaborations in real environments. In this context, the London and Paris 2011 EWG-DSS workshops' selected papers are representative of the current research activities in the area of decision support systems and addresses these challenges by considering a large number of research topics: from more static and abstract ones, such as conceptual models, to more dynamic and technical ones, such as decision support systems and software simulations and specification, from more enterprise-oriented ones, such as business knowledge management process and collaborative specification and requirements to more multi-objective and multi-criteria expert systems to support the different business behaviors in collaborative environments.

Both 2011 EWG-DSS workshops, London and Paris, considered 39 and 13 papers for oral presentation each. From the total of 52 papers, 11 papers were selected for publication in this edition by considering their content, structure and presentation quality. This led to a "full-paper" acceptance ratio of 22%, and shows the intention of preserving a high-quality forum for the next editions of EWG-DSS workshops. The proceedings selection and publication process was based on a double-blind paper evaluation method: each selected paper was reviewed by at least two internationally known experts from the EWG-DSS Program Committee.

The high quality of the London and Paris EWG-DSS workshop programs was enhanced by five keynote lectures, delivered by distinguished guests who are renowned experts in their fields, including (alphabetically): Alex Duffy (University of Strathclyde, Glasgow, UK), Philip Powell (School of Business, Economics and Informatics at Birkbeck, University of London, UK), and Rita Ribeiro (CA3 – Computational Intelligence Research Group at UNINOVA, Portugal) for the London's workshop, and (alphabetically): Denis Bouyssou (Centre National de Recherche Scientifique in Paris, France) and Sihem Amer-Yahia (Qatar Computing Research Center, Qatar) for the Paris workshop. Their lectures were very interesting and there was a high level of information exchange for further fruitful cooperation among all participants. We would like to take this opportunity to express our gratitude to all those who contributed to the EWG-DSS workshops activities in 2011, including authors, reviewers, Program Committee members, and institutional sponsors. Finally, we hope you will find the contents useful and interesting to tackle many of the collaborative challenges, in terms of research and practice activities, when addressing any of the related research areas.

Jorge E. Hernández
Pascale Zarate
Fátima Dargam
Boris Delibašić
Shaofeng Liu
Rita Ribeiro

Euro Working Group on Decision Support Systems

The EWG-DSS is a Working Group on Decision Support Systems within EURO, the Association of the European Operational Research Societies.

The main purpose of the EWG-DSS is to establish a platform for encouraging state-of-the-art high quality research and collaboration within the decision support systems (DSS) community. Additional EWG-DSS aims are to:

- Encourage the information exchange among practitioners, end-users, and researchers in the area of DSS
- Enforce networking among the DSS communities and facilitate activities that are essential for starting up international cooperation research and projects
- Facilitate professional academic and industrial opportunities for its members
- Favor the development of innovative models, methods, and tools in the field DSS and related areas
- Actively promote the interest in DSS in the scientific community by organizing dedicated workshops, seminars, mini-conferences, and conference streams in major conferences, as well as editing special and contributed issues in relevant scientific journals.

The EWG-DSS was founded during a memorable EURO Summer Institute on DSS that took place at Madeira, Portugal, in May 1989. This Summer Institute was organized by two well-known academics of the OR community: Jean-Pierre Brans and José Paixão. It enjoyed the participation of 24 young researchers of 16 different nationalities. The number of EWG-DSS members has substantially grown along the years. By the end of 2011 we were over 150 registered members, coming from various nationalities.

Through the years, quite a few well-qualified research co-operations have been established within the group members, which have generated valuable contributions to the DSS field in journal publications. Since its creation, the EWG-DSS has held annual meetings in various European countries, and has taken active part in the EURO Conferences on decision-making-related subjects.

Since the beginning of 2011, the EWG-DSS coordination board has been composed of: Pascale Zaraté (France), Fátima Dargam (Austria), Rita Ribeiro (Portugal), Jorge E. Hernández (UK), Boris Delibašić (Serbia) and Shaofeng Liu (UK).

Euro Working Group on Decision Support Systems

Organization

Conference Chairs

Fátima Dargam	SimTech Simulation Technology, Austria
Pascale Zaraté	IRIT / Toulouse University, France
Rita Ribeiro	UNINOVA - CA3, Portugal
Jorge E. Hernández	University of Liverpool, UK
Shaofeng Liu	University of Plymouth, UK
Boris Delibašić	University of Belgrade, Serbia

Program Committee

Ana Respício	University of Lisbon, Portugal
Antonio Rodrigues	University of Lisbon, Portugal
Boris Delibašić	University of Belgrade, Serbia
Csaba Csaki	University College Cork, Ireland
Dragana Becejski-Vujaklija	University of Belgrade, Serbia
Fátima Dargam	ILTC, Brazil and SimTech Simulation Technology, Austria
Frédreric Adam	University College Cork, Ireland
Isabel Nunes	Universidade Nova de Lisboa, Portugal
Jason Papathanasiou	University of Macedonia, Greece
João Clímaco	Universidade de Coimbra, Portugal
João Lourenço	IST, Technical University of Lisbon, Portugal
Jorge Freire de Souza	Engineering University of Porto, Portugal
Jorge E. Hernández	University of Liverpool, UK
Jorge Pinho de Sousa	Engineering University of Porto, Portugal
José Maria Moreno	Zaragoza University, Spain
Leonilda Varela Leonilde	University of Minho, Portugal
Nadia Lehoux	Université Laval, Canada
Pascale Zaraté	IRIT / Toulouse University, France
Peter Keenan	University College Dublin, Ireland
Philip Powel	Birkbeck, University of London, UK
Rita Ribeiro	UNINOVA - CA3, Portugal
Rudolf Vetschera	University of Vienna, Austria
Sean B. Eom	Southeast Missouri State University, USA
Shaofeng Liu	University of Plymouth, UK

Organizing Committee

EWG-DSS

Fátima Dargam — SimTech Simulation Technology, Austria
Pascale Zaraté — IRIT / Toulouse University, France
Rita Ribeiro — UNINOVA – CA3, Portugal
Jorge Hernández — University of Liverpool, UK
Shaofeng Liu — University of Plymouth, UK
Boris Delibašiæ — University of Belgrade, Serbia

London

Philip Powell — School of Business, Economics and Informatics at Birkbeck, University of London

Paris

Nadia Papamichail — Manchester Business School, UK
Alexis Tsoukias — Professor at LAMSADE CNRS, Paris-Dauphine University, France

Technical Sponsors

Working Group on Decision Support Systems
(http://ewgdss.wordpress.com/)

Association of European Operational Research Societies
(www.euro-online.org)

Organisational Co-Sponsors

Management School, University of Liverpool, UK
(http://www.liv.ac.uk/management/)

University of Toulouse, France
(http://www.univ-tlse1.fr/)

IRIT Institut de Research en Informatique de Toulouse, France
(http://www.irit.fr/)

UNINOVA - CA3 - Computational Intelligence Research Group
(www.uninova.pt/ca3/)

School of Management, University of Plymouth, UK
(http://www.plymouth.ac.uk/)

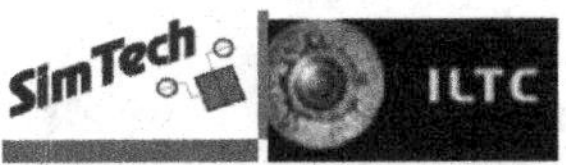

SimTech Simulation Technology, Austria
(htt#p://w#ww.SimTechnology.com)
ILTC - Instituto de Lógica Filosofia e Teoria da Ciência, RJ, Brazil
(http://#www.#iltc.br)

University of Belgrade, Serbia
(http://www.bg.ac.rs/eng/uni/university.php#)

School of Business, Economics and Informatics at Birkbeck, University of London
(http://www.bbk.ac.uk/)

Paris-Dauphine University
(http://www.dauphine.fr/)

LAMSADE – CNRS
(http://www.lamsade.dauphine.fr/)

Table of Contents

Collaborative Network Platform for Multi-site Production

António Arrais-Castro[1], Maria Leonilde R. Varela[1], Goran D. Putnik[1], and Rita A. Ribeiro[2]

[1] Department of Production and Systems, School of Engineering, University of Minho, Azurém Campus, 4800-058 Guimarães, Portugal
[2] UNINOVA - CA3, Campus FCT/UNL, 2829-516 Caparica, Portugal
arraiscastro@gmail.com,
{leonilde,putnikgd}@dps.uminho.pt, rar@uninova.pt

Abstract. The Competition in the global economy is intensifying the implementation of web-based collaboration platforms to improve the personalized interaction between clients and producers. Agility in the order-production-delivery cycle is a key element for industrial enterprises as a means to meet the requirements of this paradigm. Agile/Virtual Enterprise based scenarios are characterized by large product variety dependent on product specific requirements of individual customers. Therefore, to enable an enriched network based tool for Virtual Enterprise specification and configuration, there is a need to define a collaborative environment for dynamically enable candidate business partners to integrate it. In this paper, we propose a web platform and describe its main functionalities for interactive multi-site production network integration.

Keywords: Collaboration, Agile/ Virtual Enterprise, multi-site production network, web-based integration platform.

1 Introduction

Fast change, uncertainty, and strong competition are challenges of the actual worldwide economic context. Competitiveness is a main requirement of enterprises, whose satisfaction requires the definition of new organizational concepts, with extremely high performances that are strongly time-oriented while highly focused on cost and quality. Several factors appear as supreme factors of competitiveness: (1) the organizations' capability to achieve and explore competitive advantages in synergy, by using or integrating the optimal available resources for performing their tasks; (2) the capability for fast adaptability to the market; together with (3) the capability of managing all business processes independently of distance.

Agile/ Virtual Enterprises (A/VE) play a growing role in today's global market scenario, allowing companies to enhance collaboration and thus maximize scale and capture market opportunities. It is becoming increasingly more important to be able to easily and dynamically configure and re-configure an Agile/ Virtual Enterprise

J.E. Hernández et al. (Eds.): EWG-DSS 2011, LNBIP 121, pp. 1–13, 2012.

(A/VE), in terms of collaborative members, so that the existing manufacturing networks are maintained updated and synchronized with business goals.

In this paper we propose a platform for A/VE synthesis and present the underlying architecture and main expected functionalities.

Section 1 introduces the key concepts and some existing approaches for A/VE synthesis. Next a brief literature revision is presented, about some important and more or less closely related work. On sections 3 and 4 the proposed A/VE model and platform are described, including the underlying main functionalities. Finally, section 5 presents some concluding remarks.

Agile/Virtual Enterprises (A/VE) [14] play a permanently growing important role in the today's global market scenario, therefore it is increasingly more important to easily and dynamically be able to configure and re-configure an Agile/ Virtual Enterprise, to ensure updated existing manufacturing networks and better support management for the collaborative members. This recognition was the main motivation for this work, i.e. to contribute to putting forward a platform for A/VE synthesis.

The implementation of a multi-site production network integration platform (MSPNIP) will allow the creation of a central communication channel for distributing and sharing information between simple and complex enterprises and their corresponding products. Furthermore, it allows supporting customers and potential business partners with their production plans configurations and product requirements and specifications. Implementing MSPNIP design using a set of configurable modules allows the system to ensure support for the implementation of collaboration strategies [14] and [15] with the aim of generating value from an optimized interaction with business partners and extended partnership relations with customers. This distributed production network may be integrated with front-end systems that support interaction with customers and other commercial agents. The integration platform can be used to automatically feed distinct point of sale (POS) systems, including websites, interactive product configurators (for physical points of sale) and promotional interactive media. Additionally, the system may connect these POS systems with management back-end software, including CRM (Customer Relationship Management) and Production Management Systems.

The A/VE model [6] and [14] relies on dynamically reconfigurable collaborative networks, with extremely high performances, strongly time-oriented while highly focused on cost and quality, in permanent alignment with the market, and strongly supported by information and communication technology. Networking and reconfiguration dynamics are the main characteristics of this model, which aim for enabling and supporting business environments, assuring cost-effective integration in useful time and preventing the risk of leakage of private information about products or processes. Some existing technologies and Internet-based environments [8], [9], [10] and [13] can partially support this organizational model, but the reconfiguration dynamics can only be assured by environments able to manage, control, and enable virtual enterprise creation, operation and reconfiguration.

Hence, in this paper we propose a model for aiding organizations to collaborate in terms of business partners' integration, in meta-organization environment contexts. Such environment includes the integration of several manufacturing systems, which have to be remotely supervised and controlled through distinct business partners, connected and integrated in the context of Ubiquitous Manufacturing System (UMS) based, namely, on Internet Technology (IT), as well as other monitoring and communication devices and tools.

With the proposed IT-based platform, organizations interested on embracing a meta-organization model will be able to successfully collaborate, since the partnering enterprises will work as a seamless extended enterprise, all following a single unified process and not disjointed and fragmented processes that are only integrated via data bridges with no process or information intelligence.

2 Related Work

Globalization introduces new challenges for companies, such as facing a potentially large number of business competitors and new requirements that have to be fulfilled to ensure market share and improve customer retention.

The implementation of competitive strategies and process optimization procedures is, nowadays, an essential requirement for companies' survival. Thus, ensuring efficient, cost-effective and error-free integration of front-office and back-office processes is an essential task. Besides, companies need to adopt differentiation strategies because having the lowest prices is no longer enough: companies need to dynamically adapt their business trends, partners and products to meet the specific needs of customers.

An agile response to market trends and better support for customer individual needs and demands frequently requires agile production methods and approaches, like Agile and Lean Manufacturing [1], [2] and [3]. Lean Manufacturing method aims at eliminating waste, targeting for elimination of any activities that do not create value for the end customer. The method has two pillar concepts: automation and JIT - Just In Time. JIT was introduced by Taiichi Ohno, chief engineer at Toyota in the 1950s, as a method for fulfilling customers' needs with minimum delays, while reducing finished and in-process inventory (see, for instance, [1], [2], and [3]). With JIT, inventory is seen as just incurring costs and waste, instead of stored value. It all comes to having "the right material, at the right time, at the right place, and in the right amount". JIT make-to-order philosophy implies minimization of the risk of having unsold products. Web based product configurators may be used to improve agility - when capturing sales orders and converting them into production orders - thus helping to implement more efficient JIT processes.

On the other hand, agile manufacturing [2] and [3] was designed to make businesses more flexible and versatile, by providing: greater agility from production operations; setup and lead-time reduction; and more efficiency in managing production and product information. An Agile company needs to determine customer needs quickly and continuously reposition itself against its competitors [3]. This means that it also needs to design products and manufacture them quickly, based on customers' individual needs. Reduction on time to market of customized products requires flexible production systems, imposing additional planning challenges that may have a significant impact on the business relation with business partners.

Business to Business (B2B) agility will frequently imply a transition from self-centered to open business models. Increasing cooperation among enterprises during the product life cycle is a trend in the global market [4]. Collaborative Networks consist of groups of entities (organizations and people), largely autonomous, geographically distributed and heterogeneous, collaborating to achieve a common or compatible goal [4], [5] and [6]. A Virtual Organization is a collaborative network of organizations that comprises a set of independent organizations that share resources and skills to achieve a mission or goal [4], [5] and [6].

An Agile/Virtual Enterprise (A/VE) is a dynamically reconfigurable global networked organization, or network of enterprises, sharing information and/or knowledge, skills, core competencies, market and other resources and processes; it is configured (or constituted) as a temporary alliance (or network) to meet a (fast changing) market window of opportunity, presenting as main characteristics agility, virtuality, distributivity and integrability [5] and [6].

A multi-site production network (MSPN) – a specific collaborative network - aims at integrating various processes and phases from concepts, design, prototypes, developments, manufacturing, markets, selling, services up to re-cycles, reengineering and reverse-engineering processes [5] and [6].

The main task of a MSPN is to support business partners (BP) and associated B2B processes. Business partners may dynamically integrate this production network in order to satisfy a given set of objectives. A MSPN management system will support the implementation of Business integration workflows, for instance by deciding which partners are going to be chosen for accomplishing some production orders, in a certain specified time horizon.

Decisions about MSPN configuration concern the entire MSPN process and are important strategic decisions. For example, on the production side, decisions about the location and capacity of plants are typical tasks. On the distribution side, the locations of warehouses have to be determined, among other important and fundamental decisions.

A dynamic and reconfigurable supply chain is a critical tool for the implementation of Agile/Virtual Enterprises and for supporting mass customization business models, where products are created on a build-to-order basis [6] and [7]. Synchronization at the supply chain level is required to support customer driven business operations, where the unique circumstances associated with each ordering and production scenario are considered, instead of adopting mechanical and automated workflow procedures, which are essentially process driven. Ghiassi and Spera [8] classify synchronized supply chain management as a new paradigm to provide a competitive strategy for customer-centric business environments. Lu and Wang [9] also address the benefits of synchronized supply chain management systems.

Chen, et al. [10] propose a multi-tier multi-agent architecture for collaborative production. They use tier agents to represent enterprises and site agents to represent local production units. The authors illustrate the application of this model in the TFT-LCD industry, typically divided into three segments (TFT array, cell and module assembly). At each segment different manufacturing sites are involved. Each segment is in fact an instance of a multi-site production system. The authors propose handling each enterprise using tier agents. Each tier agent interacts with other tier agents to handle order acceptance, order coordination and order cancelation.

Ghiassi and Spera [8] propose LEAP, a distributed system for companies that may have many plants spread over a wide geographic region, making many products, which they sell in many different markets. The authors developed a mathematical model that updates demand quantities continuously using forecasting techniques. The production plan is continuously updated to reflect the revised demand data up to the final scheduling of the production run.

Rabelo and Camarinha-Matos [11] developed HOLOS, a distributed multi-agent system that uses cooperation to schedule production inside an enterprise. The system was integrated with the federated information management DIMS/FIMS [12], extending the approach to virtual enterprises.

Moreover, Malucelli, Rocha and Oliveira [13] introduce a platform for facilitating the partner's selection automatic process – ForEV. The platform is implemented through a Multi-Agent System and includes a negotiation protocol – Q-Negotiation - through multi-criteria and distributed constraint formalisms. The platform also includes a reinforcement learning algorithm.

3 Background on Dynamic A/VE Reconfiguration

Configurability dynamics and business alignment as requirements for the A/VE model responsiveness to the market demands requires shorter product life cycles and shorter time to market. Companies are forced to include frequent redesigns in product life cycle, which imply the requirement for increased dynamics to the A/V E model. Even A/VE tend to last shorter and shorter in time, while simultaneously addressing a highly dynamic reconfiguration; an A/VE can have as many instantiations as required either by product changes or as a requirement of quality and competitiveness improvement, to assure a permanent alignment with such market demands [14] and [15].

The main critical aspects associated to the recent concept of dynamically reconfigurable global networked structures, corresponding to the A/V E model - precisely based on networking and configurability dynamics - are the transaction costs and the leakage of private information [5], [6] and [16]. Transaction costs, i.e. the firm reconfiguration cost, are associated to business partners search, selection, negotiation and integration as well as permanent monitoring and the evaluation of the partnership performance. The preservation of firm's knowledge on organizational and management processes, as they are important firm's competitive factors, is also critical. The main tools suggested in the BM_Virtual Enterprise Reference Model (BM_VEARM) [16] and [17], for managing, controlling and enabling networking and dynamics and thus overcome the two critical factors, are [18] and [19]:

- Network market of resources, which is the environment for enabling and managing efficient configuration, and assuring virtuality, at low transaction costs and reduced risk of knowledge leakage.
- The broker or organization configuration manager, which is the main agent of agility and virtuality, acting either between two operations of the A/VE (off-line configurability, providing agility only) or on-line with the operation (on-line configurability, providing virtuality and a higher level of agility).

- Virtuality makes possible the transition from one physical structure (instance) to another in a way that the enterprise or process owner is not affected by the system reconfiguration and is not aware of the reconfiguration - the underlying service structure and reconfiguration process are hidden.

Dynamic organizational models represent solutions for highly customized products, small series, in highly competitive and changing environments where permanent business alignment is crucial. Partnership stability is low (sometimes very low), dependency between partners is very weak and reconfiguration dynamics should be as high as possible. Permanent monitoring of the structure is needed, to traduce the most competitive solution at every moment of the product life cycle [16] and [17].

Reconfiguration, meaning substitution of resources providers, generating a new instantiation of the network, can happen mainly from three reasons [5] and [6]:

1. Reconfiguration during the network company life cycle is a consequence of the product redesign in the product life cycle, to keep the network aligned with the market requirements.
2. Reconfiguration as a consequence of the nature of the particular product life cycle phase (evolutionary phases).
3. Reconfiguration can happen also as a consequence of the evaluation of the resources performance during an instantiation of the network, or voluntarily by rescission of participating resources, wiling to disentail from the network.

Dynamic reconfiguration requisites are essential when implementing a collaborative network that needs to assist business partners working as an integrated organization, supporting them on the decision making processes, making use of present and past information.

4 Proposed Platform for A/VE Synthesis

4.1 Platform Architecture

Figure 1 illustrates a proposed general architecture for the platform for A/VE synthesis, therefore called Collaborative Network Platform for Multi-site Production (CNPMSP). The platform implements a ubiquitous manufacturing system network, [15], [18] and [19]. The platform's main components are the web service layer, which handles incoming requests from customers, and software agents, which process orders and implement production management information flows, based on a multiple-attribute decision model [20], [21], [22], [23] and [24]. These autonomous agents are capable of directing their behavior to accomplish their specific goals in the system's context. Several distinct software agents are available, each having a specific purpose in the workflow: order agents, that process orders received from customers; production agents, that identify outsourcing/ supplier candidates and perform negotiation with them; local agents, that implement a communication interface between local business partner systems and production agents and data brokers, that control how data import and export is managed, promoting system encapsulation [25], [26], [27] and [28].

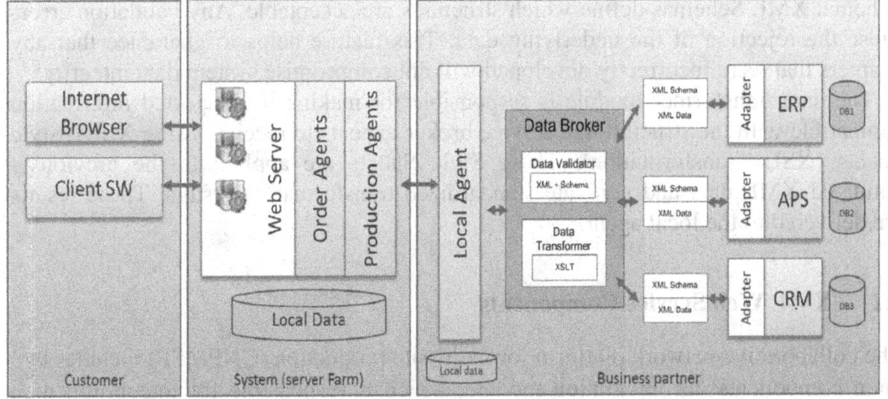

Fig. 1. General architecture for the proposed platform for A/VE synthesis

In order to optimize platform's reusability customers will interact with the platform using HTTP for data transfer. A set of web services is available for servicing customer applications. These applications can range from locally installed software packages (that post order information by calling web service methods) to server pages that are viewed using standard browser clients. Messages will be formatted using SOAP and they will be written in XML. Proxies will be used to support the integration of mobile equipment.

Integration with local systems from constituent business partners is a key component of a dynamic and distributed platform. The proposed architecture includes integration modules that support the integration of heterogeneous production management systems in the distributed management process. These modules provide a consistent abstraction of the actual data structure and functional details of each local system. As long as each business unit system can accept the input data, process it and return output data, it can be integrated in the proposed architecture. By allowing each business unit to integrate their existing systems, the proposed architecture supports maintaining each factory's autonomy. The abstraction also allows for the sharing of limited amounts of information, using controlled software components. Business units can join or leave the network without changing their internal systems.

Integration with local systems will be built using connection modules called adapters. Several adapters will be available for reading and writing information from/ into external systems (ERP, SCM, APS, among others). These modules feature read and write connectors. Each read connector is responsible for reading the information available in a backend system and transform this information into XML. Write connectors receive XML data and convert it to a format that is adequate for the associated system. XML Schemas (XSD) will be used to help validate the information and check its completeness and integrity.

The data broker component is the central data processing module and controls how import and export data are managed. The module is isolated from the details of each external system, accepting only XML information.

It includes two sub-components: data validator and data transformer. The data validator maps the information received by the broker to the corresponding XML

Schema. XML Schemas define which structures are acceptable. Any validation errors cause the rejection of the underlying data. This feature helps to guarantee that any adapters that were incorrectly developed will not compromise system data integrity.

The data transformer module is responsible for making the imported information compatible with the structure the service broker expects to receive, using XSLT Style Sheets (XSL Transformation). These Style Sheets are applied to the previously validated XML data and generate standardized transformation results. These results are delivered to the local agent.

4.2 XML Web Service Components

The collaborative network platform for multi-site production (CNPMSP) includes two main components: an integration module, which is responsible for integration with existing information systems, and a service module, which interacts with external systems (client and server applications).

Integration will be built using connection modules called connectors. Several connectors will be available for reading and writing information from/ into external systems. Each read connector is responsible for reading the information available in a backend system and transform this information into XML. Writing connectors receive XML data and convert it to a format that is adequate for the associated system. XML Schemas (XSD) will be used to help validate the information and check its completeness and integrity.

The data broker component is the central data processing module and controls how data import and export are managed. It includes two sub-components: data validator and data transformer. The data broker is isolated from the details of each external system, accepting only XML information. Data validator maps the information received by the broker to the corresponding XML Schema. Any validation errors cause the rejection of the underlying data.

The data transformer module is responsible for making the imported information compatible with the structure the service broker expects to receive. It uses XSLT style sheets (XSL Transformation), applying them to the previously validated XML data, and forwarding the transformation results to the web service layer. The data broker component can be replaced by a third party middleware solution, like TIBCO (www.tibco.com) or BizTalk Server (www.microsoft.com/biztalk). These solutions will help modeling business rules at the integration level.

The web services layer is responsible for the implementation of functionalities that support the collaborative network for multi-site production and information publishing.

The only requirement a client application has to fulfill is the ability to call web methods using HTTP and SOAP protocols and process the XML data that is returned.

4.3 Platform Main Functionalities

Figure 2 illustrates the main expected functionalities of the proposed platform for A/VE synthesis.

Customers will submit orders to the platform using available web services or server web pages. This paper assumes that order format and product description follow a base XML schema definition, mapped to a shared catalog of valid product references. To improve readability we consider that each system' task is represented by an agent and all agents collaborate between themselves to achieve the A/VE synthesis.

Whenever an order is received by the system a new order agent is associated to it. The agent starts by analyzing the order and available data to identify the list of ordered products. Each product may have different production requirements. Once the products have been defined, the order agent performs material planning in order to identify how many finished goods or components have to be produced. It then builds an activity sequence made of (Component/ Service, Start Date, Due Date, Qty) nodes, mapped to order delivery dates. The agent also identifies production dependencies and parallelism opportunities then it instantiates one production agent for each component that must be produced. The order agent next enters a monitoring cycle, analyzing feedback from production agents, checking for completion and handling exceptions. When production completes, the agent performs the closing steps associated with shipping and invoicing procedures.

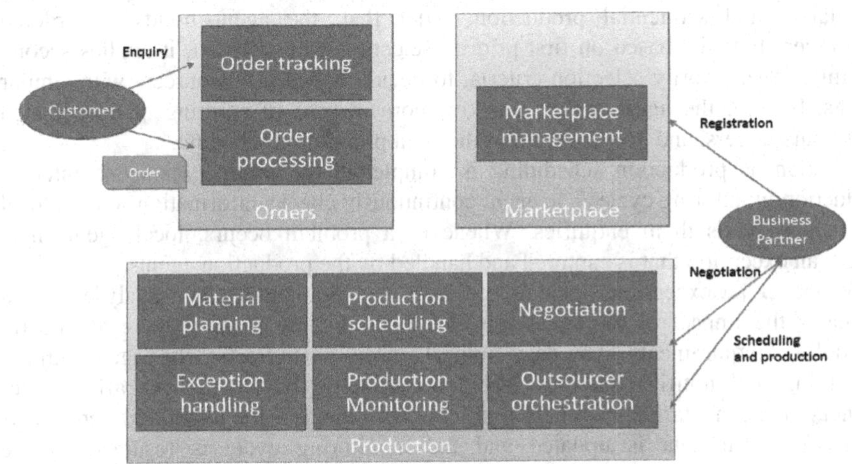

Fig. 2. Main functionalities of the proposed platform for A/VE synthesis

The production agents receive production assignments from the order agents. The agents perform a second phase of material planning, if needed, further decomposing components in production units. For each activity the agents define free slack (amount of time it may be delayed without affecting the next task) and total slack values (the amount of time the activity can be delayed without affecting the production deadline). Next they build a list of potential suppliers for each of the components or materials. For each of the components the agents initiate a bidding session, inviting registered business partners to place a bid in the system. The bid is made through local agents that are available on each of the registered business partners. These local agents are assigned to the business partners/ suppliers when they register in the system. After receiving bid proposals from invited local agents, the production agents first evaluate production capacities. Each business partner that has enough production capacity is included in a list of qualified outsourcers for the associated component. If none of the business partners has enough capacity during the request period, the agent tries to coordinate the production order, checking dependencies and trying to change production schedule, trying to create compatibility with available capacities. If the coordination process is possible, the agent notifies business partners about proposed changes. If coordination is not possible, the agent tries to split production of the associated components between multiple producers, according to reported capacity availability from compatible partners. It then asks for updated bids according to proposed schedule and capacity allocation. If splitting is not successful, the agent triggers the reject order process. This process involves the order agent and, optionally, asks from further human approval to perform order rejection.

If there was enough capacity among bidders or production coordination was successful or even if production splitting occurred, the agent ends the process with a list of qualified outsourcers. For each entry on the list the agent evaluates and updates first level bidding factors (like cost, delivery, quality ratios and previous information). Next it evaluates transportation costs between suppliers that need to perform cumulative and sequential production. After that, the agent builds an ordered outsourcer short list based on first priority selection criteria. Next, it applies second and third level priority selection criteria, to decide between outsourcers with similar ratings. Finally, the agent selects one (or more in case of splitting or coordinated work) outsourcers, and notifies them of the final production schedule.

As soon as production scheduling is completed, the production agent enters a production monitoring cycle. The agent continuously checks information sent by local agents and sends them enquiries. Whenever a problem occurs, local agents may trigger an exception that is captured and handled by the production agents.

Whenever an exception signal is received, the production agent analyses it and evaluates the impact of the exception on the production plan. If there are no re-scheduling requirements that may impact other outsourcers, the agent adjusts scheduling and notifies the local agent accordingly. If the changes affect other partners the agent starts a negotiation process with them. If the negotiation process is successful local data is updated and the monitoring cycle is resumed. If the negotiation was not successful and may compromise a final production deadline, the production agent interacts with the order agent, which will validate if the delay is acceptable. If it is not, the production may be cancelled. In this case, the production agent waits for formal production cancel approval, and informs local agents accordingly. During regular production monitoring cycle the production agent sends enquiries to local agents. In reply they send status reports and time estimates. If the production agent detects production delays it evaluates if they compromise production schedule, analyzing dependencies and total/ free slack values. If scheduling is compromised, the agent checks with the order agent to see if the delay is acceptable, when matched with order delivery dates. If the delay is not acceptable, the agent starts the replace outsourcer process. After notifying the local agent from the outsourcer, the production agent starts a new bidding session for the work that was previously assigned to it.

Finally, it should be noted that since our description of the platform functionalities follows a typical multi-agent system model [25], [26], [27] and [28] it has the advantage of being implemented using known techniques and concepts.

5 Final Comments

Agile/Virtual Enterprise (A/VE) integration is still a major concern of current manufacturing organizations that are worried about overcoming concurrency and surviving difficulties.

In this paper we propose a framework for A/VE synthesis, allowing business partners to take part on a collaborative environment, dynamically reconfigurable, that supports feasible integration with their existing system.

The proposed framework showed how technology can serve the needs of an expanding and increasingly competitive A/VE organizational model. Agile/ Virtual Enterprises were addressed in this work as a highly dynamic, reconfigurable agile network of independent enterprises sharing all resources, including knowledge, market, and customers - while using specific organizational architectures that introduce the enterprises' true virtual environments. In addition, our framework took in consideration that agility, distributivity, virtuality, integrability, scalability and evolutionary capability are the main requirements for competitiveness that new organizational models must address. Finally, the proposed platform architecture also included support A/VE operations assuming that participating business partners may have heterogeneous information systems and legacy systems.

By using the proposed framework, a group of companies may integrate themselves on a collaborative network increasing their scale and achieving competitive advantages typically exclusive of global companies. Being structured in a modular way and facilitating integration with existing systems, the platform will be a cost effective solution, with a good potential of value creation. Without such a tool, companies will have more difficulties aggregating their capabilities and collaborating to achieve common business goals.

Future work includes the implementation of a more elaborated multi-agent system mechanism to incorporate demand forecast in the order scheduling and negotiation processes. The adoption of a peer-to-peer architecture, without any central server mediation, will also be evaluated. Additionally, the authors plan to test the system using a selected industry segment, simulating its application in a real production environment.

Acknowledgments. The authors wish to acknowledge the support of: 1) The Foundation for Science and Technology – FCT, under the scope of the financed Project on "Ubiquitous oriented embedded systems for globally distributed factories of manufacturing enterprises" - PTDC/EME-GIN/102143/2008, and 2) EUREKA, under the Project E!4177-Pro-Factory UES.

References

1. Goddard, W.E.: Just-In-Time: Surviving by Breaking Tradition. Oliver Wight Ltd. Pub. (1986)
2. Kidd, P.T.: Agile Manufacturing Forging New Frontiers. Addisson-Wesley, Reading (1994)
3. Nagel, R., Dove, R.: Twenty-first Century Manufacturing Enterprise Strategy—An Industry Led Review, Iacocca Institute, Leigh University, USA, vol. 1, 2 (1991)
4. Camarinha-Matos, L.M., Afsarmanesh, H.: Collaborative networks: a new scientific discipline. Journal of Intelligent Manufacturing 16, 439–452 (2004)
5. Cunha, M.M., Putnik, G.D.: Discussion on Requirements for Agile/ Virtual Enterprises Reconfigurability Dynamics: The Example of the Automotive Industry. In: Camarinha-Matos, L.M. (ed.) Collaborative Business Ecosystems and Virtual Enterprises, pp. 527–534. Kluwer Academic Publishers, Boston (2002)
6. Cunha, M.M., Putnik, G.D., Ávila, P.: Towards Focused Markets of Resources for Agile / Virtual Enterprise Integration. In: Camarinha-Matos, L.M., Afsarmanesh, H., Erbe, H. (eds.) Advances in Networked Enterprises: Virtual Organisations, Balanced Automation, and Systems Integration, pp. 15–24. Kluwer Academic Publishers, Berlin (2000)
7. Campanella, G., Ribeiro, R.A., Varela, L.R.: A Model for B2B Supplier Selection. In: Melo-Pinto, P., Couto, P., Serôdio, C., Fodor, J., De Baets, B. (eds.) Eurofuse 2011. AISC, vol. 107, pp. 221–228. Springer, Heidelberg (2011)
8. Ghiassi, M., Spera, C.: Defining the Internet-based supply chain system for mass customized markets. Computers & Industrial Engineering 45, 17–41 (2003)
9. Lu, L., Wang, G.: A study on multi-agent supply chain framework based on network economy. Computers & Industrial Engineering 54, 288–300 (2008)
10. Chen, W.-L., Huang, C.-Y., Lai, Y.-C.: Multi-tier and multi-site collaborative production: Illustrated by a case example of TFT-LCD manufacturing. Computers & Industrial Engineering 57, 61–72 (2009)
11. Rabelo, R., Camarinha-Matos, L.M.: Towards Agile Scheduling in Extended Enterprise. In: Balanced Automation Systems II: Implementation Challenges for Anthropocentric Manufacturing. Chapman and Hall, London (1996)
12. Afsarmanesh, H., Garita, C., Ugur, Y., Frenkel, A., Hertzberger, L.O.: Design of the DIMS Architecture in PRODNET (1999)
13. Malucelli, A., Rocha, A.P., Oliveira, E.: B2B Transactions enhanced with ontology-based services (2004)
14. Cunha, M.M., Putnik, G.D.: Business Alignment in Agile/ Virtual Enterprise Integration. In: Khosrow-Pour, M. (ed.) Advanced Topics in Information Resources Management, vol. IV. Idea-Group Publishing (2005)
15. Putnik, G.D., Cunha, M.M., Sousa, R., Avila, P.: Virtual Enterprise Integration: Challenges of a New Paradigm (2005)
16. Putnik, G.D.: BM_Virtual Enterprise Architecture Reference Model. Technical Report RT-CESP-GIS-2000-<GP-01>. University of Minho, Portugal (2000)
17. Putnik, G.D.: BM_Virtual Enterprise Architecture Reference Model. In: Gunasekaran, A. (ed.) Agile Manufacturing: 21st Century Manufacturing Strategy, pp. 73–93. Elsevier Science Publ., UK (2001)
18. Cunha, M.M., Putnik, G.D., Gunasekaran, A.: Market of Resources as an Environment for Agile/ Virtual Enterprise Dynamic Integration and for Business Alignment. In: Khalil, O., Gunasekaran, A. (eds.) Knowledge and Information Technology Management in the 21st Century Organisations: Human and Social Perspectives, pp. 169–190. Idea Group Publishing, London (2002)

19. Cunha, M.M., Putnik, G.D.: Business Alignment in Agile/ Virtual Enterprise Integration. In: Khosrow-Pour, M. (ed.) Advanced Topics in Information Resources Management, vol. IV. Idea-Group Publishing (2005)
20. Chen, S.-J., Hwang, C.L., Hwang, F.P.: Fuzzy Multiple Attribute Decision Making: Methods and Applications. Lecture Notes in Economics and Mathematical Systems, vol. 375. Springer (1992)
21. Triantaphyllou, E.: Multi-Criteria Decision Making Methods: A Comparative Study. Applied Optimization, vol. 44. Springer (2000)
22. Sucky, E.: A dynamic model for strategic supplier selection. In: Operations Research Proceedings, vol. 2004, pt. 4, pp. 118–126 (2005), doi:10.1007/3-540-27679-3_15
23. Campanella, G., Ribeiro, R.A.: A framework for dynamic multiple criteria decision making. Decision Support Systems 52(1), 52–64 (2011), doi:10.1016/j.dss.2011.05.003
24. Blattberg, R.C., Glazer, R.: Marketing in the Information Revolution. In: Blattberg, R.C., et al. (eds.) The Marketing Information Revolution, pp. 9–29. Harvard Business School Press, Boston (1994)
25. Nwana, H.S.: Software Agents: An Overview. Knowledge Engineering Review 11(3), 1–40 (1996)
26. Genesereth, M.R., Ketchpel, S.P.: Software Agents. Communication of the ACM 37(7) (July 2004)
27. Rocha, A.P.: Metodologias de Negociação em Sistemas Multi-Agentes para Empresas Virtuais. PhD thesis, Faculty of Engineering, Porto University (2001)
28. Jennings, N.R.: On Agent-Based Software Engineering. Artificial Intelligence 117(2), 277–296 (2000)

A Conceptual Model for MRP IV

Manuel Díaz-Madroñero, Josefa Mula, and David Peidro

Research Center on Production Management and Engineering (CIGIP)
Universitat Politècnica de València, Escuela Politécnica Superior de Alcoy
Plaza Ferrándiz y Carbonell 2, 03801, Alcoy, Alicante, Spain
{fcodiama,fmula,dapeipa}@cigip.upv.es

Abstract. In current supply chains where there is a considerable offshoring of raw materials and parts suppliers, production planning can no longer be considered a separate and independent process from transportation planning. However, current systems only focus on production decisions, regardless of the transport considerations. This means that proposed production plans could be suboptimal, and even infeasible. In these cases, manual replanning is a common practice in companies until production plans are made feasible as far as available transport capacity is concerned. For the purpose of avoiding the suboptimization of these plans, we present a conceptual model, the MRP IV, which serves as a reference to develop a new production technology and integrates material planning, production resource capacities and supply chain transport decisions, and acts as a baseline to propose resolution models and algorithms required to develop MRP IV as a decision-making system.

Keywords: MRP, integration, production planning, transport planning.

1 Introduction

In the current context, characterized by globalization of economy and offshoring of supply chain members, production planning systems present several deficiencies. This is because the core of these systems was developed in the 70s, when the need to increase productivity in manufacturing plants in a local environment dominated. In these years, Orlicky [1] presented the MRP (Material Requirement Planning) system, and nowadays it continues to be the most widely used production planning system. The evolutions of the MRP were reflected in the MRP II (Manufacturing Resource Planning) [2] system, which considers productive capacity constraints and a variety of interrelated functions such as business planning, sales and operations (production planning), a master production schedule and MRP. Later, MRP III (Money Resource Planning) [3] introduces the financial function; and the MRP evolved into the ERP (Enterprise Resource Planning) [4], which incorporates all the company functions into a unique decision system. Moreover, these systems have been adapted to the current economic context characterized by adding new information and communication technologies and developing other functions such as supply chain management or transport, among others [5]. However, despite the various features added, the main component of ERP and MRP II systems is still based on the logic of the original MRP

J.E. Hernández et al. (Eds.): EWG-DSS 2011, LNBIP 121, pp. 14–25, 2012.

systems and they only focus on material requirements and on production capacities planning. This represents an important limitation in global supply chains where the optimization of transport costs subject to logistical constraints must be also considered given their impact on production planning decisions. That is, current production planning systems calculate the production and procurement planning decisions based on MRP systems and its variants, as well as transport planning systems based on graph theory, mathematical programming models or spreadsheets, although not in an integrated way. In this context, production plans must generally be replanned or rescheduled (sometimes manually) because they do not contemplate transportation planning issues. This work aims to develop a conceptual model, the MRP IV, which integrates the material, production resource capacities and transport planning (type of transport, form of collection, etc.) decisions in the supply chain to avoid the suboptimization of these plans which, nowadays, are usually generated sequentially and independently.

The rest of the paper is arranged as follows: Section 2 offers a problem description related to MRP and transport planning problems. Section 3 presents a literature review about MRP and integrated production and transport planning models. Section 4 shows the conceptual model for MRP IV. Section 5 illustrates the potential use of MRP IV in an automobile seat assembler. Finally, the last section provides conclusions and directions for further research.

2 Problem Description

There are two main problems faced by manufacturers of finished goods (FG) in assembly supply chains: the optimization of their production plans and procurement processes. On the one hand, manufacturers determine their production plans to meet customer demand by taking into account their inventory levels and the different production costs. On the other hand, the manufacturers have to optimise their procurement processes by determining the purchasing plan of parts (PA) and raw materials (RM) and their collection at the suppliers' facilities. The first problem corresponds to a production multi-level lot-sizing problem, or MRP, while the second is a specific vehicle-routing problem (VRP) to determine the set of products that should be sent in a vehicle and the route it is to travel.

The described problem considers a finite and discrete planning horizon and a supply chain formed by a manufacturer of FG, with a single production facility, a set of PA and RM suppliers and a set of transport suppliers. The production facility is characterized by a production capacity, which comprises the available capacity of own production resources and subcontracted resources. In accordance with the characteristics of the available manufacturing resources, production batch sizes, setup times and production times required to produce each FG are defined. Also, production resources can run in regular time, overtime hours, or can otherwise involve idle hours. On the other hand, demand can be backlogged in accordance with the availability of resources in each period and the predefined safety stocks. Finally, the production system is characterized by a set of function costs: production costs, inventory of PA, RM and FG costs, backlogged demand costs, undertime hours of productive resources, overtime hours of productive resources and subcontracting costs.

The bill of material (BOM) expresses the quantity of each PA and RM needed to produce one unit of each FG. Each PA and RM is characterized by its physical dimensions and special shipping units needed to deliver them, such as pallets or special racks. Moreover, the supplier of each PA and RM can arbitrarily determine an order lot size, which may or may not coincide with the production lot size of FG at the manufacturer.

According to Fleischmann [6], transport planning is usually the responsibility of the supplier, but there are important exceptions, e.g. in the automobile industry, where the manufacturer controls the transports from suppliers and determines the quantities of the required PA and RM to be collected in each supplier. The transport network characteristics are defined by the geographical distribution of PA and RM suppliers, the transport capacity offered by the fleet of the available vehicles and the different costs functions related to transport issues (e.g. costs related to occupied volume, discounts, costs for using extra transport capacity, costs incurred by urgent deliveries, waiting truck costs, etc.) Also, different shipment modes, such as full-truckload or FTL, less-than-truckload or LTL and milk-run, are considered to transport PA and RM from supplier to the manufacturer. The shipment mode and the shipment delivery frequency, which consists in the frequency of materials arriving from different suppliers to manufacturer, are determined by the geographical distribution of PA and RM suppliers and order lot sizes. Transport capacity, shipment modes and shipment frequency can be regulated by means of contracts drawn by with transport suppliers.

However, despite the fact that production and transport planning problems are closely related and should be solved simultaneously to achieve an optimal solution, in practice, they are usually solved separately and independently. The most habitual procedure is master production schedule (MPS) calculation and MRP, used to determine the quantities of each FG to be produced in a given planning horizon, as well as the requirements of the associated PA and RM. If the quantities to be ordered to suppliers can be transported with the available transport capacity, the corresponding orders are firmly placed. On the other hand, if the results obtained with MRP are infeasible in relation to the existing transport network, they need to be manually amended until they become feasible, otherwise it is necessary to increase the existing transport capacity and to rerun MRP. In most cases in this context, transportation planning is based on planners' experience and personal judgments by using spreadsheets, which implies obtaining suboptimal results.

We hypothesize that a new production technology, called MRP IV, is required, which integrates decision making relating to materials planning, production resources capacities and transport in the supply chain to avoid suboptimal plans which, currently, are normally generated sequentially and independently.

3 Literature Review

Material Requirement Planning (MRP) system is an essential component of the current production planning and control systems in manufacturing enterprises. In order to achieve optimal production decisions, aspects such as minimization of total costs and constraints related to supply, demand or available resources were gradually incorporated into mathematical programming optimization models which consider the original MRP issues. In this sense, in the seminal work of Karni [7] a general integer programming formulation was developed, covering conditions on lot sizes and time phasing; conditions on storage and production capacities; and changes in production and storage costs per unit. Another early contribution to model MRP problems was by Billington et al. [8] who formulated a capacity-constrained MRP system as a mixed integer program (MIP). Their model was for general product structures with production lead times, overtime and capacities of work centres. Later, Clark [9] studies the approximate modelling and optimization of capacity utilization in MRP multi-level systems, by formulating and solving a mathematical model using two approaches based on model approximation and sequential decomposition. More recently, Yenisey [10] addresses the optimization of material flows in MRP systems with a flow network with a side constraints approach and by solving the related MIP model. Moreover, Noori et al. [11] develop a fuzzy multi-objective linear programming model to extend the work proposed by Yenisey [10] which considers the minimization of total costs and time. However, one of the major drawbacks of these formulations is to ignore the uncertainty associated with any production environment. The literature reports different approaches to consider uncertainty in MRP systems, such as simulation [12, 13], stochastic inventory control [14], fuzzy logic [15], fuzzy mathematical programming [16–19], fuzzy programming with resources based on the credibility theory [20] and MRP parameterization [21–23], among others. Other approaches to consider uncertainty in MRP systems can be found in several reviews [24–26].

Several developments have been proposed in the literature related to original MRP logic. In this sense, Kim [27] and Barba-Gutierrez [15] plan the disassembly of multi-level products based on the reverse MRP (RMRP) [28]. Moreover, DePuy [29] presents a methodology to determine production plans for facilities involved in the remanufacture of products, that is, those that accept inoperable units, salvage the good or repairable components from those units, and then re-assemble good units to be re-issued into service. On the other hand, in order to adapt MRP systems to new manufacturing environments several works redefine the traditional bill of materials (BOM) concept. Chen et al. [30] include customization features by generating a BOM for each customized product, adjusting the traditional MRP approach for the make-to-order philosophy. Other approaches take into account the customer preferences by using a flexible BOM [31] to deal with possible shortages when using MRP to plan the requirements of dependent demand items and an alternative BOM (ABOM) [32] to optimize the purchase quantity from suppliers, while they satisfy demand using specific characteristics from the TFT-LCD industry, such as the customer preferences for ABOM and the purchase quantity ratio.

On the other hand, standard MRP calculations are based on the dynamic multi-level capacitated lot-sizing problem (MLCLSP). Both production planning in the form of lot sizing problems and vehicle routing have attracted the scientific community's attention in recent decades and several literature reviews like [33–36], for capacitated production problems, and like [37–39], for VRP, among others, have been published.

However, to tackle these problems in an integrated way is not common in the literature despite the influence of transport activities on the performance of supply chains. In this sense, in the literature review by Mula et al. [40], any proposal is identified that simultaneously optimize transport and production planning beyond considering the costs and capacities associated with a limited transport resource without modeling its own characteristics such as shipment modes or associated restrictions. Moreover, the transportation planning aspects treated in combination of production planning problems in supply chains are related commonly to distribution activities. Boudia and Prins [41] propose a memetic algorithm which simultaneously deals with production and distribution decisions with the aim of minimizing total production setups, inventories and distribution costs. Bilgen [42] addresses the production and distribution planning problem in a supply chain system that involves the allocation of production volumes among the different manufacturing plants, and the delivery of the products to the distribution centers with an integrated optimization model. Jolai et al. [43] propose a multi-objective linear programming problem for integrating production–distribution, which is solved by applying a genetic algorithm, particle swarm optimization and a hybrid genetic algorithm. Readers are referred to [40, 44–46] for literature reviews about production-distribution planning. In relation to inbound logistics, Yung et al. [47] propose a tactical model which simultaneously determine, through a two-layer decomposition (TLD) method that combines several heuristics, the annual production quantity and lot size to be assigned to the suppliers, and the annual shipment amounts and order quantities from each supplier to individual destinations to meet their respective total demands at a minimum total cost. Moreover. Kuhn and Liske [48] present a static model, based on the Economic Lot Sizing Problem, which assumes an infinite time horizon and a common cycle policy to determine simultaneously production plans at manufacturing plants and vehicle routes from suppliers. To the best of our knowledge, there is no research work in the literature integrating production planning in a MRP system and transport planning for procurement from suppliers. Hence, in this paper we present a conceptual model, the MRP IV, which serves as a reference to develop new production technology and integrates material planning, production resource capacities and procurement transport decisions in the same decision-making system.

4 Conceptual Model for MRP IV

In this article, a conceptual model that addresses the planning problem explained in the previous section is presented. Our proposal, called MRP IV, integrates those aspects related to production planning and provisioning transport the same model. For this purpose, MRP IV contemplates various inputs (which could be considered in generic MRP and provisioning transport planning models) that generate different outputs to minimize total costs. Figure 1 illustrates the proposed model. Figure 1 includes the input parameters associated with MRP systems and transport decision-making processes. Those parameters which can be used simultaneously for aspects relating to both production and transport planning are presented as elongated rectangles overlapping both areas. The MRP IV inputs and outputs are described in Table 1 and Table 2, respectively.

Table 1. MRP IV inputs

MRP IV Inputs	
General inputs	Planning horizon which is divided into equal periods and with an equivalent extension to the suppliers' maximum lead time.
	Customer demand of the FGs to be produced
	Bill of Materials. It represents the list of subassemblies, PA and RM needed to manufacture a FG.
	Initial inventory and initial delayed demand of finished goods, PA and RM.
	Safety stocks of each finished good, PA and RM
	The supply lead time of each PA and RM as it is considered null for finished goods. It comprises the supplier production time, the transport time and the safety time.
	Programmed receptions for each PA and RM
Production system inputs	Function costs: variable production costs, inventory holding costs, delayed demand costs, undertime hour costs and overtime hour costs of productive resources and subcontracting costs.
	Production capacity of available productive resources
	Production time. This is the time required to produce each product with the available productive resources
	Setup time. It represents the capacity lost due to cleaning, machine adjustments, calibration, inspection, change in tooling, etc., when production for a new product starts
	Production batch size
Suppliers inputs	PA and RM dimensions
	Order lot size of each PA and RM. The quantities to order are multiple integers of this lot size, and it may, or may not, coincide with the production lot size, depending on the supplier's preferences.
Transport system inputs	Function costs: fixed per vehicle costs, variable costs according to occupied volume, costs for using extra transport capacity, costs incurred by urgent deliveries, etc.
	Transport capacity. This corresponds to the capacity of the transport network between the suppliers of PA and RM and the manufacturer of finished goods. This transport network is formed by the set of vehicles with different capabilities that logistics suppliers offer to the manufacturer and the conditions for their use regulated by means of contracts.

Table 1. (*continued*)

	Shipment modes. The shipment modes considered in this model are full truck load (FTL), milk-run and less than load (LTL). For each supplier of PA and RM different shipment modes can be selected depending on the volume of PA and RM to transport. FTL deliver large order sizes to the plant via either JIT or direct delivery. For milk-run, several medium-sized loads from suppliers are bundled and transported directly to the plant. With LTL, small orders are directed to a cross-docking point and consolidated into a single vehicle, which transports the PA and RM to the plant.
	Shipment frequency. This consists in the frequency of PA and RM arriving from different suppliers. This frequency influence on the inventory levels at the plant and on the size of shipments. For example, if the reception frequency is low, the orders received will be large, and therefore they will increase the inventory significantly. However, if the shipment frequency is high, the order sizes will be small and adjusted to the net requirements, thus the inventory on hand will be lower.
	Shipping units which are required for transporting PA and RM; for example, special containers, racks, pallets, etc.

Table 2. MRP IV Outputs

MRP IV Outputs
Master Production Schedule which specifies the quantity to produce of each finished good
Overtime and undertime hours of productive resources and subcontracting hours
Planned ordering of RM and PA, which specifies the quantities to order of each PA or RM to each supplier
Number of vehicles employed and routes for each shipping mode and the number of shipping units that each vehicle transports.
Inventory of FG, PA and RM, at the end of each planning period
Delayed demand at the end of each planning period

After obtaining the outputs for the MRP IV model, they have to be evaluated in terms of feasibility of solutions given. If outputs are infeasible, this may be due to causes relating to the production or transport system design. In this case, it is necessary to examine production and transport systems and specially their capacities, and to adjust them suitably before rerunning the MRP IV. Moreover, if outputs are feasible, it is necessary to economically evaluate the solution obtained in relation to the different costs associated with the model because they may not be acceptable from the financial, productive or logistic viewpoint even though they are feasible. Moreover, possible changes in the environment can imply the need to redesign the overall system or some of its parts so that the results obtained through the MRP IV model are valid. For this reason, MRP IV model should include a period that reviews the transport network and the production system.

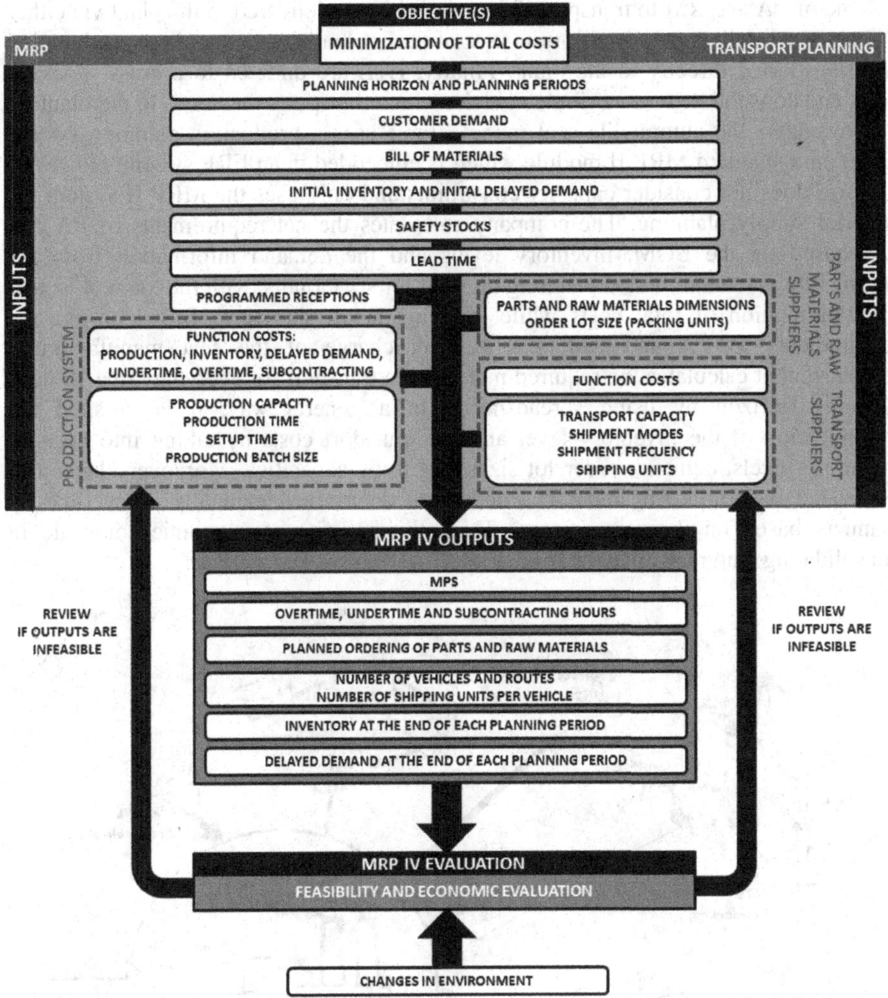

Fig. 1. Conceptual model for MRP IV

5 Application in an Automobile Seat Assembler

The proposal of the conceptual model for MRP IV is motivated by the problem of optimization of production planning and procurement transport in an automobile seat manufacturer. The company is an assembly plant for car seats belonging to a multinational group leader in the supply of seats in the automobile sector. In turn, the seat manufacturer has a broad base of suppliers that supply PA and RM manufacturing FG. These suppliers of PA and RM may be in the vicinity of the plant or be located a long distance. In both cases, the shipment modes may be different for each supplier depending on the order size of PA and RM. Figure 2 shows the different shipment modes depending on the thickness of the arrows, which represents the volume of PA and RM to transport. FTL are full loads delivered to the plant via either JIT or direct delivery. For milk-run, several partial loads from suppliers are bundled and transported directly to the plant. Finally, LTL are directed to a cross- docking point and consolidated into a single vehicle, which transports the goods to the plant.

Nowadays, the automobile seat manufacturer uses a production planning system based on a standard MRP II module which is embedded in an ERP system. However, the firm does not consider capacity constraints and only uses the MRP II system for material supply planning. The company calculates the net requirements of PA and RM based on the BOM, inventory levels and the demand information from the automobile assembler with a planning horizon for six months, with the main objective of minimization of total costs while avoiding stock shortages. Based on the net requirements of PA and RM, the staff in charge of the seat manufacturer's replenishment calculates the required materials to transport for every day in a 10 days planning horizon by using spreadsheets. In a general way, it is pursued the minimization of the inventory level and the transport costs by taking into account inventory levels, demand, order lot sizes and truck capacities. Moreover, the routes associated with milk-run and LTL modes are determined manually every time by planners based on their experience. Thus, the benefits of economies of scale in consolidating shipments may be lost.

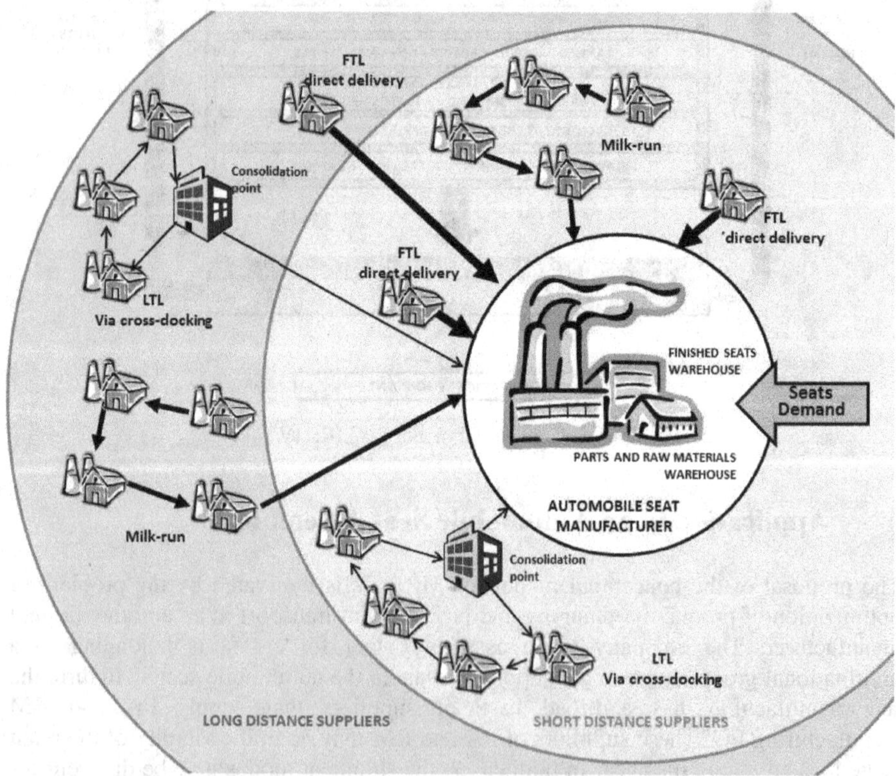

Fig. 2. Shipment modes from suppliers to seat manufacturer

Therefore, the MRP system is, mainly, used in the short-term as an inventory repository and the transport planning process may offer frequently sub-optimal results. Besides, due to restrictions imposed by transportation providers and high logistics costs, sometimes, production plans may be infeasible, so rescheduling is necessary to make them feasible. This example illustrates the potential use of our proposal in this real-world company. The calculations of the MRP IV should include jointly the inputs detailed in Figure 1, corresponding to the present production system, PA and RM and transport suppliers with the aim of getting realistic and feasible outputs for the short term related to integrated production and procurement transport plans.

6 Conclusions

In this paper, we propose a conceptual model, called MRP IV, in order to avoid the independent and sequential production and transport planning decision-making processes. MRP IV model acts as a reference to develop a new production technology which integrates transport planning and MRP systems in the same decision-making system. For this purpose, the main inputs and outputs of the MRP IV model have been identified. A forthcoming work is related to the modeling and solution approaches for the proposed conceptual model and the validation of the obtained solutions in real-world environments.

References

1. Orlicky, J.: Material Requirements Planning. McGraw-Hill, New York (1975)
2. White, O.W.: MRP II—Unlocking America's Productivity Potential. CBI Publishing, Boston (1981)
3. Schollaert, F.: Money resource planning, MRP-III: the ultimate marriage between business logistics and financial management information systems. Library Albert (1994)
4. Wylie, L.: ERP: A vision of the next-generation MRP II. Computer Integrated Manufacturing 300, 1–5 (1990)
5. Stadtler, H., Kilger, C.: Supply chain management and advanced planning: concepts, models, software and case studies. Springer, Berlin (2008)
6. Fleischmann, B.: Distribution and Transport Planning. In: Stadtler, H.Y., Kilger, C. (eds.) Supply Chain Management and Advanced Planning, pp. 229–244. Springer, Heidelberg (2005)
7. Karni, R.: Integer linear programming formulation of the material requirements planning problem. Journal of Optimization Theory and Applications 35, 217–230 (1981)
8. Billington, P.J., McClain, J.O., Thomas, L.J.: Mathematical programming approaches to capacity-constrained MRP systems: review, formulation and problem reduction. Management Science. 1126–1141 (1983)
9. Clark, A.R.: Optimization approximations for capacity constrained material requirements planning. International Journal of Production Economics 84, 115–131 (2003)
10. Yenisey, M.M.: A flow-network approach for equilibrium of material requirements planning. International Journal of Production Economics 102, 317–332 (2006)

11. Noori, S., Feylizadeh, M.R., Bagherpour, M., Zorriassatine, F., Parkin, R.M.: Optimization of material requirement planning by fuzzy multi-objective linear programming. Proceedings of the Institution of Mechanical Engineers, Part B: Journal of Engineering Manufacture 222, 887–900 (2008)
12. Tavakoli-Moghaddam, R., Bagherpour, M., Noora, A.A., Sassani, F.: Application of fuzzy lead time to a material requirement planning system. In: Proceedings of the 8th International Conference on Fuzzy Systems, vol. 8, pp. 208–213. World Scientific and Engineering Academy and Society (WSEAS) (2007)
13. Sun, L., Heragu, S.S., Chen, L., Spearman, M.L.: Simulation analysis of a multi-item MRP system based on factorial design. In: Proceedings of the Winter Simulation Conference (WSC), pp. 2107–2114. IEEE (2009)
14. Inderfurth, K.: How to protect against demand and yield risks in MRP systems. International Journal of Production Economics 121, 474–481 (2009)
15. Barba-Gutiérrez, Y., Adenso-Díaz, B.: Reverse MRP under uncertain and imprecise demand. The International Journal of Advanced Manufacturing Technology 40, 413–424 (2009)
16. Mula, J., Poler, R., Garcia, J.P.: MRP with flexible constraints: A fuzzy mathematical programming approach. Fuzzy Sets and Systems 157, 74–97 (2006)
17. Mula, J., Poler, R., Garcia-Sabater, J.P.: Material Requirement Planning with fuzzy constraints and fuzzy coefficients. Fuzzy Sets and Systems 158, 783–793 (2007)
18. Mula, J., Poler, R., Garcia-Sabater, J.P.: Capacity and material requirement planning modelling by comparing deterministic and fuzzy models. International Journal of Production Research 46, 5589–5606 (2008)
19. Mula, J., Poler, R.: Fuzzy Material Requirement Planning. In: Kahraman, C., Yavuz, M. (eds.) Production Engineering and Management under Fuzziness. STUDFUZZ, vol. 252, pp. 39–57. Springer, Heidelberg (2010)
20. Li, T., Lin, P., Sun, G.J., Liu, H.H.: Application of Fuzzy Programming with Recourse in Material Requirement Planning Problem. In: Proceedings of International Conference on Measuring Technology and Mechatronics Automation, pp. 546–549. IEEE (2009)
21. Hnaien, F., Dolgui, A., Ould Louly, M.A.: Planned lead time optimization in material requirement planning environment for multilevel production systems. Journal of Systems Science and Systems Engineering 17, 132–155 (2008)
22. Louly, M.A., Dolgui, A., Hnaien, F.: Optimal supply planning in MRP environments for assembly systems with random component procurement times. International Journal of Production Research 46, 5441–5467 (2008)
23. Louly, M.A., Dolgui, A.: Optimal time phasing and periodicity for MRP with POQ policy. International Journal of Production Economics 131, 76–86 (2011)
24. Mula, J., Poler, R., Garcia-Sabater, J.P., Lario, F.C.: Models for production planning under uncertainty: A review. International Journal of Production Economics 103, 271–285 (2006)
25. Dolgui, A., Prodhon, C.: Supply planning under uncertainties in MRP environments: A state of the art. Annual Reviews in Control 31, 269–279 (2007)
26. Wazed, M., Ahmed, S., Nukman, Y.: A review of manufacturing resources planning models under different uncertainties: state-of-the-art and future directions. South African Journal of Industrial Engineering 21(1), 17–33 (2010)
27. Kim, H.J., Lee, D.H., Xirouchakis, P.: Two-phase heuristic for disassembly scheduling with multiple product types and parts commonality. International Journal of Production Research 44, 195–212 (2006)

28. Gupta, S.M., Taleb, K.N.: Scheduling disassembly. International Journal of Production Research 32, 1857–1866 (1994)
29. DePuy, G.W., Usher, J.S., Walker, R.L., Taylor, G.D.: Production planning for remanufactured products. Production Planning and Control 18, 573–583 (2007)
30. Chen, Y., Miao, W.M., Lin, Z.Q., Chen, G.L.: Adjusting MRP for dynamic differentiation of identical items for process customisation. Production Planning and Control 19, 616–626 (2008)
31. Ram, B., Naghshineh-Pour, M.R., Yu, X.: Material requirements planning with flexible bills-of-material. International Journal of Production Research 44, 399–415 (2006)
32. Lin, J.T., Chen, T.L., Lin, Y.T.: Critical material planning for TFT-LCD production industry. International Journal of Production Economics 122, 639–655 (2009)
33. Karimi, B., Fatemi Ghomi, S.M.T., Wilson, J.M.: The capacitated lot sizing problem: a review of models and algorithms. Omega 31, 365–378 (2003)
34. Jans, R., Degraeve, Z.: Modeling industrial lot sizing problems: a review. International Journal of Production Research 46, 1619–1643 (2008)
35. Quadt, D., Kuhn, H.: Capacitated lot-sizing with extensions: a review. 4OR: A Quarterly Journal of Operations Research 6, 61–83 (2008)
36. Buschkühl, L., Sahling, F., Helber, S., Tempelmeier, H.: Dynamic capacitated lot-sizing problems: a classification and review of solution approaches. Or Spectrum 32, 231–261 (2010)
37. Laporte, G.: The vehicle routing problem: An overview of exact and approximate algorithms. European Journal of Operational Research 59, 345–358 (1992)
38. Toth, P., Vigo, D.: Models, relaxations and exact approaches for the capacitated vehicle routing problem. Discrete Applied Mathematics 123, 487–512 (2002)
39. Eksioglu, B., Vural, A.V., Reisman, A.: The vehicle routing problem: A taxonomic review. Computers & Industrial Engineering 57, 1472–1483 (2009)
40. Mula, J., Peidro, D., Díaz-Madroñero, M., Vicens, E.: Mathematical programming models for supply chain production and transport planning. European Journal of Operational Research 204, 377–390 (2010)
41. Boudia, M., Prins, C.: A memetic algorithm with dynamic population management for an integrated production–distribution problem. European Journal of Operational Research 195, 703–715 (2009)
42. Bilgen, B.: Application of fuzzy mathematical programming approach to the production allocation and distribution supply chain network problem. Expert Systems with Applications 37, 4488–4495 (2010)
43. Jolai, F., Razmi, J., Rostami, N.: A fuzzy goal programming and meta heuristic algorithms for solving integrated production: distribution planning problem. Central European Journal of Operations Research 19, 547–569 (2011)
44. Sarmiento, A.M., Nagi, R.: A review of integrated analysis of production-distribution systems. IIE Transactions 31, 1061–1074 (1999)
45. Erengüç, Ş.S., Simpson, N.C., Vakharia, A.J.: Integrated production/distribution planning in supply chains: An invited review. European Journal of Operational Research 115, 219–236 (1999)
46. Bilgen, B., Ozkarahan, I.: Strategic tactical and operational production-distribution models: a review. International Journal of Technology Management 28, 151–171 (2004)
47. Yung, K.L., Tang, J., Ip, A.W., Wang, D.: Heuristics for joint decisions in production, transportation, and order quantity. Transportation Science, 99–116 (2006)
48. Kuhn, H., Liske, T.: Simultaneous supply and production planning. International Journal of Production Research 49, 3795–3813 (2011)

Conceptualising the Mass Customisation Decision-Making Process in Collaborative Supply Chain Networks

Andrew C. Lyons, Jorge E. Hernández, Lucy Everington, and Dong Li

University of Liverpool Management School,
Chatham Street, Liverpool L69 7ZH, UK
{A.C.Lyons,J.E.Hernandez,L.Everington,dongli}@liverpool.ac.uk

Abstract. Mass customisation processes inevitably lead to complex environments where raw materials, modules and assemblies, finished goods and services are planned to meet the needs of individual customers by co-ordinating resources within and across organisational boundaries. Furthermore, collaborative approaches are necessary components of the process of managing mass customisation regimes and dampening the inherent complexities of mass customisation environments. These collaborative approaches are information-sharing processes that facilitate decision-making at every supply chain node. These nodes include product design, production planning, transport and logistics and resource management. Moreover, within small/medium companies, the information flows and requirements often change due to the high variability of customer requirements. A generic integrated view which considers the critical aspects of mass customisation is needed to support the necessary decision-making processes. These generic solutions will lead to a model that can be reused in different environments. In this paper, an example in the aerospace industry is given to illustrate the conceptualisation of the model in a small/medium company.

Keywords: Collaborative decision-making, mass customisation, framework supply chain networks, aerospace case study.

1 Introduction

Managing the supply chain network (SCN) has become a way of improving competitiveness by reducing uncertainty and enhancing customer service [10]. A supply chain network is a network of autonomous or semi-autonomous business entities involved, through upstream and downstream links, in the different processes and activities that produce goods or services to customers [12]. In this context, a SCN is composed of several autonomous or semi-autonomous business entities, in which each entity has the capability and capacity to take on certain types of tasks, according to its organisational roles in the network. These capabilities, capacities, and organisational roles can be modeled by individual-based models [13]. Moreover, it is possible to say that it is necessary (in a SCN) to consider collaborative approaches to solve conflicts between several decentralized functional units, because each unit tries to locally optimise its own objectives, rather than the overall SCN objectives [6].

J.E. Hernández et al. (Eds.): EWG-DSS 2011, LNBIP 121, pp. 26–41, 2012.

Hence, SCN´s are generally characterised by multiple products, several manufacturing sites and distribution warehouses, and a wide variety of operations, in which the product design and customisation decision-making are key topics. The production management in such networks, along with the uncertainty at the various levels of a SCN in terms of demand, processing, supply and transportation result in a high complexity in the management of material flows. A number of strategic planning and operational decisions should be made: (i) design and location of manufacturing sites, (ii) design of logistics systems, (iii) the appropriate inventory levels for components and finished products, (iv) the stocking policies, (v) the safety factors for each stock-keeping unit (SKU), (vi) the specification of customer service and performance priorities. [24].

Thereafter, this paper presents the conceptualisation of the mass customisation decision-making process for a particular collaborative SCN based on the REMPLANET INTERATED FRAMEWORK (RIF) which has been developed in the European REMPLANET project [17]. The conceptual model describes the ideal network structure, strategic considerations, operational considerations and information and decision flows. The purpose of this model is to allow companies to be cognisant of the ideal practices for their network type and how such practices can be achieved through collaborative initiatives. The conceptual model provides a route map for companies to 'move' from one collaborative strategy to another to support different customer and suppliers decision-making requirements that are associated with differing degrees of customisation in the SCN. Hence, an example from the aerospace industry is considered to illustrate the key customisation decisions in the network.

Thus, in order to present the subject matter related to this work, this paper is set out as follows. Firstly, the main concepts related to mass customisation decision making in SCN's are addressed. Secondly, the mass customisation decisions to support collaborative SCN are conceptualised to highlight the key MC decisions and their relationships within the network under a collaborative environment basis. Following this, the conceptual model and key parameters to support mass customisation in collaborative SCN's are defined based on (IRF) [17]. Following on from this, the model is used to conceptualise the collaborative decision-making for MC in the aerospace SCN industry. Finally, the conclusions and further research are presented.

2 Background

Supply chain management is becoming increasingly difficult due to the complexity of supporting the provision of products in increasingly demanding and volatile markets. Furthermore, the combination of globalisation and digitalisation have had a tremendous economic impact and have radically transformed the environment in which companies operate. Companies are responding to their customers even when the requirements are highly focused and personalised [10]. In such a scenario, the information flow among the SCN nodes must be pertinent, timely and robust. For instance, as established by Lyons et al. [14], information transparency allows information to be made accessible upstream in a SCN and helps to dampen the demand amplification which occurs when information is transmitted sequentially to lower-tier suppliers. Thereafter, the process in where fulfilling the specific requirements from specific customers will be commonly known as mass customisation (MC). In this context, the provision of customer specific products can be undertaken through MC, which is defined by Tseng et al. [20], as being concerned with the production of "customized products in order to meet individual customer's needs with mass production efficiency". Moreover, since MC implies not only the business process management from every specific order from every specific customer, but also implies the implementation of the proper information technologies to support the proper demand information flow, under an MC environment it is necessarily to encompass all of the different types of system requirements from the manufacturing operations within the SCN's environments. Hence, MC introduces a high number of variables including, small batch sizes, random order arrivals and a spread of due dates. Moreover, from the study undertaken by Tseng e al. [19], the definition of the product family architecture must consider meta-level design process integration in order to support MC. By considering this, product design optimisation for reusability and commonality can be achieved. This method, in order to minimise the variability or distortion of the demand, might also include the definition of the SCN decoupling point as the main buffer within the supply chain. In an MC environment, there are two different approaches that can be used in determining the position of the decoupling point. The strategic approach, which provides guidelines based on knowledge-based systems, and the conceptual models to define and select the decoupling points [8]. In this same context, Jiao and Tseng [9] establish that MC in the SCN should consider three customisability aspects. These aspects are oriented to support the intrinsic nature of product design, the economic latitude of (production) process variations due to product customisation and the value of customisation as perceived by the customers. This means that the design of the MC system implies the co-ordination of customer requirements, product characteristics, production processes, and logistics networks, in order to achieve rapid response to customer orders [5].

Da Silveira et al. [3] identified the following levels of product customisation : standardisation, usage, packaging and distribution, additional services, additional custom work, assembly, fabrication and design. It is important to highlight that the success of the mass customisation systems depends on a series of external and internal factors which justify the application of mass customisation as a competitive weapon. The principal six factors most commonly presented in the literature are as follows: (1) customer demand for variety and customisation must exist, (2) the market conditions must be appropriate, (3) the value chain should be ready, (4) appropriate technology must be available, (5) products should be customisable and (6) knowledge must be shared. By adopting such a MC approach, Potter et al. [15] established that the companies may be rewarded with a competitive advantage. However, this becomes difficult for the companies when a MC dynamic production environment is being considered or is present in the companies. Hence, as has been established by Poulin et al. [16], manufacturers need to develop capabilities to fulfil these personalisation requirements while still respecting price, quality and service constraints. This is an enormous challenge since there are many possible personalisation offers that a firm could propose, up to the extreme of delivering completely different products with no little overlap in terms of components to each client. As defined by Poulin et al. [16], Customisation/personalisation categories include the following issues: (1) Popularising; (2) Varietising; (3) Accessorising; (4) Parametering; (5) Tailoring; (6) Adjusting; (7)

Monitoring; (8) Collaborating. For highly personalised options, customers must be involved earlier in the manufacturing process and should expect higher prices and longer delivery times.

In addition, Tseng and Radke [21] considers that the MC promotes the notion that product configuration replaces the fixed set of specifications. Due to the many different configurations being influenced by an even wider variety of parameters the defining of the solution space becomes a complicated issue. This is particularly problematic in cases where the MC strategy is based on the definition of a unique product, where the decision processes are complex, due to a huge number of possible combinations of components [4]. The key MC decisions imply that customers may be involved with the conception of the product, with its design, and working with the designers to best meet the needs of the consumer, by also selecting the appropriate suppliers. Manufacturers can make decisions based on how they can best satisfy the level of customisation required through the use of their SCN [22]. Supplier selection, as studied by Chiu and Okudan [1], is required to evaluate the SCN performance at the conceptual design stage for MC. Based on this, it is possible to highlight the fact that, during the product design stage, the product functionalities are to be generated based on the customer requirements but, in addition, the main components from those products will be validated in terms of design by customers. This will produce bi-directional MC decision-making process attempting the collaboration between customer and suppliers in terms design and MC processes.

Thereafter, it is possible to highlight that MC needs to be addressed with a particular SCN case in order to understand and measure its behaviour. This will also influence the information flow and planning and control of the MC processes. Hence, every SCN tier must be identified and linked to its own decisions to support the MC process. The following section is oriented towards identifying the main MC decisions in the particular case of collaborative SCN's. Based on this, the main MC information and decision flows will be characterised from a generic point of view.

3 Mass Customisation Decisions in Collaborative Supply Chains

Based on Lambert and Cooper [2], the SCN configuration considers nodes such as supplier, manufacturer, distributor and customer. Decisions in collaborative supply chains are referred mainly to the information exchange process, thus every decision-maker, irrespective of the SCN tier to which it belongs, will consider the following information:

- **Suppliers**
  - *Transactional relationships with suppliers of rarely used parts.*
  - *Some parts needed at modification plant supplied directly by suppliers.*
  - *Close relationships with nearby suppliers for common components.*
- **Manufacturers**
  - *Order details and production schedules.*
  - *New product information, feedback and suggestions on new products.*
  - *Order information and order status info.*
  - *Order details and production schedules.*
  - *Delivery requests' pick up times, delivery receipts.*

- **Distributor**
  -The customer is viewed as a long term client. The customer may come to the factory for the design stage.
  -Distributor geared to rapidly deliver one of a kind products to customers' preferred location and to take products back to modification.
- **Customer**
  -Customers' needs and preferences, information on how the company can fulfil these needs.

An example of this kind of collaborative network can be seen in Figure 1. This type of network represents the case where the product is designed-to-order and is highly customised, with products for different customers only having small overlaps in terms of functionality, size and components. In addition, considering the main RIF definition, a collaborative SCN in term of the MC process can be seen as a full customisation SCN.

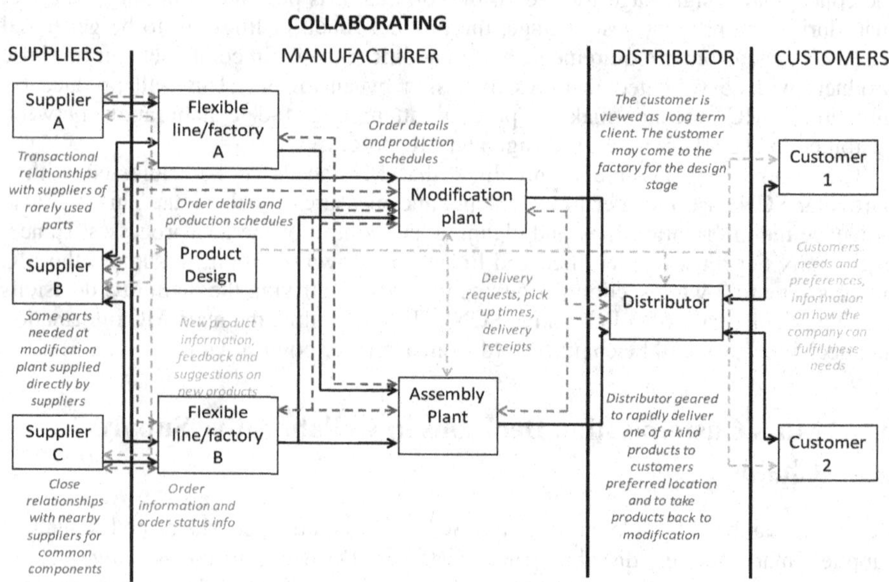

Fig. 1. Full customisation SCN (Source: REMPLANET [17])

From Figure 1, it is possible to highlight that the ability to meet the customers' functional needs will be an order winner as the products will be highly customised from suppliers and manufacturers. In this case quality may also be an order winner if the customer wants a higher standard of quality than is found in standard products or lower levels of customised products. Lead time is likely to be long, potentially over a year and the product will be designed with the customer in face-to-face meetings which may also involve input from suppliers of components. Price will be high and may be an order qualifier but is likely to be unimportant to a certain extent. This network uses the design-to-order principle which with product customisation being so high may involve the design of the product being completed collaboratively by all parties in the supply chain. Products will be made as one offs and thus done in a job shop type environment.

In this case, due to the wide range of products, processes and components, production planning and controls will need to be cognisant of the characteristics of the entire supply chain, an enterprise resource planning (ERP) may be required to integrate the different solutions from many perspectives in terms of supporting the decision-making in the SCN's. Thereafter, the methodology (Figure 2) to model the MC decision-making process in the SCN considers three main building blocks: the environment definition, the activities and actors, and the information and decision flow.

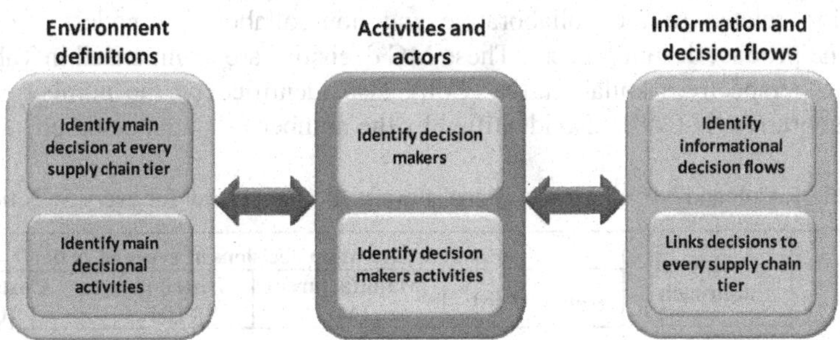

Fig. 2. Collaborative MC methodology in SCN. (Source: adapted from REMPLANET [17]).

Finally, for the MC decision flow, the information flows are likely to be aided by the customer and the manufacturer. However, the suppliers may also be involved. If the suppliers do not attend the relevant policy and communication meetings, information on planned projects will need to be communicated quickly to the suppliers to ensure they can produce the components needed and that this can be done within an acceptable time frame and price bracket.

3.1 Main Decision across the Collaborative Network at Every Decisional Level

The decision-making process related to the MC process in a collaborative SCN is concerned with the definition of those processes that are configured to obtain the relevant information to carry out a MC process. In order to support this, three decisional levels (DL) have been considered. The first one is the strategic level (DL-S) which is oriented to define the main goals and decisions acceptance ranges in order to promote validity of the information, constraints and the decision-making process. The second one is the tactical level (DL-T), which is oriented to promote the collaborative processes related to the MC process. In this context, these processes will consider the information that come from collaborative nodes and the information which belongs to the non-collaborative nodes. Finally, the operational level (DL-O) is oriented to support the decisional information relevant to the short term decision making. This level is mainly, related with the non-collaborative component of the MC process such as the firm orders sent by the non-collaborative nodes which commonly are supported by a forecasting process. Thereafter, at this level it will also be possible to identify the mains deviations of the forecasted orders which will be used as input information for the strategic and tactical levels.

Hence at the strategic level, it is possible to say that the main decisions are related to the definition of the strategic design plans. These plans define which information, customers, levels and finance matters will suit the MC process in the SCN best. Next, the tactical level considers mainly what to do with the result of the design information sharing process. In this case (with regard to the demand visibility) the forecasting process takes place at this decisional level. Moreover, the forecasting process, in order to promote collaboration among the SCN nodes, considers the demand plan as a key input that every SCN node is required to share and also the firm orders which, at the short term level, are collected from the non-collaborative nodes. Thereafter, the MC process (supported by the collaborative decision making-process) considers the main information related to the collaborative and non-collaborative nodes in order to support the product design process. These MC decisions are summarised in Table 1 in which the perspectives collaborative (Coll), also identified by the number "2" and non-collaborative (N-Coll), also identified by the number "1", are compared.

Table 1. Coll and N-Coll MC decisions at every decisional level for every SCN tier

Level	Decisional approach	Mass customisation decisions at every SCN tier			
		Supplier (S)	**Manufacturer (M)**	**Distributor (D)**	**Customer (C)**
	Strategic				
DL-S1	N-Coll	-Receiving orders management.			-Send firm orders.
DL-S2	Coll	-Receive orders and send back proposal. -Find collaborative customers	-Receive product design specifications and send proposals to its suppliers.	-Receive product design specifications and send proposals.	-Define the demand visibility to share. -Product design sharing process.
	Tactical				
DL-T1	N-Coll				-Send demand plans.
DL-T2	Coll	-Receive planned orders.	-Collaborative design planning.		
	Operative				
DL-O1	N-Coll	-Execute the process.	-Execute the process.	-Execute the process.	-Execute the process.
DL-O2	Coll	-Execute the process. -Collect information to support upper tier decision-making	-Execute the process. -Collect information to support upper tier decision-making	-Execute the process. -Collect information to support upper tier decision-making	-Execute the process. -Collect information to support upper tier decision-making

As can be seen in Table 1, there are functions to manage the processes related with the collaborative nodes and also with the non-collaborative nodes. In addition, it is possible to observe that the MC processes consider only the tactical and operational decisional levels for design planning and process execution. This is due to the fact that MC, under a collaborative network environment, will consider the best properties of both types of nodes (the collaborative and non-collaborative), and then the visibility related with mid-term information will support the MC decision-making process. This mid-term information should be related to the forecasting that the SCN considers. The demand planning function is one of the most critical functions and supports the decision-making process at almost every level. Hence, by considering these generic decisional aspects of MC in collaborative networks, the following section can conceptualise MC in collaborative networks under the IRF approach.

4 The Conceptual Model for Mass Customisation in Collaborative Supply Chain Networks

The conceptual model of MC in collaborative networks is based on the integrated REMPLANET framework (Figure 3) or IRF [17]. The IRF aims to establish clear linkages between organisational strategies, decision-making mechanisms, operational activities and the network responsiveness.

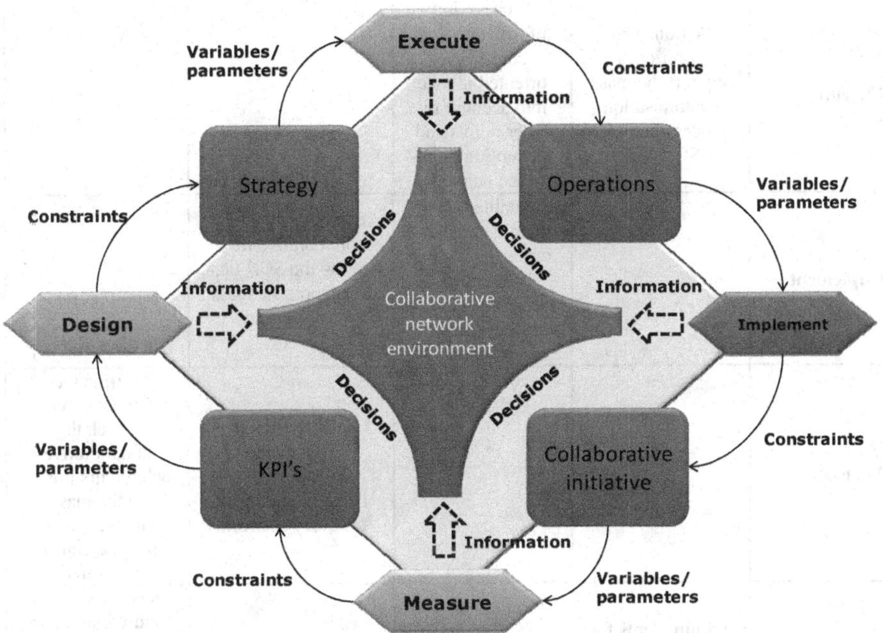

Fig. 3. IRF conceptual model for MC decisions in collaborative SCN

The four main blocks can define the IRF in the context of the main activities, information flow and network definitions. These blocks are as follows:

- **Strategy.** This is oriented to define the relevant strategic concepts for specific networks such as customisation level and type, sales channel, order qualifiers and order winners.
- **Operations.** In this block, the main operations' concepts for the specific network, including order fulfilment strategy, decoupling point, manufacturing processes and the scope of the process design are defined.

- **Collaborative initiatives.** The initiatives in this block, are essential to the success of this network and will support the network effectiveness and efficiency in the MC environment.
- **KPI's.** This block introduces the Key Performance Indicators (KPI) which are relevant to each specific network.

In addition, the main blocks will consider four main decisional activities which are oriented to support the information flow among the nodes in the collaborative network. These activities refer to the constraints and definitions of variables/parameters used to link the main blocks with every decision in the collaborative network such as: design, execute, implement and measure.

Table 2. MC comparative views for the decisions-making process in collaborative SCN

Mass customisation activity	Collaborative network building block			
	Strategy	Operations	Collaborative initiative	KPI's
Execute	Actions and definitions to support the mass customisation process in every SCN tier.	Process and information flow constraints oriented to take into account re-order points and decoupling points in the network.		
Implement		Establish the main parameters for the execution of the mass customisation process in the network.	Establish the main collaborative flow among the SCN tiers to support the mass customisation process.	
Measure			Characterisation of the main collaborative behaviour suitable for every network.	Define the dimensions in which the collaborative behaviours linked to the mass customisation process can be measured.
Design	Requirements for SCN information flow to support the mass customisation in the collaborative environment.			Key parameters and variables to measure the behaviour of the information for the mass customisation process in the collaborative network.

Under a decision-making approach for MC in collaborative networks, the decisional activities consider the following facts (Table 2). The design activity is oriented to give the main constraints for the strategy block and considers the main KPIs defined at the strategic decisional level. The executed activities consider all the inputs and outputs of every MC process in the collaborative network and define the main rules to support the MC decision- making process. The implemented activity takes into account the constraints defined in the execute activities in order to support the main operations linked to the MC process. Finally, the measure activities are concerned with the collation of different KPIs, the definition of their rank and the comparison of their application to different scenarios (collaborative and non-collaborative for instance). KPI's definition has been adapted from [7] and Related decisions are linked to what has been established in Table 1.

Table 3. Mass customisation decision in collaborative networks

Aspects	Strategy	KPI	Related decision
Reliability	Define robust MC strategies for different network types	SCN efficiency	DL-S1-M DL-S2-M DL-S1-C DL-S2-C DL-T2-M DL-T2-C
Responsiveness	Prepare the design process to support the demand variability	Lead times Back orders Delay on demand	DL-O1-S DL-O2-S DL-O1-M DL-O2-M
Flexibility	Design flexibility and quick response mechanism to avoid bullwhip effects	%Forecast error Products cycle Inventory level	DL-T1-S DL-T2-S DL-T1-M DL-T2-M DL-T1-C DL-T2-C
Cost and Financial	Ensure the right financial cycle time to maintain a continuous improvement	Managing costs Sales penalties	DL-S1-M DL-S2-M
Assets and Infrastructure	Strategies to support the customers demand	Performance assets	DL-S1-S DL-S2-S DL-S1-M DL-S2-M
Safety	Minimise the safety stocks at the supplier facilities	Inventory levels	DL-O1-S DL-O2-S
Environment	Generate a MC process considering the environmental constraints	Environmental measures	DL-S1-M DL-S2-M

Every decision might be measured in different ways (Table 3). In this context, the IRF has considered the work of Huang and Keskar [7] to classify the main KPIs appropriate to support the MC decision-making process in collaborative networks. This classification includes aspects such as reliability, responsiveness, flexibility, cost and finances, assets and infrastructure, safety and environment and is to be linked to the main decision definition from Table 1.

In addition, from Table 3 it is possible to conclude that the main IRF decisional elements have been covered within the KPI definitions. In addition, the approach of Huang and Keskar [7] leads the IRF in to a more robust measurement environment for MC decision making in collaborative networks. It is possible to highlight that those strategic MC decisions covers design matters of the MC process, while tactical and operational decisions are oriented to the planning and the optimisation processes, respectively. Hence, the IRF considers a generic-based orientation to define and model MC decisions at every decisional level in every SCN tier.

4.1 Main Implications for the Collaborative Networks in the Aerospace Industry

The supply network configuration, for one particular component or product, of the aerospace industry is shown in Fig. 4.The main SCN components consist of second and third tier suppliers which are normally SMEs, the integrator node as the first tier supplier and, the final customers, which are normally large companies who support the development of the final products. The second and third tier suppliers can be classified into four groups: Raw material (RM) suppliers, Machining companies (MachCop), Treatment (TM) companies and Service treatment companies or Subcontractors (Subcon). All of these suppliers have to be approved and controlled to meet aerospace standards. As Fig. 4 displays, both flows of information and material between these entities are been considered. Information flows, shown by the dotted lines, include the flow of request for quotation (RFQ) and the flow of purchase orders (PO).

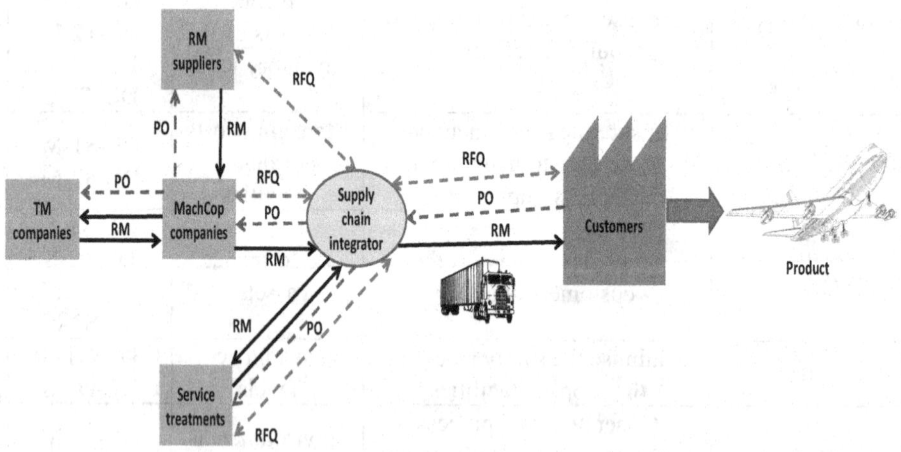

Fig. 4. Aerospace SCN (source: adapted from REMPLANET [17])

Material flow, represented by the solid arrows, occurs when the PO has been released. The process begins when a customer places a RFQ. The integrator then designs the route of each product and sends the RFQ to potential suppliers. Having received a quotation back from the suppliers, the integrator summarises all the information and sends it back to the customer. This two-way communication is represented by a double-headed arrow. After that, when repeat orders are placed with the integrator, the PO is released to a pre-defined MC supplier. It is the responsibility of the MachCop to acquire raw materials, machine parts and send parts to be heat treated. Finished parts are delivered to the integrator to be inspected. Then those parts are sent to be treated by a service treatment or subcontractors. Before dispatch to the customer, to ensure product conformity, final inspection is done by the integrator. The dispatch of goods to the customer is the responsibility of the transport service. When a customer is satisfied with the quote or is placing an existing order, they place a PO which triggers the order fulfilment process.

There are five main sub-processes involved in the order fulfilment process. It begins with the contract review in order to determine whether to accept the order. Secondly, there is the sales order processing (SOP) procedure after which the PO is released to chosen suppliers. After that, the Goods-in operations is undertaken to inspect parts and determine if the parts require a further subcontract operation. If they do, there will then be a subcontracting procedure. If not, the goods will be packed and dispatched to the customer.

4.2 Key Customisation Decision-Making Processes for Collaborative SCN Solutions

Customisation decision-making processes that support the collaboration in the network are related to the order management process. The process that a new order goes through before becoming an approved order is called the New Product Introduction process (NPI). Thereafter, the process will be extended from a standard order process (Fig. 5) to its collaborative or full customised perspective (Fig. 6). Then, NPI begins with the customers RF. Once satisfied with the quote, customers will release a PO. This is also called a FAIR PO since it requires the 'First Article Inspection Requirement (FAIR)' document to be submitted with the part.

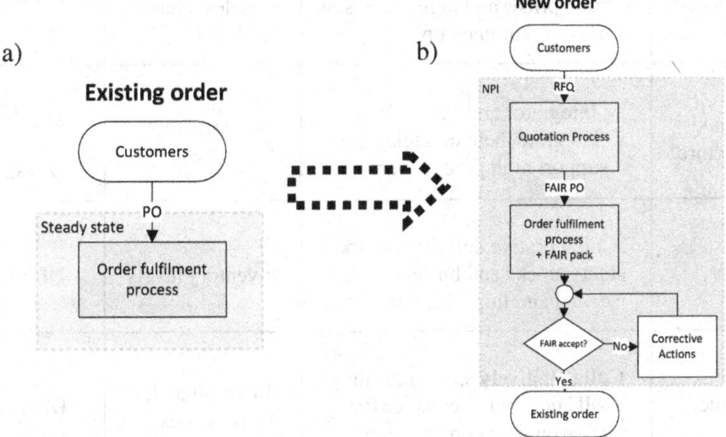

Fig. 5. Integration at the high level MC processes. a) Current process, b) collaborative solution. (source: REMPLANET [17])

The order fulfilment process includes the following five sub-processes: contract review, sales order processing (SOP), goods-in operations, subcontracting procedure and pack and dispatch. Once manufactured the FAIR batch is delivered to the customer. Once the FAIR batch is accepted then the next order of that type placed is considered to be an existing order. The main decision are addressed in Table 4.

Table 4. Mass customisation decision in SCN in the aerospace industry (adapted from [7])

Aspects	Strategy	KPI	Related decision
Reliability	Define robust information flow mechanism supporters to enhance the order fulfilment in lower SCN tiers	Order fulfilment rates	DL-S2-M DL-S2-C
Responsiveness	Customer and integrators increase demand visibility to their suppliers	Lead Times Delay on demand	DL-O2-M DL-O2-C
Flexibility	Customer and integrators share information to adjust their capacities and resources availabilities	Inventory levels	DL-T2-S DL-T2-M DL-T2-C
Cost and Financial	Total cost including product cost which is the total of RM, MC and Subcon prices and logistics cost is summed up	Penalties and sales rates	DL-S2-M
Assets and Infrastructure	Integrator and MC SME´s integrate their strategies to support high product variety	Performance assets	DL-S2-S DL-S2-M
Safety	Collaborative definition of the safety stocks and buffers for the second and third tier suppliers.	Inventory levels	DL-O2-S
Environment	Collaboratively share and study MC demand to enhance the environment contributions'.	Environmental measures	DL-S2-M

Table 4 shows the characterisation of the main decisions for MC in SCN in a collaborative environment. In the example aerospace SCN the decisions are based on the idea of enhancing the SCN performance as a whole. Related decisions such us MC SCN design, flexibility and responsiveness are meant to be collaborative decisions rather than individual decisions. In addition, in this environment the main decisions are to be centralised to the integrator node rather than decentralised. Within this, the integrator SCN node manages the order fulfilment within their suppliers.

5 Conclusions

The objective of identifying the MC decisions and allocating them within the collaborative SCN is not only to improve the accuracy of the physical material and information flows of the product design planning, but to also establish links between the internal and external information to improve the performance of supply chains. Thus, by studying MC decision making in collaborative environments, swift response to changes, reduction in inventories and, ultimately, improved service levels can be achieved. In this context, the decision-making model supports the identification of the main functions, information and constraints in terms of the MC process. The proposed model has been tested to a real aerospace SCN environment in which nodes related to this configuration are willing to collaborate to enhance their performance. Therefore, it is possible to identify the main decisions at any decisional level in order to consider the impact at any decisional centre of the decision-making model. In future research, the proposed model will be applied to different SME SCNs by considering different SCN types and their demand data and constraints. Standard frameworks such as Zachman, ToGAF, SCOR, etc will support further domain modelling processes and studies.. In addition, further simulation models supported by discrete-event based models, multi-agent systems and linear programming models will be considered in order to be included in the integrated REMPLANET framework [17]. In addition, it is expected that after more validations coming from this conceptual model, more accurate conceptualisations from the mass customisation process in collaborative SCN will be given in where the proposed model will be compared with other collaborative decision-making models.

Acknowledgments. The research leading to these results has received funding from the European Community's Seventh Framework Programme (FP7/2007-2013) under grant agreement n° NMP2-SL-2009-229333. Authors also would like to thank all the FP7 WP leaders and Companies stakeholders how has supported this study within their knowledge and useful recommendations.

References

1. Chiu, M., Okudan, G.: An Integrative Methodology for Product and Supply Chain Design Decisions at the Product Design Stage. Journal of Mechanical Design 133, 1–15 (2011)
2. Lambert, D.M., Cooper, M.C.: Issues in Supply Chain Management. Industrial Marketing Management 29(1), 65–83 (2000)

3. Da Silveira, G., Borenstein, D., Fogliatto, F.S.: Mass customization: Literature review and research directions. International Journal of Production Economics 72, 1–13 (2001)
4. Frutos, J.D., Santos, E.R., Borenstein, D.: Decision Support System for Product Configuration in Mass Customization Environments. Concurrent Engineering – Research and Applications 12(2), 131–144 (2004)
5. Helo, P.T., Xu, Q.L., Kyllonen, S.J., Jiao, R.J.: Integrated Vehicle Configuration System–Connecting the domains of mass customization. Computers in Industry 61(1), 44–52 (2010)
6. Hernández, J.E., Poler, R., Mula, J., Lario, F.C.: The Reverse Logistic Process of an Automobile Supply Chain Network Supported by a Collaborative Decision-Making Model. Group Decision and Negotiation Journal 20(1), 79–114 (2011)
7. Huang, S.H., Keskar, H.: Comprehensive and configurable metrics for supplier selection. International Journal of Production Economics 105(2), 510–523 (2007)
8. Jeong, I.: A dynamic model for the optimization of decoupling point and production planning in a supply chain. International Journal of Production Economics 131(2), 561–567 (2011)
9. Jiao, J., Tseng, M.: Customizability analysis in design for mass customization. Computer-Aided Design 36(8), 745–757 (2004)
10. Labarthe, O., Espinasse, B., Ferrarini, A., Montreuil, B.T.: Toward a methodological framework for agent-based modelling and simulation of supply chains in a mass customization context. Simulation Modelling Practice and Theory 15(2), 113–136 (2007)
11. Lau, H.C.W., Lee, W.B.: On a responsive supply chain information system. International Journal of Physical Distribution & Logistics Management 30(7-8), 598–610 (2000)
12. Lin, F., Shaw, F.J.: Reengineering the Order Fulfillment Process in Supply Chain Networks. The International Journal of Flexible Manufacturing Systems 10, 197–229 (1998)
13. Lin, F., Tan, G.W., Shaw, M.J.: Modeling Supply-Chain Networks by a Multi-Agent System. In: Thirty-First Annual Hawaii International Conference on System Sciences, HICSS, vol. 5, p. 105 (1998)
14. Lyons, A.C., Coronado-Mondragon, A.E., Bremang, A., Kehoe, D.F., Coleman, J.: Prototyping an information system's requirements architecture for customer-driven, supply-chain operations. International Journal of Production Research 43(20), 4289–4320 (2005)
15. Potter, A., Breite, R., Naim, M., Vanharanta, H.: The potential for achieving mass customization in primary production supply chains via a unified taxonomy. Production Planning & Control 15(4), 472–481 (2004)
16. Poulin, M., Montreuil, B., Martel, A.: Implications of personalization offers on demand and supply network design: A case from the golf club industry. European Journal of Operational Research 169(3), 996–1009 (2006)
17. REMPLANET, WP3, Integrated REMPLANET framework (2012), `http://www.remplanet.eu` (reviewed on February 11, 2012)
18. Selladurai, R.S.: Mass customization in operations management: oxymoron or reality? Omega 32(4), 295–300 (2004)
19. Tseng, M.M., Jiao, J., Merchant, M.E.: Design for Mass Customization. CIRP Annals - Manufacturing Technology 45(1), 153–156 (1996)
20. Tseng, M.M., Lei, M., Su, C., Merchant, M.E.: A Collaborative Control System for Mass Customization Manufacturing. CIRP Annals - Manufacturing Technology 46(1), 373–376 (1997)

21. Tseng, M.M., Radke, A.M.: Production Planning and Control for Mass Customization – A Review of Enabling Technologies. In: Mass Customization. Springer Series in Advanced Manufacturing, Part III, pp. 195–218. Springer (2011)
22. Senanayake, M.M., Little, T.J.: Mass customization: points and extent of apparel customization. Journal of Fashion Marketing and Management 14(2), 282–299 (2010)
23. Seuring, S.: The product-relationship-matrix as framework for strategic supply chain design based on operations theory. International Journal of Production Economics 120(1), 221–232 (2009)
24. Srinivasan, M., Moon, Y.B.: A comprehensive clustering algorithm for strategic analysis of supply chain networks. Computers & Industrial Engineering 36(3), 615–633 (1999)

Combining FDSS and Simulation to Improve Supply Chain Resilience

Isabel L. Nunes[1,2,*], Sara Figueira[3], and V. Cruz Machado[1,3]

[1] Departamento Engenharia Mecânica e Industrial, Faculdade de Ciências e Tecnologia / Universidade Nova de Lisboa, Campus de Caparica, 2829-516 Caparica, Portugal
[2] Centro de Tecnologia e Sistemas, UNINOVA, 2829-516 Caparica, Portugal
[3] UNIDEMI, Campus de Caparica, 2829-516 Caparica, Portugal
{imn,ssf15698,vcm}@fct.unl.pt

Abstract. This work presents an application of the Supply Chain Disturbance Management Fuzzy Decision Support System designed to support decision-making processes aimed at improving the performance/resilience of Supply Chains. The Fuzzy Decision Support System analyses the effects of Supply Chain disturbances and the effects of implementing mitigation (proactive) and/or contingency (reactive) plans set to counter such disturbances, reducing their negative impacts. This paper illustrates the application of the Fuzzy Decision Support System in real life support of Supply Chain management using an academic case study where four scenarios related with an automotive Supply Chain are presented. The analysis of the *Performance Index* of each Supply Chain entity and the analysis of the *Supply Chain Performance Index* allow the selection of the operational policy whose implementation ensures best Supply Chain resilience.

Keywords: Fuzzy Decision Support System, Supply Chain Disturbances Management, Mitigation plan, Contingency plan, Performance Index.

1 Introduction

A supply chain disturbance (SCD) can result from acts or events that are originated inside of the Supply Chain (SC) (e.g., supplier failures, equipment breakdown, employees' absenteeism) or may result from extrinsic events (e.g., social turmoil, terrorist attacks, or acts of God such as volcanic eruptions, hurricanes or earthquakes) [1]. The likelihood of occurrence of a SCD is enhanced nowadays by the increased use of outsourcing of manufacturing and R&D, globalization, reduction of supplier base, more integrated processes between companies, reduced buffers, increased demand for on-time deliveries in shorter time windows and shorter lead times or shorter production life cycles [2].

Although a specific disturbance may occur in one entity of the SC, the interdependencies of the various entities in the network often cause the propagation of the disturbance along the SC, which will probably result in unfulfilled customers' orders.

* Corresponding author.

J.E. Hernández et al. (Eds.): EWG-DSS 2011, LNBIP 121, pp. 42–58, 2012.

Thus, SC should be as resilient as possible to potential disturbances, because any disturbance can have long-term negative effects on companies' financial performance [3]. Resilience is the ability of a system to return to its original or desired state, after being disturbed [4]. To achieve this objective it is crucial the selection and implementation of adequate operational policies, namely mitigation or contingency plans to counter the effects of disturbances [5].

Companies are not limited to choosing a single measure, and in many circumstances a combination of measures might be the appropriate strategy. However, implementation of mitigation and contingency plans is not free. Therefore passive disturbance acceptance may be appropriate in certain circumstances [6].

The integration of modelling and simulation functionalities in a Decision Support System (DSS) is an adequate approach to deal with the SC disturbances management activities. DSS are interactive computer-based information systems whose objective is to assist decision-makers in using data and models to solve unstructured problems [7]. A DSS supports business or organizational activities [8].

Therefore, the purpose of this paper is to discuss the analysis of the effects of SC disturbances and of the implementation of mitigation and/or contingency plans to reduce the negative impacts of the disturbances, using a Fuzzy Decision Support System (FDSS), named Supply Chain Disturbance Management Fuzzy Decision Support System (SCDM FDSS). The SCDM FDSS was applied to study the improvement of the resilience of an automotive SC. Due to confidentiality clauses agreed with the automotive SC a portion of the original study was adapted as a case study used for academic purposes. The case study SC is composed by the focal firm, two 1st tier suppliers and three 2nd tier suppliers. The case study objectives are, first, to analyze the effects of disturbances in entities of the SC and their propagation throughout the SC; and, second, to support the decision-making process in the selection of the most adequate operational policies that counter disturbances in complex SC.

The FDSS operates laying on two main pillars, one is the use of Fuzzy Set Theory (FST) to model the uncertainty associated with the disturbances and their effects on the SC; the other is the use of computer simulation to study the behaviour of the SC subject to disturbances, and the effects resulting from the implementation of mitigation or contingency plans. For this latter purpose the system uses discrete-event simulations performed by the ARENA software, which is a commercial simulation tool. ARENA integrates the SCOR methodology [9], [10], [11]. FST [12] provides appropriate logical/mathematical tools to deal with and represent knowledge and data, which are uncertain, complex, imprecise, vague, incomplete or subjective.

The use of the SCDM FDSS in real life environments helps the information sharing and the situational awareness among the entities of a SC, improving their collaboration and contributing to the resilience of the SC.

The paper is organized as follows: after this introduction, in the second section the SCDM FDSS model is described with focus on the inference process. The third section presents the case study and describes the different scenarios that were simulated using ARENA. A fourth section presents the results and discusses the FDSS application. At the end of the paper, some conclusions are drawn from the presented work.

2 Fuzzy Decision Support System Model

The SCDM FDSS was designed to assess SC and organizations based on their performance considering different scenarios (e.g. normal, when a disturbance occurs and when mitigation and/or contingency plans are implemented). The aim of the FDSS is to assist managers in their decision process related with the choice of the best operational policy (e.g., adoption of mitigation and/or contingency plans) to counter disturbance effects that can compromise SC performance.

To make this possible the following basic requirements were settled [13]:

1. The system must offer decision support, at managerial level, on how to improve the performance/resilience of a SC, considering alternative operational policies;
2. The system must be adaptable to different SC configurations;
3. The system must provide means for users to:
   a. assess estimates of the impact of a disturbance in the SC performance at SC entity and global levels. This is done through the analysis of a *Performance Index* (PI) for each SC entity and the analysis of the *Supply Chain Performance Index* (SCPI) derived from key performance indicators (KPI);
   b. assess estimates of the impact of the adoption of alternative operational policies that counter SC disturbances;
   c. rank the merit of alternative operational policies by comparing their PI and SCPI;
4. The system must able to model uncertainties inherent to the SC and to the disturbances;
5. The system must present high usability standards, allowing its easy exploitation by users that are not experts in simulation tools, namely through the use of natural language in user interfaces.

The block diagram of the proposed SCDM FDSS is illustrated in Fig. 1 [13].

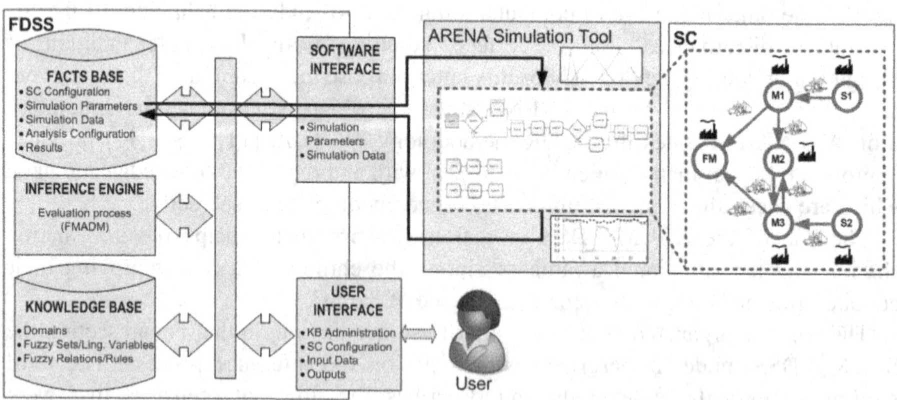

Fig. 1. Schematic of relationship between SCDM FDSS and ARENA (adapted from [13])

The FDSS has the four basic blocks that are common to any DSS (i.e., Knowledge Base, Inference Engine, Facts Base and User Interface) and a fifth block, the Software Interface, which provides for the necessary interface between the FDSS and the simulation tool (ARENA software):

- Knowledge Base – contains the necessary knowledge elements about the domains (e.g., disturbance types, operational policies, KPI), and the elements that are required for the inference process (e.g., fuzzy sets, linguistic variables, fuzzy relations);
- Inference Engine – runs an inference process that offers the reasoning capability of the system. It performs the FDSS analysis using a Fuzzy Multiple Attribute Decision Making (FMADM) model, and fuzzy data that characterizes the analyzed situation (e.g., fuzzified KPI);
- Facts Base – stores the user inputs (e.g., SC configuration, disturbance data, selection of operational policies, simulation parameters) and results from simulations;
- User Interface – by plugging to the Knowledge Base offers the user a set of options for configuration of the SC and of the analysis (e.g., disturbance types, disturbance levels, alternative operational policies). The results of the analysis (i.e., performance indexes) are presented to the user in the User Interface;
- Software Interface – provides the necessary interface between the SCDM FDSS and ARENA. When a simulation is required the Simulation Parameters related with a specific scenario (e.g., SC disturbance, implementation of a mitigation plan) are sent to the Simulation Tool on an adequate format through the Software Interface. As the simulation ends the Simulation Data are returned to the SCDM FDSS through the Software Interface and stored in the Facts Base.

To represent the SC processes the ARENA simulation software based on the SCOR model was used [11]. This model involves three types of participants – Costumers, Manufactures and Suppliers – each one with its set of processes – Source, Production and Delivery. The behaviour of the SC was simulated with Arena using injects that reflect a chronological sequence of events, some of them corresponding to disturbances. Each simulation comprises a warm-up-period followed by a steady-state period. The discrete time data (i.e., the data send to the SCDM FDSS) are collected during the steady-state period.

Despite this paper describes a specific setting of the SCDM FDSS in terms of analysis model and the interface with ARENA simulation software, the adoption of a fuzzy approach for developing the decision support system introduces a high degree of flexibility for the configuration and evolution of the analysis model. In fact, Fuzzy Set Theory is a generalization of Classical Set Theory, which means that a fuzzy model can integrate or combine meta-heuristic approaches with classical approaches (e.g. stochastic models). Therefore the SCDM FDSS can accommodate different analysis methodologies and tools in the inference process, and interface with different simulation tools offering alternative simulation techniques.

2.1 Inference Process

In the SCDM FDSS, the inference process was designed to assess SC based on its performance. The assessment includes the evaluation of SC performance considering different scenarios, the ranking of the different solutions, and their classification according to some defined criteria. Based on this assessment, a recommendation about an advisable line of action can be offered, for instance, the implementation of a specific type of mitigation or contingency plan. The inference process includes 7 steps [13]:

1 - *Computing the KPI for each scenario and SC entity for each discrete simulation time period.* The KPI are obtained in the end of each ARENA SC simulation. The KPI expressions and the description of the same expressions are presented in Table 1;

2 - *Synthesizing the time discrete KPI into an equivalent KPI for the relevant period considered.* The equivalent KPI is obtained through the mean function;

3 - *Fuzzifying the equivalent KPI into a fuzzy KPI (FKPI).* Fuzzy sets convert KPI in normalized FKPI, i.e., fuzzy values in the interval [0, 1], where a fuzzy value close to 0 means a bad performance and a fuzzy value close to 1 means a good performance. The most adequate fuzzy sets for the fuzzification of the KPI are Z-shaped, S-shaped and trapezoidal. The fuzzification is done using a parametrically defined membership function *membf* that converts data input values (x) in membership degree $\mu(x)$ (adapted from [14]). The parameters are specified according to the following expression:

$$\mu(x) = membf(x, minr, maxr, maxf, minf, linear) \tag{1}$$

where:

minr – rise minimum: abscissa value where a section of a membership function curve stops being 0, starting to rise up to 1;

maxr – rise maximum: abscissa value where a rising section of a membership function curve reaches the value 1;

maxf – fall maximum: abscissa value where a section of a membership function curve stops being 1, starting to fall dawn to 0;

minf – fall minimum: abscissa value where a falling section of a membership function curve reaches the value 0;

linear – parameter that indicates if the membership function is of a linear (1) or quadratic (0) type.

The definition of the parameters *minr, maxr, maxf,* and *minf* for specific fuzzy sets is customized for each SC entity in decision meeting with management and their value can be adjust to the evolution of the organization's objectives.

4 - *Computing of a fuzzy performance Category Indicator (CI)* for each scenario and SC entity using weighted aggregations of FKPI, through the following expression:

$$\mathrm{CI}_{ik} = \sum_{j=1}^{n} w_{ijk} \times \mathrm{FKPI}_{ijk} \tag{2}$$

where:

CI_{ik} – is the fuzzy performance *Category Indicator* for i^{th} category of KPI and for k^{th} SC entity;

FKPI_{ijk} – is the jth *Fuzzy Key Performance Indicator* of the ith category of KPI and the kth SC entity;

w_{ijk} – is the weight of jth Fuzzy Key Performance Indicator of the ith category of KPI and the kth SC entity.

Table 1. Key Performance Indicators' expressions

Key Performance Indicator	Expression
1) Order Fulfilment Rate	$OFR(t) = 1 - \frac{[a(t) - b(t)] - [c(t) - d(t)] + e(t)}{f(t) - b(t)}$
Description: - Percentage of orders delivered on time - The anticipated orders are not considered, only the delayed orders - $a(t)$ is the sum of the orders with delivery time equal to t - $b(t)$ is the sum of the anticipated orders with delivery time equal to t	- $c(t)$ is the sum of the orders delivered in t - $d(t)$ is the sum of the orders with delivery time greater than t - $e(t)$ is the sum of delayed orders delivered in t - $f(t)$ is the sum of the orders with delivery time smaller or equal to t
2) Mean Lead Time	$MLT(t) = T1(t) + T2(t) + T3(t) + T4(t)$
Description: sum of average production (T1), warehousing (T2), release (T3), and delivery (T4) cycle times	
2.1) Average production cycle time	$T1(t) = \frac{\sum Start\ build\ data(t) - \sum Order\ receipt\ data(t)}{Number\ of\ total\ orders(t)}$
Description: Average time between order reception and beginning of production	
2.2) Average warehousing cycle time	$T2(t) = \frac{\sum Finished\ goods\ inventory\ data(t) - \sum Start\ build\ data(t)}{Number\ of\ total\ orders(t)}$
Description: Average time between beginning of production and warehousing	
2.3) Average release cycle time	$T3(t) = \frac{\sum Release\ for\ delivery\ data(t) - \sum Finished\ goods\ inventory\ data(t)}{Number\ of\ total\ orders(t)}$
Description: Average time between warehousing and release to delivery	
2.4) Average delivery cycle time	$T4(t) = \frac{\sum Delivery\ at\ customer\ site\ data(t) - \sum Release\ for\ delivery\ data(t)}{Number\ of\ total\ orders(t)}$
Description: Average time between release to delivery and delivery to customer	
3) Total Production Cost	$TPC(t) = [MCost(t) \times PQ(t)]) + IPCost(t) + PTCost(t) + PCost(t) + SPCost(t)$
Description: Includes the material cost used in the production (MCost) multiplied by the production quantity (PQ) and the operational costs of all production resources (IP – issue product, PT – produce and test, P – package, SP – stage product)	
4) Total Inventory Value	$TI(t) = RM(t) + WIP(t) + FGI(t)$
Description: Includes the raw material stock value (RM), the work-in-process stock value (WIP) and the finished goods inventory stock value (FGI)	
4.1) Raw Material Value	$RM(t) = Number\ of\ RM\ units(t) \times RM\ unit\ cost(t)$
Description: Stock value of raw material	
4.2) Material in Process Value	$WIP(t) = Number\ of\ WIP\ units(t) \times WIP\ unit\ cost(t)$
Description: Stock value of material in process	
4.3) Finished Goods Value	$FGI(t) = Number\ of\ FGI\ units(t) \times FGI\ unit\ cost(t)$
Description: Stock value of finished goods	
5) Transportation Cost	$TCost(t) = \frac{Delivery\ Time(t) \times Delivery\ Cost(t)}{Lot\ Size(t)}$
Description: Transportation Cost	

5 - *Computing of a fuzzy Performance Index (PI)* for each scenario and SC entity using a weighted aggregation of CI, using the following expression:

$$\mathrm{PI}_k = \sum_{i=1}^{m} w_{ik} \times \mathrm{CI}_{ik} \quad (3)$$

where:

PI_k – is the *Performance Index* of kth SC entity for the current scenario;
CI_{ik} – is the fuzzy performance *Category Indicator* for i^{th} category of KPI and for k^{th} SC entity;
w_{ik} – is the weight of the ith category of KPI and the kth SC entity.

6 - *Computing of a fuzzy Supply Chain Performance Index (SCPI)* for each scenario using a weighted aggregation of PI, using the following expression:

$$\mathrm{SCPI} = \sum_{k=1}^{p} w_k \times \mathrm{PI}_k \quad (4)$$

where:

SCPI – is the *Supply Chain Performance Index* of the SC for the current scenario;
PI_k – is the *Performance Index* of kth SC entity for the current scenario;
w_k – is the weight of the kth SC entity.

7 – *Ranking alternatives*. Scenario results for each entity and for the SC are ranked based on their PI and SCPI, respectively, in order to identify the operational policy with more merit.

3 Case Study

3.1 Characterization of the SC

Recent news reported that an industrial accident in a member of a foreign automotive SC affected the production activity forcing a stoppage of approximately 5 days. Considering this event, the management of a national automotive SC decided to study if the mitigation plan that is already implemented would be effective if a similar situation occurred in their installations and to test alternative operational policies. The SCDM FDSS was used to help choosing the best policy to face disturbance effects in the SC. The SC analyzed in this study, which is illustrated in Fig. 2, corresponds to part of an automotive SC, and the case study addressed in this paper focuses in entities SU2 and M3.

The SC is constituted by the Final Manufacturer (FM), Manufacturers 1 and 3 (M1 and M3) which correspond to the 1st tier suppliers, and Suppliers 1 and 2 and Manufacturer 2 (SU1, SU2 and M2), the 2nd tier suppliers.

The material flow within the SC is illustrated in Fig. 2 and complementary information is presented in Table 2.

FM orders ten units of products 1 and 2 with a two hour periodicity to M1 and M3. FM has a JIT production policy. Therefore the 1st tier suppliers are located in the same industrial area. On the other hand, M1 has one supplier (SU1) located in a different location and the material transportation takes, on average, six hours. M1 orders product 3 and product 4 once a week to SU1, delivering product 1 to FM four times a day and product 5 to M2 once a day. M3 orders product 6 once a day to SU2 outsourcing its production to M2, i.e. M3 daily forwards product 6 to M2. In turn, M2 orders product 5 to M1 once a day and then combines it with product 6 to manufacturer product 7. M3 also orders product 7 to M2 once a day, delivering product 2 to FM four times a day. M3 has one supplier (SU2), which is not co-located with him and materials transportation takes about 5.5 hours to get to M3.

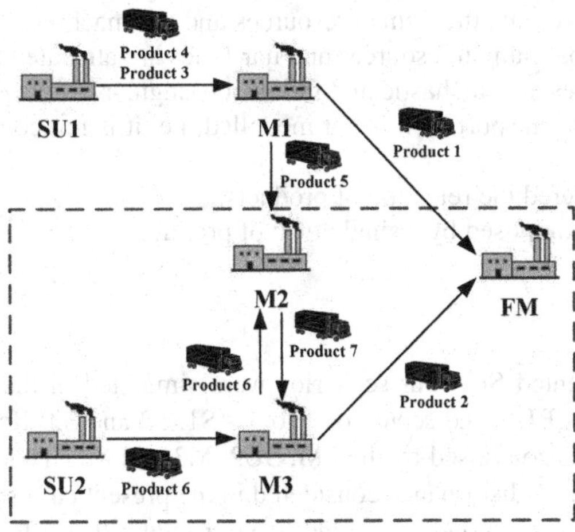

Fig. 2. Schematic of the Supply Chain

Table 2. Characteristics of the SC entities

Entity	Product	Promised Lead Time	Customer Demand (units/day)	Transportation Time (hours)	Safety Stock (days)
M1	1	2 hours	40	About 0.5	3
	5	1 day	80	About 0.5	3
M2	7	1 day	80	About 0.5	1
M3	2	2 hours	40	About 0.5	3
	6	1 day	80	About 0.5	3
SU1	3	2 days	40	About 6	0
	4	3 days	80	About 6	
SU2	6	2 days	80	About 5.5	0

The assumptions made to manage the ARENA simulation complexity were the following:

- There is an independent relationship between the model and the FM behaviour, which means that FM waits for a delivery even when a rupture of stock exists on the supply;
- FM demand is not affected by SC performance;

- Orders are scheduled to production and to delivery using a FIFO (first in, first out) rule;
- Production planning is ruled by a make-to-order policy;
- Materials sourcing follow a policy of periodic revision;
- FM only has the Source process. It only places and receives orders from his suppliers;
- SU1 and SU2 do not have the Source process, because they have stock on hand to satisfy their customer's orders;
- Process costs are proportional to the corresponding resource time;
- A resource represents the human resources and the machines. The resources time includes the time that human resources and machines are allocated to a process;
- Processing times are stochastic and follow a triangular distribution;
- Return time of transportation is not modelled, i.e. it is not considered the reverse flow of materials;
- It is not considered the rejection of products;
- Each order is composed by a single type of product.

3.2 Scenarios

Based on the presented SC, four scenarios were simulated in the ARENA software (baseline scenario – BL – and scenarios 1 to 3 – S1, S2 and S3). In Fig. 2 a sub-SC is underlined, which is composed by the FM, SU2, M3 and M2. This sub-SC groups the SC entities affected by disturbance considered in the present case study.

The disturbance corresponds to an industrial accident that affects SU2 production process (scenario 1 - S1). The industrial accident renders the facilities inoperative for about 5 days and the production stops during this time. After this period the production resumes its activity and the delayed orders are the first to be produced. In this scenario it is expected that SU2 will not be able to deliver product 6 to M3 during the production stoppage. This will have an effect in M3 deliveries to M2 and consequently in M3 deliveries to the FM.

S2 tests an alternative operational policy assuming that the one which is currently in place (i.e. existence of safety stock) does not exist. This scenario considers the same disturbance as S1 and the implementation of a contingency plan four hours after the occurrence of the industrial accident. The contingency plan consists of increasing the production volume in another factory belonging to the same company group of SU2. The alternative manufacturer takes the same time to produce one unit as SU2. However, since it is located in a different geographic area, the transportation time is higher. As in S1, when the production resumes the delayed orders are the first to be manufactured. The implementation of the contingency plan has costs. These costs are associated with the increase of the production volume in the alternative manufacturer, the utilization of resources that enable this increase, and with the use of a different transportation company. Although these costs are associated with the production and transportation activities of the factory group, they are imputed to SC entity that suffers the disturbance (SU2). It can be anticipated that, in this scenario, SU2 will be able to make deliveries to M3, and thus, the disturbance effects will not be propagated through the SC. On the other hand, SU2 transportation and production costs will increase.

In S3 the disturbance occurs and a mitigation plan is implemented by the client (M3) of the SC entity that is affected by the disturbance (SU2). This mitigation plan is twofold: (1) M3 has a 3 days safety stock, and (2) an alternative supplier is preselected to place orders when the safety stock is not enough to mitigate SU2 disturbances. The costs associated with the first part of this mitigation plan (i.e. raw material stock value) are incurred in all four scenarios. In this scenario, contrary to S2, neither the production nor the transportation suffers alterations. The costs associated with the mitigation plan correspond to an increase of the selling price practiced by M3 supplier, which means that the selling price of the alternative supplier is higher than of the usual supplier (SU2). In this case it is believed that the disturbance effects will not be felt by M2 and FM, since the mitigation plan is implemented by M3. M3 production costs are expected to increase with the increase of the material production price.

All four scenarios were analyzed using the SCDM FDSS interfaced with the ARENA software.

4 Results

This section presents the results and a discussion of the case study considering the application of the SCDM FDSS inference process described in Section 2.1.

The simulation of each scenario by ARENA covered a period of time of 35 days, after the steady-state was reached, considering an 8 hours working day.

On the first step of the inference process the different KPI for each scenario and SC entity were computed for each discrete simulation time period. Fig.3 illustrates the time discrete data resulting from the computation of the KPI "Order Fulfilment Rate" for the four scenarios regarding Manufacturer 2. Due to lack of space the graphs of the other KPI are not presented in this paper.

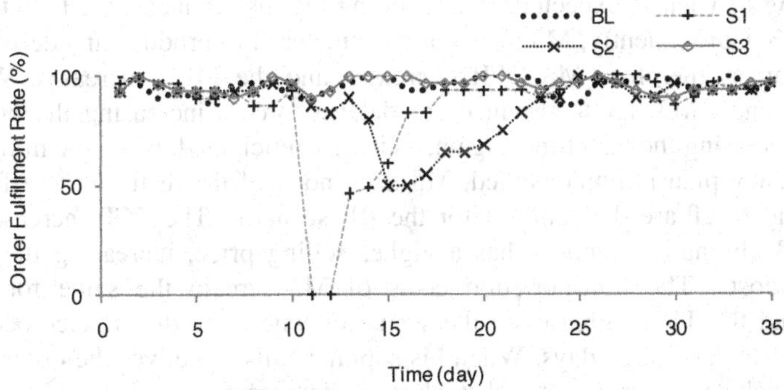

Fig. 3. Example of a KPI computed based on time-discrete simulation data: Order Fulfilment Rate of Manufacturer 2

The next step is synthesizing the time discrete KPI values into an equivalent KPI single value. Table 3 presents the following equivalent KPI data for each SC entity and scenario: Order Fulfilment Rate (OFR), Mean Lead Time (MLT), Total Production Cost (TPC), Transportation Cost (TC) and Total Inventory Value (TIV).

The equivalent KPI of M1 and SU1 are the same for all scenarios, given that these two entities are not affected by the disturbance. In S3, SU2 does not take any measure to counter the disturbance; as a result, the equivalent KPI are the same for S1 and S3.

Under the disturbance effect, SU2 MLT increases because, when the disturbance ends, SU2 has to produce the delayed orders, increasing the production resource rate and consequently increasing the lead time. The equivalent OFR value decreases, because of the production stoppage of about 5 days. The production and transportation costs increase with the contingency plan implementation. The TIV value of SU2 increases in S1 and S2. In the first case, when the disturbance ends the work-in-process (WIP) and the finished goods inventory (FGI) values increase. With the aim of producing the delayed orders, the production rate increases, which means that the WIP and FGI values also increase. In S2, with the increase of the transportation time and the limitation of the transportation resources, FGI increases.

Table 3. Equivalent KPI data for a period of time of 35 days for each SC entity

		OFR (%)	MLT (days)	TPC (MU)	TC (MU)	TIV (MU)
M1	**All scenarios**	99.8	0.07	63	4	297
M2	**BL**	95.1	0.28	348	1	297
	S1	80.2	0.52	370	1	343
	S2	86.3	0.35	355	1	311
	S3	95.7	0.28	348	1	296
M3	**BL**	100	0.07	584	4	2219
	S1	79.2	0.13	584	4	1985
	S2	99.9	0.07	584	4	1951
	S3	99.7	0.07	589	4	2170
SU1	**All scenarios**	100	1.77	77	12	82
SU2	**BL**	100	1.26	108	12	108
	S1/S3	78.2	1.84	108	14	111
	S2	61.4	2.32	115	23	115

According to what is expected, in S1, during the disturbance SU2 fails to deliver orders to M3. Consequently, M3 does not have material to produce and deliver orders to his customer; therefore M3 OFR decreases and the MLT increases. When the disturbance ends, M3 has to produce the delayed orders increasing the production rate, thus increasing the lead time. Again, as it was anticipated, when the mitigation or the contingency plan is implemented, M3 does not feel the disturbance effects, and the OFR and MLT are the same as for the BL scenario. The TCP increases in S3, because M3 alternative supplier has a higher selling price, increasing the material production costs. The transportation costs of M3 remain the same for all four scenarios and the TIV decreases in the scenarios where the disturbance occurs. M3 has a safety stock of three days. When his supplier fails to deliver the orders he uses the safety stock and the raw material stock value decreases.

In S1 and S2 the equivalent OFR of M2 decreases because, in both scenarios, M2 is affected by the disturbance in SU2. Since he does not receive material he cannot produce and consequently he is not able to fulfil the orders on time. The same situation affects the equivalent MLT value for scenarios S1 and S2 whose value increases. These results are consistent with the expected ones described when the description of the scenarios in section 3.2. The TPC increases in S1 and S2 because, when the disturbance ends, M2 produces the delayed orders increasing the production time and consequently, the production costs. The transportation costs of M2 remain the same for all scenarios. The TIV increases in scenarios S1 and S2, because of the raw material cost increase. In S3, M2 is not affected by the disturbance, therefore the KPI values are the same as in the BL scenario.

The third step is fuzzifying each equivalent KPI into a fuzzy KPI. The FKPI are obtained using the parametric membership function *membf* (1). The costs indicators were fuzzified using a Z-shaped fuzzy set, the OFR indicator using a S-shaped fuzzy set and the MLT indicator using a trapezoidal-shaped fuzzy set. Table 4 presents the parameter values for each fuzzy set curve (per SC entity). The parameters were defined in decision meetings with the SC entities' management.

Table 4. membf parameters used for the fuzzification of the KPI (per SC entity)

		OFR (%)	MLT (days)	TPC (MU)	TC (MU)	TIV (MU)
M1	*minr*	50	0.01	-	-	-
	maxr	100	0.07	-	-	-
	maxf	-	0.17	65	3.5	300
	minf	-	0.23	90	5	400
M2	*minr*	40	0.1	-	-	-
	maxr	100	0.3	-	-	-
	maxf	-	0.7	350	1	300
	minf	-	0.9	600	2	550
M3	*minr*	50	0.01	-	-	-
	maxr	100	0.07	-	-	-
	maxf	-	0.11	600	3.5	2000
	minf	-	0.17	700	5	3000
SU1	*minr*	40	1.5	-	-	-
	maxr	100	1.7	-	-	-
	maxf	-	2.1	70	10	80
	minf	-	2.3	110	25	120
SU2	*minr*	40	0.5	-	-	-
	maxr	100	1.3	-	-	-
	maxf	-	1.7	100	10	100
	minf	-	2.5	200	25	200

The parameters selection was defined considering the reality of each SC entity. For instance, the OFR *minr* value of M2, SU1 and SU2 is lower than for M1 and M3, since the M1 and M3 customer (FM) has a JIT production policy which means that any delays severely affect FM performance. The same situation is valid for the MLT indicator: the MLT values of M1 and M3 are lower than the MLT values of M2, SU1 and SU2, because the last three entities have a higher lead time. The costs also differ among SC entities, situation reflected by the parameters used. Table 5 presents the FKPI values per SC entity.

The final step of the inference process is the computation of the fuzzy performance indicators (CI, PI and SCPI). These computations require the definition of weights reflecting the preferences of the decision-makers regarding the importance to each type of FKPI, KPI category and SC entity in the SC. The weight values defined by the managers of SC entities regarding this case study are presented in Table 6.

Table 5. Fuzzy KPI (FKPI) per SC entity

		OFR	MLT	TPC	TC	TIV
M1	**All scenarios**	1	1	1	0.67	1
M2	**BL**	0.92	0.89	1	1	1
	S1	0.67	1	0.92	1	0.83
	S2	0.77	1	0.98	1	0.96
	S3	0.93	0.90	1	1	1
M3	**BL**	1	1	1	0.67	0.78
	S1	0.58	0.67	1	0.67	1
	S2	1	1	1	0.67	1
	S3	0.99	1	1	0.67	0.83
SU1	**All scenarios**	1	1	0.83	0.87	0.95
SU2	**BL**	1	0.95	0.92	0.87	0.92
	S1/S3	0.64	0.83	0.92	0.73	0.89
	S2	0.36	0.23	0.85	0.13	0.85

Table 6. Weight of each SC entity (w_k), KPI category (w_{ik}) and fuzzy KPI (w_{ijk})

	w_k	**KPI categories**	w_{ik}	**FKPI**	w_{ijk}
M1	0.3	Delivery Performance	0.8	OFR	0.5
				MLT	0.5
		Costs	0.2	TPC	0.3
				TC	0.2
				TIV	0.5
M2	0.2	Delivery Performance	0.6	OFR	0.6
				MLT	0.4
		Costs	0.4	TPC	0.4
				TC	0.2
				TIV	0.4
M3	0.3	Delivery Performance	0.7	OFR	0.5
				MLT	0.5
		Costs	0.3	TPC	0.3
				TC	0.2
				TIV	0.5
SU1	0.1	Delivery Performance	0.6	OFR	0.6
				MLT	0.4
		Costs	0.4	TPC	0.4
				TC	0.2
				TIV	0.4
SU2	0.1	Delivery Performance	0.6	OFR	0.6
				MLT	0.4
		Costs	0.4	TPC	0.35
				TC	0.30
				TIV	0.35

The weights assigned to the SC entities are related with their criticality and uniqueness as supply sources and with their position in relation to FM. M1 and M3 are first tier suppliers and their products are not easily replaceable, therefore they receive a high weight. The criticality and uniqueness of their supplies justifies that both entities have mitigation plans implemented (3 days of safety stock). Second tier suppliers receive a weight smaller than first tier suppliers. However, M2 supplies a product that is more critical and difficult to replace than the ones supplied by SU1 and SU2. As a result the weights of SU1 and SU2 in the SC are smaller than M2 weight.

The difficulty of replacing M2 by an alternative source of supply justifies that this SC entity has a mitigation plan implemented (1 day safety stock). This is not the case for the other second tier suppliers, which do not need to have measures in place to counter the occurrence of eventual disturbances.

The values of the promised lead time of M2, SU1 and SU2 are higher than for M1 and M3, consequently the first three entities MLT received weights which are smaller than M1 and M3 weights.

For M1 and M3, the OFR and the MLT have the same weight, since their client (FM) has a JIT production policy. Therefore, for FM is as important not to receive delayed orders as it is not to receive anticipated orders. This does not happen for the rest of the SC entities, which present a lower MTL weight, because they have high lead times (M2 lead time is 1 day, SU1 lead time is 2/3 days and SU2 lead time is 2 days) and their customers have a batch policy.

All SC entities have higher weights for the delivery performance category than for the costs category.

M2, SU1 and SU2 have a higher weight value associated to the TPC and to the TIV than the weight value associated to the TC, since the first two costs are much higher than the TC. In case of M1 and M3, the TIV is higher than the other two costs, so it has a higher weight associated.

Based on these weights the values of the CI and the PI for each SC entity and scenario, and the SCPI for each scenario were computed. Table 7 presents the results. The best operational policy to adopt by a SC entity corresponds to the implementation of the scenario that presents the highest PI value considering the highest SCPI.

Table 7. Fuzzy performance *Category Indicator* (CI) and *Performance Index* (PI) for each scenario and SC entity, and *Supply Chain Performance Index* (SCPI) for each scenario

		BL	S1	S2	S3
M1	CI_{DP}	1	1	1	1
	CI_C	0.93	0.93	0.93	0.93
	PI	**0.99**	**0.99**	**0.99**	**0.99**
M2	CI_{DP}	0.91	0.80	0.86	0.92
	CI_C	1	0.90	0.98	1
	PI	**0.94**	**0.84**	**0.91**	**0.95**
M3	CI_{DP}	1	0.63	1	1
	CI_C	0.82	0.93	0.93	0.85
	PI	**0.95**	**0.72**	**0.98**	**0.95**
SU1	CI_{DP}	1	1	1	1
	CI_C	0.89	0.89	0.89	0.89
	PI	**0.95**	**0.95**	**0.95**	**0.95**
SU2	CI_{DP}	0.98	0.72	0.31	0.72
	CI_C	0.91	0.85	0.63	0.85
	PI	**0.95**	**0.77**	**0.44**	**0.77**
SC	**SCPI**	**0.96**	**0.85**	**0.91**	**0.94**

A short analysis of the CI values offers some insight about the differences in the results of the several scenarios.

M1 and SU1 have the same values for all indicators in all scenarios since they are not affected by the disturbance in SU2.

The disturbance effects propagate through the SC affecting the delivery performance of M3 to FM ($CI_{DP\_S1} = 0.63$) and M2 ($CI_{DP\_S1} = 0.80$).

The mitigation plan is implemented by M3 while the contingency plan is implemented by SU2. Therefore, SU2 indicators are the same for S1 and S3. When the disturbance occurs in SU2 his delivery performance (DP) drops, but is even worst when SU2 implements the contingency plan, since the transportation time increases when this happens ($CI_{DP\_BL}= 0.98$, $CI_{DP\_S1/S3}= 0.72$ and $CI_{DP\_S2}= 0.31$).

The costs for SU2 are higher when he implements the contingency plan than when the disturbance occurs and no measures are taken ($CI_{C\_S1/S3} = 0.85$ and $CI_{C\_S2} = 0.63$). This is due to an increase of transportation and production costs.

M3 costs increase when he implements the mitigation plan, since the selling price of his alternative supplier increases. On the other hand, in all four scenarios, M3 have 3 days of safety stock which means a high raw material stock value. When his supplier fails to deliver, M3 uses the safety stock to mitigate the failures and consequently his raw material stock value decreases ($CI_{C\_BL} = 0.82$, $CI_{C\_S1/S2} = 0.93$ and $CI_{C\_S3} = 0.85$).

The last step of the inference process is ranking the alternatives based on PI and SCPI values, in order to identify the best operational policy to deal with the disturbance. The next paragraphs will discuss the ranking of the policies from a SC entity perspective, based on the PI values, followed by a discussion about the best operational policy from a SC perspective, based on the SCPI.

The overall performance of SU2 (the SC entity affected by the disturbance) decreases more when he implements the contingency plan (S2) than in the other scenarios. Thus, from its own perspective passive acceptance of the disturbance effects should be considered ($PI_{S1/S3} = 0.77$ and $PI_{S2} = 0.44$). However, from M3's perspective when the contingency plan is implemented by SU2 (S2) his overall performance is better than in the scenarios where no measures are taken by SU2 ($PI_{S1} = 0.72$, $PI_{S2} = 0.98$ and $PI_{S3} = 0.95$). In fact, the overall performance of M3 is better with the contingency plan than with the mitigation plan. This is because the costs increase in S3 and the delivery performance is equal in S2 and S3.

Regarding M2, his overall performance is better when the mitigation plan is adopted by M3 ($PI_{S2} = 0.91$and $PI_{S3} = 0.95$).

The synthesis of the PI analysis is that the mitigation plan (S3) should be adopted by M3 to counter the effects of the disturbance in SU2. In fact, for M2 scenario 3 offers the best overall performance; and for M3, although the contingency plan presents a better overall performance, the PI results are close to each other for both policies.

Regarding the entire SC, the overall performance drops when the disturbance occurs ($SCPI_{BL} = 0.96$ and $SCPI_{S1} = 0.85$). Considering the effect of the alternative operational policies it is possible to conclude that the implementation of the mitigation plan leads to a better SC performance than the adoption of the contingency plan ($SCPI_{S2} = 0.91$ and $SCPI_{S3} = 0.94$). This reinforces the conclusions reached when the PI were analyzed.

The ranking of the results allows the conclusion that the passive acceptance of the disturbance by the SC is not adequate because its performance drops significantly; and when the two operational policy alternatives are confronted, the mitigation plan already implemented in the SC (which was tested in S3) is more adequate than the contingency plan (which was tested in S2).

5 Conclusions

A supply chain disturbance can result from acts or events that are originated inside of the SC (e.g., supplier failures, equipment breakdown, and employees' absenteeism) or may result from extrinsic events (e.g., social turmoil, terrorist attacks, or acts of God such as volcanic eruptions, hurricanes or earthquakes).

Although a specific disturbance may occur in one entity of the SC, the interdependencies of the various entities in the network often cause the propagation of the disturbance along the SC, which will probably result in unfulfilled customers' orders. Thus, SC should be as resilient as possible to potential disturbances, because any disturbance can have long-term negative effects on companies' financial performance. To achieve this objective it is crucial the selection and implementation of adequate operational policies, namely mitigation or contingency plans to counter the effects of disturbances.

Therefore, the objective of this paper was to study the effects of different disturbances and the implementation of mitigation and/or contingency plans to reduce the negative impacts of disturbances using a decision support system named SCDM FDSS.

The SCDM FDSS, coupled with a simulation software such as ARENA, helps decision-makers to choose the best operational policy to counter the disturbance effects by calculating and analyzing the PI for each SC entity and the SCPI for the all SC. The fuzzy model is flexible allowing the integration or combination of meta-heuristic approaches with classical approaches, accommodating different analysis methodologies and tools in the inference process. On the other hand the FDSS can also interface with other simulation tools using alternative simulation techniques.

The case study presented in this paper is an academic version of part of a real world analysis performed on an automotive SC, whose original data and results cannot be presented due to confidentiality clauses of the study. The case study was used to test the existing operational policy (i.e., a mitigation plan) against an alternative operational policy (i.e., a contingency plan). In the case study presented a disturbance affecting a SC entity was simulated and analyzed in terms of the local effects in the SC entity and of the propagation throughout the SC. Four scenarios were evaluated using the SCDM FDSS. The analysis of the *Performance Index* of each SC entity and of the *Supply Chain Performance Index* showed that the existing mitigation plan was the one that ensured the best performance of the SC when affected by the disturbance that was considered in the scenarios tested.

The use of the SCDM FDSS in real life environments helps the information sharing and the situational awareness among the entities of a SC, improving their collaboration and contributing to the resilience of the SC. The results of the SCDM FDSS and the advice about operational policies to implement can be made accessible to all SC entities in an immediate and transparent way if they share common IT platforms or if the results are shared through some web-based tool. An alternative approach is the use of the SCDM FDSS in support of SC entities' coordination meetings.

Tools such as the SCDM FDSS can be valuable in supporting decision-makers selection of best operational policy, namely to counter disturbance effects propagation throughout the SC, contributing to better performance, not only at entity level, but also of the SC as an all, therefore contributing to the increase of SC resilience.

Directions for future work include the evolution of the SCDM FDSS to a fuzzy expert system that provides advice to decision-makers, and the creation of a web platform that supports further research on the issues related with shared decision-making among the SC entities.

Acknowledgments. This work was funded by the Portuguese Foundation for Science and Technology, project number MIT-Pt/EDAM-IASC/0033/2008.

References

1. Nunes, I.L., Machado, V.C.: A Fuzzy Expert System Model to Deal with Supply Chain Disturbances. International Journal of Decision Sciences, Risk and Management 4, 127–151 (2012)
2. Norrman, A., Jansson, U.: Ericsson's proactive supply chain risk management approach after a serious sub-supplier accident. Int. J. of Physical Distribution & Logistics Management. 34, 434–456 (2004)
3. Tang, C.S.: Perspectives in supply chain risk management. International Journal of Production Economics 103, 451–488 (2006)
4. Chopra, S., Sodhi, M.S.: Managing Risk To Avoid Supply-Chain Breakdown. MIT Sloan Management Review 46, 53–62 (2004)
5. Peck, H.: Drivers of supply chain vulnerability: an integrated framework. International Journal of Physical Distribution & Logistics Management 35, 210–232 (2005)
6. Tomlin, B.: On the Value of Mitigation and Contingency Strategies for Managing Supply Chain Disruption Risks. Management Science 52, 639–657 (2006)
7. Sprague, R.J., Watson, H.J.: DSS - Putting Theory Into Practice. Prentice-Hall, Inc. (1986)
8. Turban, E., Sharda, R., Delen, D.: Decision Support and Business Intelligence Systems, 9th edn. Prentice-Hall (2010)
9. Persson, F., Araldi, M.: The development of a dynamic supply chain analysis tool - Integration of SCOR and discrete event simulation. Int. J. Production Economics 121, 574–583 (2009)
10. Pundoor, G., Herrmann, J.W.: A hierarchical approach to Supply Chain simulation modelling using the Supply Chain Operations Reference model. International Journal of Simulation and Process Modelling 2, 124–132 (2007)
11. Supply-Chain Council – Supply-Chain Operations Reference-model, Version 9.0, `http://supply-chain.org/f/SCOR90OverviewBooklet.pdf`
12. Zadeh, L.A.: Fuzzy sets. Information and Control 8, 338–353 (1965)
13. Nunes, I.L., Figueira, S., Machado, V.C.: A Supply Chain Disturbance Management Fuzzy Decision Support System (in review)
14. Nunes, I.L.: Knowledge Acquisition for the Development of an Upper- Body Work-Related Musculoskeletal Disorders Analysis Tool. Human Factors and Ergonomics in Manufacturing 17, 149–162 (2007)

Training Clinical Decision-Making through Simulation

Cecilia Dias Flores[1], Marta Rosecler Bez[2], Ana Respício[3], and João Marcelo Fonseca[1]

[1] Pós-Graduação em Ciências da Saúde, Universidade Federal de Ciências da Saúde de Porto Alegre (PPGCS/UFCSPA), Rua Sarmento Leite, 245, Porto Alegre, Brazil
[2] Universidade FEEVALE, Novo Hamburgo, Brazil
[3] Departamento de Informática/Centro de Investigação Operacional, Universidade de Lisboa, Lisboa, Portugal
{dflores,joaomf}@ufcspa.edu.br, martabez@feevale.br, respicio@di.fc.ul.pt

Abstract. Clinical decision making faces relevant uncertainties, outcomes and trade-offs. It has to deal with diagnosis uncertainties, the choice of diagnostic tests, the selection of prescriptions and procedures, and the treatment follow up, many times facing severe budget limitations and lack of sophisticated equipment. This paper presents a multi-agent learning system for health care practitioners: SimDeCS (Simulation for Decision Making in the Health Care Service). This system relies on simulations of complex clinical cases integrated in a virtual learning environment, and has been developed within a program offering continuous education, training and qualification to professionals in the Brazilian health care service. SimDeCS will be made available on the Internet, thus providing access to professionals working throughout the country. The main contribution is the system architecture and the model knowledge.The learning environment has been designed as a multi-agent system where three intelligent agents are included: Domain Agent, Learner Agent, and Mediator Agent. The knowledge model is implemented by the Domain Agent through probabilistic reasoning, relying on expert human knowledge encoded in Bayesian networks. A clinical case is presented and discussed.

Keywords: clinical decision making, simulation, reasoning, knowledge modelling, multi-agent systems, Bayesian networks.

1 Introduction

The UnA-SUS (Open University of the Health Care System) is a project carried out by the Brazilian Ministry of Health with the Pan-American Health Organization, along with the National School of Public Health, that tends to build up conditions for the operation of a Brazilian network for permanent education in health care, integrating academic institutions that composes it with health services and the SUS management. UnA-SUS was created, by the year 2008, to fulfil the request in the formation of human resources in the Brazilian health care system.

The UnA-SUS is a collaborative network of academic institutions and, among its specific objectives, has as a purpose to virtually offer qualification to those who work

J.E. Hernández et al. (Eds.): EWG-DSS 2011, LNBIP 121, pp. 59–73, 2012.

in the health domain. The Universidade Federal de Ciências da Saúde de Porto Alegre (UFCSPA) in Brazil is one of the teaching institutions that integrate UnA-SUS.

Simulation of real cases in a Web environment, based on probabilistic reasoning, has a strategic importance to support the continuing formation of professionals at service, as it allows for training diagnostic reasoning in a safe environment facing complex and challenging clinical cases.

This paper introduces SimDeCS (Simulation for Decision Making in the Health Care Service) which is a multi-agent intelligent learning environment developed according to the following features.

- The learner elaborates his own knowledge model through his interaction with the proposed clinical case and the system continuously asks for actions and decisions.
- Feedback and additional information is permanently available.
- Whenever necessary, a negotiation process[1] among the agents[2] and the learner will take place as a way to review his model.

For the principle of medical education, medical students should carry out the practice of two skills: the hypothetical model construction and diagnostic reasoning, which both are problem-solving tasks. Apart from diagnosis, the learner should have an opportunity to actively construct models of diseases that include the possible causes of disease, associated symptoms, and evaluate the model application. This way, the learner can attain and make use of the necessary knowledge in diagnostic reasoning.

SimDeCS supports learning by using a constructivist approach to perform diagnostic reasoning. The learner is provided with the possibility of applying and evaluating different courses of action while progressing in the process of diagnostic reasoning, relying on his previous knowledge. Thus, knowledge is built through the learner-simulation. Initially, it was designed just to allow knowledge modelling to support clinical decision making. It has hereby gained a broader function: it provides the final user (student) a virtual reality interface where he can interact with the characters in the story (patients and relatives) while investigating the proposed clinical case and obtaining assistance to guide the next clinical action. Therefore, SimDeCS accompanies step-by-step the student's decision making from its domain built-in model and whenever the course of action takes the student to a conclusion different from the expected, the environment promotes a negotiation process based on pedagogical strategies to induce the user to review decisions.

---

[1] The basic requirement of a negotiation process is that the interaction among agents shares a common goal so that an agreement is reached with respect to the negotiation object. Usually, different dimensions of the negotiation object will be negotiated simultaneously. The initial state for a negotiation to take place is the absence of an agreement, which can include a conflict or not. In the case of a teaching and learning process, a point of conflict is the relation of beliefs about the knowledge domain between teachers and students. A process of teaching and learning is a way of reducing the asymmetry between the teacher's and the student's confidence on the topic studied. [1].

[2] An agent is a program that can work autonomously, interacts with other agents and services, lives in an environment, and performs a task in the name of a person or an organization [2].

The user may further evaluate, specify and review his decisions under the guidance of SimDeCS. Training of strategies for diagnosis will be supported qualitatively, i.e. the system will be able to identify which information becomes necessary to support a given hypothesis or to differentiate two different ones. Diagnostic reasoning will also be supported quantitatively, as the system should be able to quantify the influence of some gathered information on a diagnostic hypothesis, and to identify which is the most important information to acquire to carry on. The Bayesian network approach was chosen to deal with uncertain knowledge as it is mathematically principled.

Although the literature proposes several studies and simulation tools for the medical field [3][4][5][6], there is a lack of proposals focusing on constructivist systems, representing clinical guidelines into BNs.

Next section will be devoted to present general concepts on Bayesian networks and simulation. Section 3 presents SimDeCS with special emphasis on its architecture and the communication between agents. A clinical case concerning a network for adult migraine is presented and discussed in section 4. Finally, the paper ends with some final remarks and future work perspectives.

2 Context

Bayesian networks have been widely used all over the world to model uncertain domains [7]. Uncertainty is represented by probability and the basic inference is the probabilistic reasoning, that is, the probability of one or more variables assuming specific values giving the available evidence. Another important reason for choosing the Bayesian network approach is in its two-fold feature that enables qualitatively and quantitatively domain modelling. The qualitative domain model is represented by the set of variables and their causal relationship, which can be easily built by using a Directed Acyclic Graph. The quantitative model expresses the strength of the causal pair-wise relationships, by conditional probability distribution.

We follow the hypothesis that a physician engaged in medical diagnosis implicitly performs probabilistic reasoning. The physician's practice corresponds to taking full advantage of the probabilistic relationship between the variables present in a Bayesian network that models the medical domain of interest. Reviews of published case studies in the domain of environmental medicine support this hypothesis [8, 9, 10, 11] Moreover there is empirical evidence that the probabilistic reasoning, when supported by Bayesian networks, corresponds closely to the human reasoning pattern [12].

Definition (Bayesian Network). A Bayesian network (BN) is a direct acyclic graph where nodes are random variables, and arcs represent direct probabilistic dependence relations among the nodes they connect. The strength of the relationship of x_i with $pa(x_i)$, its parents (nodes with arcs that arrive in x_i), is given by $P(x_i|pa(x_i))$, the conditional probability distribution of x_i given its parents. The joint probability distribution of all variables is given by $P(x_1, ... ,x_n)$. If $pa(x_i)$ is an empty set, $P(x_i|pa(x_i))$ is reduced to the unconditional distribution of x_i.

A simulation can be understood as a simplified reproduction or representation of a real scenario, event or process. It attempts to assemble all the main components that compose a real scenario in a coherent and integrated way to modulate the corresponding environment and evaluate its evolution with or without interference from a decision making agent. Medical simulations have their origin in anesthesiology [13] in groups that made use of this resource in training with the idea to reduce risks in real situations. Emergency training situations by means of immersion courses such as Basic Life Support (BLS), Advanced Cardiac Life Support (ACLS), Advanced Trauma Life Support (ATLS), and Pediatric Advanced Life Support (PALS) make use of simulated scenarios for learning, training and student evaluation to those who will exercise this knowledge in real environments with real patients in life threatening situations.

Medical teaching simulation tools can therefore be comprehended in an ample way as tools that permit educators to keep total control in pre-selected clinical scenarios, outlining in this phase of learning all the real patient's potential risks and annoyances [14].

According to Kincaid et al [15], simulation brings consistent advantages for the learning environment in general with applicable specificities for medical teaching such as:

- aids the student to comprehend complex relations that in another way would demand costly equipment or potentially dangerous experiments;
- grants the application of scientific and technical knowledge in an integrated and simultaneous manner;
- permits the student to search for new methods and strategies for the solution of the study case;
- provides an environment close to reality for training and the reinforcement of acquired knowledge;
- reduces the risk in authentic situations.

The use of a simulation tool is consolidated in the formation of new professionals in civil and military aviation as well as in the recycling of knowledge or acquisition of new abilities. Virtual simulated environments, just like in the medical area, grant the binomial student-teacher the opportunity to revoke the risks in the initial learning stages and in the consolidation of decision processes.

Mainly in the health care area, simulation tools generally permit with ease the parallel consideration in decision making in the economic impact on utilized strategies. Parallel trees of decision can be evaluated with overlapped final results and regard the economic impact of each one separately. Teaching ranges not only attendance decisions, but completes itself with more restricted real scenarios or not of resources and the economic viability of simulated decisions.

The foremost objective in teaching medicine should be attaining patterns of excellence with the measurable results of the learning process [14]. The overlapping of "first not to cause harm" allied with the possibility of teaching in controlled scenarios makes the medical simulation a desirable tool if proved to be efficient for the purpose it is intended for.

A specific subtype of simulation tends to carry out the evaluation of competence [16]. Once consolidating the student to a knowledge domain in a medical area, the next stage in extraction from this same domain with pertinent conducts to the proposed situation in a correct planning order and regarding technical practicability make part of fundamental learning. The simulation environment delivers ways to quantify this competence acquisition process. For this much it is necessary to assure a golden-pattern in which the student will be compared and will work as a mark in case of conflict between different decision algorithms used by different decision makers.

Among different types of simulators and dissimilar objectives during its use, we encounter the High Fidelity Simulators [17] that were subsequently reviewed [18] and are distinguished from the rest for not being static. Questions and answers change according to the interaction between the student and the simulation tool.

BNs are well fit to model diagnosis processes [19] and BN reasoning is quite manageable computationally, as it is based on two simplifying assumptions that reasoning could not be cyclic and that the causality supporting a child state would be expressed in the links between it and its parent states [20]. In addition, the authors have extensive experience with modelling diagnosis using BNs in related previous works [1], from which this project could benefit.

3 SimDeCS

The SimDeCS is a multi-agent computational environment aimed to support learning by using a constructivist approach. We tend to focus on medical reasoning in order to describe the SimDeCS. The development of this environment is in accordance with the physician process on technical education and specialization, which in general occurs through the following activities: medical appointments, class attendance, and round sessions. Medical students and instructors discuss real cases and current topics of their specialties during round sessions. They also make use of classes to discuss papers previously handed out by the professor and read by the students. The medical student can use the SimDeCS as a complementary tool to ease his technical skill development on formulated diagnoses at his own pace.

The process of formulating a definite medical diagnosis can be seen as being composed of the following steps: medical interview, Current Disease History (CDH), formulation of a differential diagnosis, formulation of preliminary diagnosis, and definite diagnostic formulation. If suitable, after the formulation of a preliminary diagnosis and before the definite diagnostic formulation, the physician can review the technical literature and request complementary lab tests. In medical interviews, the physician consults the patient to be aware of the history of his previous diseases. To obtain the CDH, the physician inquires the patient about main complaints. Then, the physician examines the patient visually in order to determine his condition while searching for physical signs and keeps record of the symptoms mentioned by the patient. The physician proceeds to examine the patient physically, oriented by detected signs and symptoms.

The physician, with the gathered information, commences a differential diagnosis in which he selects a set of pathologies (diseases) compatible with the collected data and tries to get new results that can exclude a number of hypothetical pathologies. By reducing the set of hypothetical pathologies, it is possible to establish the preliminary diagnosis to determine the most probable pathology. If there is need for confirming preliminary diagnosis, the physician may request supplementary clinical exams. While waiting for lab results, the physician can review technical literature concerning the pathology he suspects the patient might be suffering from. The lab test analysis can substantiate the preliminary diagnosis, making it definitive or supply new information for a new preliminary diagnostic formulation.

The SimDeCS follows the decisions carried out by the student starting from its domain built-in model and if the student's decisions point towards a different conclusion from the expected, the environment starts a negotiation process based on pedagogical strategies in order to induce the learner to review his decisions.

The SimDeCS is composed of three agents: Learner Agent, Domain Agent, and Mediator Agent. The Domain Agent represents the expert knowledge domain while the Learner Agent represents learner knowledge. The student will learn by means of the SimDeCS support with the development of diagnostic reasoning and in making hypothesis. If the decisions made by the student are different from the expected in the environment, the system's Mediator Agent motivates the leaner to review his model qualitatively (when the learner follows a line of reasoning different from the expected) or quantitatively (when the learner values an aspect in detriment more than the other aspects analysed). The Mediator Agent guides the learner based on pedagogical strategies.

3.1 SimDeCS Architecture

SimDeCS is a multi-agent learning environment in development for the health learning area. Its utilization comes from the formulation of clinical cases by the instructor or expert with variable levels of complexity through the Web, making use of a high level Domain Specific Language (DSL) known as VR-MED [21]. This was conceived so that programmers and planners supported by a simple and proper notation can specify the characteristics of a study case. It is carried out by a graphic notation that attempts to represent the characteristics encountered in the domain of clinical cases and provide support for its execution through simulations in the health care area. Therefore modelling of the problem (clinical case) by a domain expert (physician, dentist, health agent, etc.) is carried out by the VR-MED, making use of a visual notation in the shape of a diagram that dismisses knowledge in the area of informatics by the expert. It becomes possible to specify in this diagram all the details of the clinical case at matter, just as the characters (patients, physicians, relatives, etc.) that make part of the case. Fig. 1 presents an example of a clinical case model.

Each generic clinical situation is expressed in the form of a Bayesian network. The VR-MED language provides the necessary interface for the identification of Bayesian networks, previously created in a repository, which will be linked to the simulation tool user.

In each network there are resources defining the importance of nodes in the identification of the modelled diagnosis (essential, complementary, excluding, and null effect nodes). The evaluation of a student/user is done through perception and selection of nodes regarded essential and non essential, in disregarding the null effect nodes, in a time concomitant evaluation required by the choice of the student/user, and in the accumulated costs of successive decisions. The randomly dispersed motors, according to the pertinence of its presence in different networks, permit variations in the consecutive course of cases.

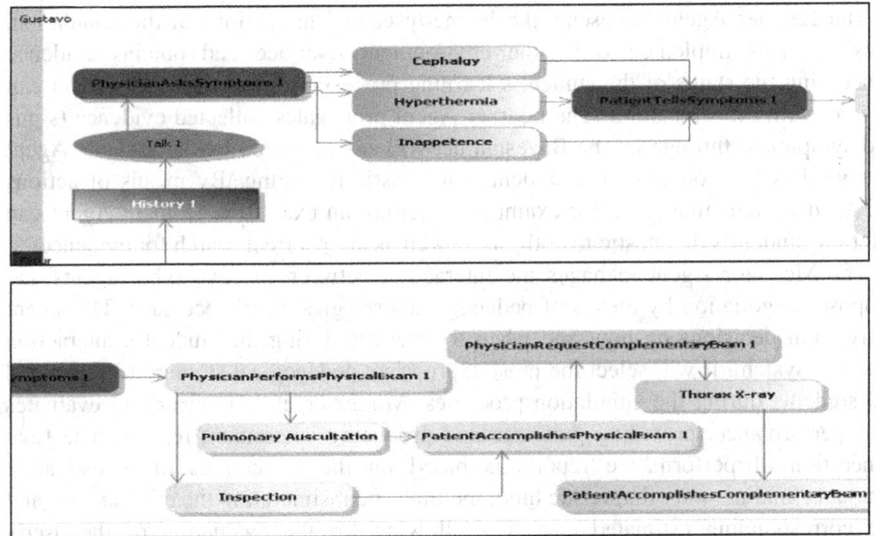

Fig. 1. Medical case diagram modeled by the VR-MED. Part a) physician asks for symptoms and patient reports cephalgy, hiperthermia and innapetence. Part b) represents the result of physician performs exam (inspection, pulmonary auscultation) and Complementary exam (Torax X-ray).

As mentioned before, the SimDeCS is composed of three artificial agents and its interaction is represented in the Figure 2.

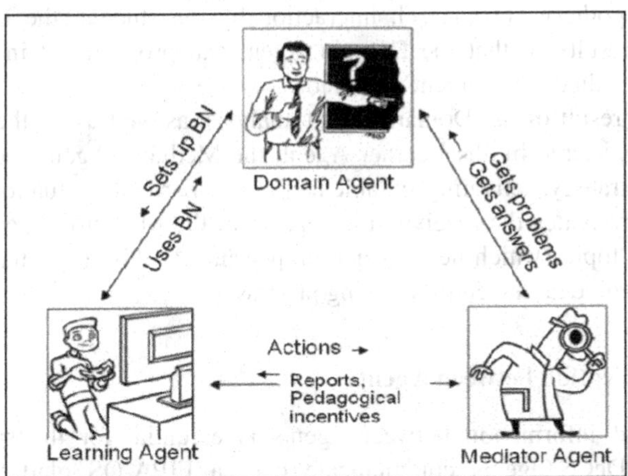

Fig. 2. SimDeCS agents

The Domain Agent is responsible for knowledge management and, therefore, represents the domain expert. It is based on clinical cases of varying degrees of complexity which have modelled as Bayesian networks, by expert clinicians, and collected in a repository.

The Learner Agent represents the learner/user and his actions in the simulation. This agent is implemented by the environment interface and obtains evidence concerning the status of the student's learning process in a way that the student can interact with the simulation. The Learner Agent propagates collected evidence (signs and symptoms) throughout the Bayesian network administered by the Domain Agent that verifies the course of the student's diagnostic reasoning. By means of actions executed by the student as, for example, soliciting an exam, the Domain Agent can infer the student's diagnostic hypothesis as well as an incorrect search for evidence.

The Mediator Agent manages the interaction between the two other agents and proposes negotiation by means of pedagogical strategies when necessary. This agent carries out decisions on how and when to interfere during the student's interaction with the system. It will select the most appropriate pedagogical strategy to query and aid students during the simulation processes. Moreover, it supervises and evaluates user performance, providing guidance and producing assessment reports. The final generation of performance reports is based on the corrections of investigative conducts (and not only diagnostic hits), the time spent simulating the clinical case and the corresponding estimated cost thus allowing for the evaluation of the user's performance in the SimDeCS.

The communication between agents follows a cycle of interactions that obey the following protocol:

1. The Domain Agent presents the user (learner) with a case study through a virtual reality interface with virtual characters (playing patients and relatives). The Learner Agent only takes notes on the example and passes it on to students.
2. The Domain Agent makes available case studies where students model the diagnostic hypothesis. From each interaction by the student, the Learner Agent presents the results so that the Domain Agent can propagate it in the Bayesian network and evaluate the student's decision.
3. Based on the result of the Domain Agent analysis, as well as on the trajectory of the student registered by the Learner Agent, the Mediator Agent chooses the best pedagogical strategy, activating suitable tactics to a particular situation.
4. The student evaluates the received message from the Mediator Agent and tries to reflect on the topics which he considers important. At this stage, the student may also decide to give up the entire learning process.

3.2 Communication between Agents

The exchange of information between agents is essential for the success of the simulation. SimDeCS agents communicate over a FIPA-OS platform [22]. The Foundation for Intelligent Physical Agents (FIPA) has put forward an Agent Communication Language (ACL), which is based on Speech Act Theory. FIPA assumes the existence of an agent management system, yet not part of the language, and abstracts the low-level communication details. Currently, the inform, request, query-if and query-ref acts are being used through the FIPA Request and Query Interaction Protocols. Bayesian networks are represented, for communication purposes, in a XML-based format (XBN), and FIPA-SL0 is used as content language for communicative act messages. To establish communication between agents there is a need for a common frame of reference or shared ontology which determines how particular message content is to be interpreted.

This communication in the SimDeCS is established by using a JADE (JAVA Agent Development) framework. JADE is developed in JAVA implementing the FIPA patterns for intelligent agents [23]. JADE provides a series of patterned resources for the development of technologies based on agents, considerably accelerating the development process.

Figure 3 displays a sequential diagram representing the exchange of messages between SimDeCS agents.

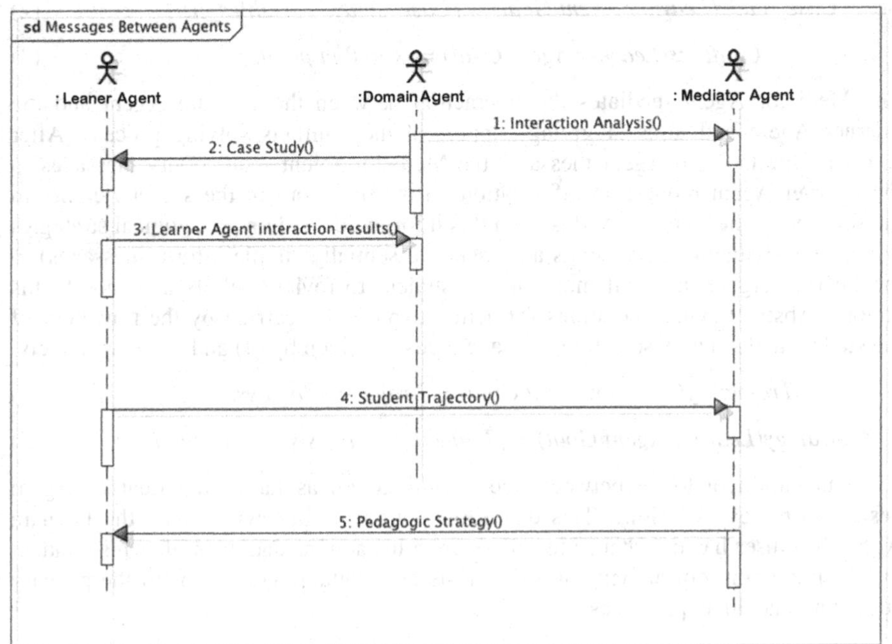

Fig. 3. Sequential diagram showing messages exchanged between agents

The Learner Agent sends request messages to the Domain Agent with the state of the instance variables of the case at matter informing the decisions made by the student for a review. The Learner Agent "observes" the actions carried out by the student such as ready questions, received replies and decision making. The abstract syntax notation for action expressions carried by this message content type is given by (1).

$$SimulationParameters(Learner\ Agent\ State) = \{State\_variables\} \quad (1)$$

The Domain Agent has medical domain knowledge depicted through Bayesian networks. It makes available the knowledge domain and explanation resources to the student, which is enough to aid in the learning process. The Domain Agent sends inform messages to the Learner Agent with the case study to be solved, including the list of variables (medical interview, current disease history, main complaint, etc.) in which the student can make use of it in the construction of his diagnostic hypothesis. Providing variables that are sensitive for the case study context will help to maintain common ontology among agents during the learning process. As the Domain Agent receives the variables directed by the student (*State_variables*), it begins an action (program) that reviews the student's belief through the propagation of these variables by the Bayesian network expert. Once a search for some mistaken evidence or tendency to find diagnoses that is different from the expected is found, the Domain Agent sends inform messages to the Mediator Agent presenting the conflict points. Abstract syntax notations for action expressions carried by case-study and conflict message types are, respectively, (2) and (3).

$$\textit{Case\_study(Learner Agent Goal)} = \{\textit{Case\_study, Variables\_list}\} \tag{2}$$

$$\textit{Conflicts(Learner Agent Goal)} = \{\textit{Conflict points}\} \tag{3}$$

The Mediator Agent mediates the interaction between the Domain Agent and the Learner Agent and aims at giving support in the conflicts solving process. After receiving the Domain Agent message, the Mediator Agent sends query messages to the Learner Agent requesting information on the trajectory of the student/learner in the solution of the study case. Based on this information and on pedagogical strategies in use, the Mediator Agent sends arguments (essentially simple inform messages) to the Learner Agent that will motivate the student to review beliefs and modify his actions. Abstract syntax notations for action expressions carried by the trajectory of the student and strategy selection message types are given by (4) and (5), respectively.

$$\textit{Trajectory(Learner Agent Goal)} = \{\textit{trajectory\_analysis}\} \tag{4}$$

$$\textit{Strategy(Learner Agent Goal)} = \{\textit{Trajectory\_analysis; Arguments}\} \tag{5}$$

Communication dialogue between agents will go on as far as the Learner Agent desires to review decisions. This can allow actions to be reviewed by the Domain Agent. The user has the chance to reflect upon his actions and even alter his conduct in the simulation tool arriving at a diagnosis or a suitable conduct with the primary attention in health experiences.

4 A Clinical Case: The Adult Migraine

The Brazilian Society of Family Medicine and Community (SBMFC / Sociedade Brasileira de Medicina de Família e Comunidade) [24], founded in the year of 1981, with national extent, counts with several working groups. One of the SBMFC working groups coordinates the production of clinical guidelines to be delivered to health care professionals. These guidelines attempt to compile the best available evidence in pertinent clinical problems towards primary attention and are made available through the SBMFC in the shape of texts, tables and/or flux sheets. Some of the SBMFC guidelines have been adopted to be modelled by Bayesian networks within the SimDeCS project. The resulting networks specified in VR-MED language provide the foundations for the simulation tool development.

Once a guideline is chosen to be diagrammed as a Bayesian network, a study of the entire formative content of the text goes into process to extract variables that compile the state of knowledge for the problem at issue. Afterwards, these variables are linked to structure a Bayesian network.

When there is a correct identification of the set of variables and the corresponding relationships between them, the occurrence probability for each variable is quantified. It becomes necessary to point out that the nodes and the network probabilities both primordially seek an adequate simulation in a way that the concepts present in the guidelines may remain didactically representative for the expert that models the case study.

Proposing a migraine case to be attended in a primary attention level, as an example, the expert may choose to model a network for a typical clinical situation. Within the most prevailing possibilities in a primary attention level, there are the tension-type headache, the migraine, the cluster headache, the articulation dysfunction temporomandibular, and sinusitis. Each nosologic entity is associated with some particular signs and symptoms which, however, overlap broadly. While modelling a presentation upon another in the VR-MED level, the expert makes the diagnosis more probable. To exemplify: when modelling a migraine network with the objective to favour a migraine diagnosis over others, nodes as a hemicranial pain presentation, pulsating pain, and rest relief will have greater weight over the remaining, such as nasal discharge or an unilateral red eye. Figure 4 displays a Bayesian network fragment based on the clinical guideline for the diagnosis and treatment of adult migraine.

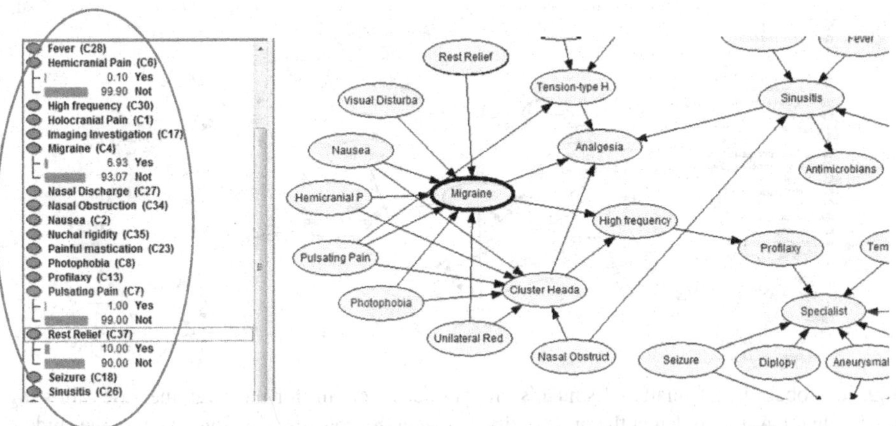

Fig. 4. A Bayesian network representing adult migraine

The initial probabilities (Fig 4) in a modelled network suffer with the propagation of signs and symptoms that are fortified or weakened by the clinical expert (Fig 5).

In the hypothesis of a user's choice during the execution of a simulation to develop a clinical suspicion of sinusitis and direct an investigation or a treatment pertinent to this diagnostics hypothesis (for instance an antibiotic therapy) makes the Mediator Agent perceive the discrepancy between the user's choice and the probabilities of the modelled network (Fig 6).

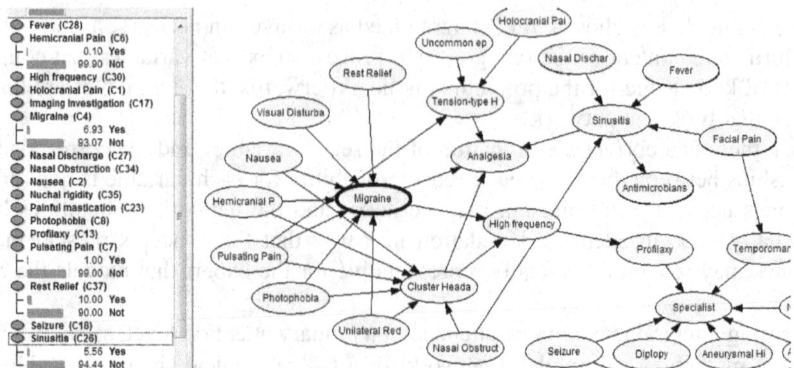

Fig. 5. A Bayesian Network representing migraine, extended from Fig 4 to include the occurrence of clinical signs suggesting migraine (after the modelling by the clinical expert)

The detection of this difference makes the Mediator Agent intervene in selecting the best tactic in the pedagogical strategy library for the situation. The selected intervention, for instance, could be a reading suggestion from the guideline as to the nature of the common presentation of sinusitis (facial pain, nasal secretion) compared to the signs of a typical migraine as described above. Another example of possible intervention could be the option in discussing the case with a virtual tutor that can carry out the analysis of the simulation that implies a review of the wrong diagnostic.

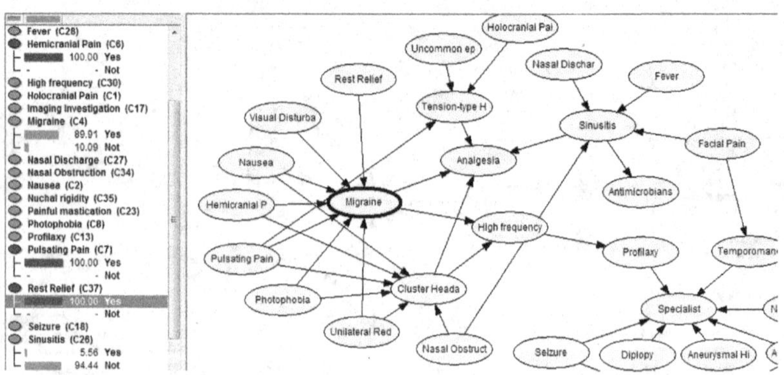

Fig. 6. Probability of unaltered sinusitis after initial modeling for the migraine case, allowing the Mediator Agent to detect the dissociation between the courses of action taken by the student on the best probability proposed

Besides the modelling of variables and the probabilistic quantification of each node of a Bayesian network in the SimDeCS, the expert is responsible to bring on possible questions and answers relevant to the envisaged knowledge building. Such properties will be responsible for the structuring of a dialog between the student and the patient during the simulation.

The interaction between the user and the simulation tool is done by means of a virtual environment where the "dialog" simulates a real-life situation involving the user and the patient (played by their corresponding avatars). The patient shows his symptoms and significant characteristics through a previous inquiry. Figure 7 displays a screen of the SimDeCS interface.

Moreover, at any stage of the simulation, the process can be revised to include additional facts, thus allowing the introduction of patient feedback and, therefore, enhancing the user decision-making process.

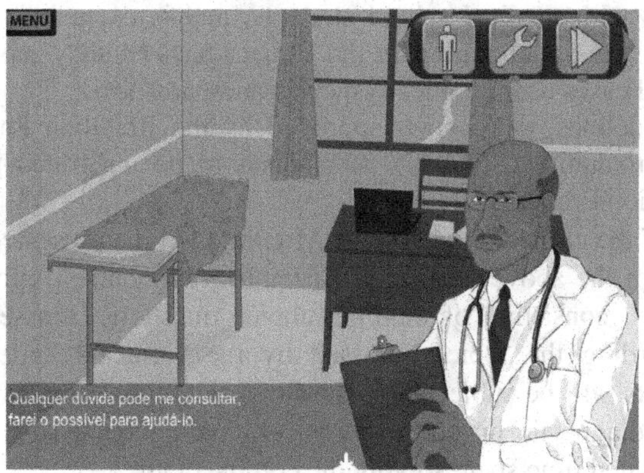

Fig. 7. A screen of the SimDeCS interface

5 Final Remarks and Future Work

Simulators have become widely adopted support tools for the education and continuing medical development of health care professionals. Several aspects contribute to this, namely, the simulation model is close to the clinical experience, users can interact with virtual characters (avatars) representing real life characters involved in a clinical history, and the interactive clinical case simulation directly observes and records clinical decision-making in real time. Moreover, interactive clinical case simulation can provide a safe environment for problem based learning as it simulates virtually the diagnosis and treatment phases of the real clinical process.

The SimDeCS simulation tool has been developed to offer monitoring of the user/learner during the simulation process, providing feedback and guidance on the clinical decisions made, by means of intelligent agents, in order to discharge pedagogical tactics, and recording automatically the clinical reasoning of the user/learner as well as the time spent, thus allowing for assessment of the user/player performance.

Bayesian networks are adequate to model knowledge and to support reasoning under uncertainty knowledge modelling, under the purposes of the project. The kernel of the simulation tools is therefore composed by Bayesian networks where knowledge is modelled by professionals in the health care area through clinical guidelines set up by the Brazilian Society of Family Medicine and Community.

The use of a multi-agent architecture in this type of situation makes its implementation possible, mainly in Web developing environments, modularizing development and generating a final product of greater quality and scientific relevance.

Several works have been devoted to this purpose counting with professionals in the health care area to model the specific knowledge in Bayesian networks, which also includes experts in the computational area generating the VR-MED language domain and modelling agents, and specialists in education, all working with pedagogical tactics to forward along with professionals in the area of simulators in the front-end development or friendly user interface.

The system is under development moving forward into the validation phase which will include tests, with medical school students, and is expected to occur in June 2012. Clinical experts collaborating in the project have already modelled networks concerning clinical cases of migraine, dyspepsia and parasitosis.

A Clinical Guidelines component, approved by the Brazilian Society of Family Medicine and Community (SBMFC), is planned to be integrated into the Family Health Specialization Program.

The contents of the clinical guideline on Migraine will be presented to 120 doctors who are students of the above mentioned Specialization course. A formal evaluation will be carried out, consisting of multiple choice questions to assess the student's performance regarding the topic discussed by the Clinical Guideline. After this evaluation, students will be subjected to the SimDeCS simulation, which will assess them in terms of diagnostic hit and coherent clinical conduct, cost of the proposed research and simulated time spent solving the complex case.

In order to avoid the bias of one evaluation succeeding another (in that this could incur in "training" and change the performance of the following stage), groups will be crossed over so that half the students carry out the formal evaluation before the simulation and the other half start with the system and then do the formal evaluation.

The simulation tool will require students to practice simulation in three complex cases. The first evaluation will be discarded, as it will be a practice task allowing participants to get familiar with the system and therefore its results should not be considered for user evaluation.

After this evaluation process, the system will be made available through the Internet, as a Web service, to all the UnA-SUS partners.

Acknowledgments. The authors gratefully acknowledge the Brazilian agencies, CAPES and UnA-SUS, and the National Funding from FCT - Fundação para a Ciência e a Tecnologia, under the project: PEst-OE/MAT/UI0152, for the partial support to this research project.

References

1. Flores, C.D., Seixas, L.J., Gluz, J.C., Vicari, R.M.: A Model of Pedagogical Negotiation. In: Bento, C., Cardoso, A., Dias, G. (eds.) EPIA 2005. LNCS (LNAI), vol. 3808, pp. 488–499. Springer, Heidelberg (2005)
2. Luiz, M., Helder, C.: On tailoring teams of software agents tuned for tasks. In: Proceedings of the Workshop on Multi-Agent Systems: Theory and Applications (MASTA 2001). 10th Portuguese Conference on Artificial Intelligence. Porto, Portugal (2001)

3. Holzinger, A., Kickmeier-Rust, M.D., Wassertheurer, S., Hessinger, M.: Learning performance with interactive simulations in medical education: Lessons learned from results of learning complex physiological models with the HAEMOdynamics SIMulator. Computer and Education 52, 292–301 (2009)
4. Botezatu, M., Hult, H., Fors, U.G.: Virtual patient simulation: what do students make of it? A focus group study. BMC Medical Education 10, 91 (2010)
5. Bradley, P.: The history of simulation in medical education and possible future directions. Medical Education 40, 254–262 (2006)
6. Kneebone, R.: Simulation in surgical training: educational issues and practical implications. Medical Education 37(3), 267–277 (2003)
7. Jensen, F.V., Olsen, K.G., Andersen, S.K.: An algebra of Bayesian belief universes for knowledge-based systems. Networks 20, 637–659 (1990)
8. Suebnukarn, S., Haddawy, P.: A Bayesian approach to generating tutorial hints in a collaborative medical problem-based learning system. Artif. Intell. Med. 38(1), 5–24 (2005)
9. Suebnukarn, S.: Intelligent tutoring system for clinical reasoning skill acquisition in dental students. J. Dent. Educ. 73(10), 1178–1186 (2009)
10. Athanasiou, M., Clark, J.Y.: A Bayesian network model for the diagnosis of the caring procedure for wheelchair users with spinal injury. Comput. Methods Programs Biomed. 95(suppl. 2), S.44–S.54 (2009)
11. de Oliveira, L.S., Andreão, R.V., Sarcinelli-Filho, M.: The use of Bayesian networks for heart beat classification. Adv. Exp. Med. Biol. 657, 217–231 (2010)
12. Pearl, J.: Belief networks revisited. Artificial Intelligence 59, 49–56 (1993)
13. Chakravarthy, B.: Medical Simulation in EM Training and Beyond. Newslett. Soc. Acad. Resid. 18(1), 18–19 (2006)
14. Ziv, A., Ben-David, S., Ziv, M.: Simulation Based Medical Education: an opportunity to learn from errors. Medical Teacher 27(3), 193–199 (2005)
15. Kincaid, J.P., Hamilton, R., et al.: Simulation in Education and Training. In: Modeling and Simulation: Theory and Applications, ch. 19. Kluver, Boston (2004)
16. Scalese, R.J., Obeso, V.T., Issenberg, S.B.: Simulation Technology for Skills Training and Competency Assessment in Medical Education. J. Gen. Intern. Med. 23(suppl. 1), 46–49 (2008)
17. Issenberg, S.B., McGaghie, W.C., Petrusa, E.R., Gordon, D.L., Scalese, R.J.: Features and uses of high-fidelity medical simulations that lead to effective learning: a BEME systematic review. Med. Teach. 27, 10–28 (2005)
18. Nishisaki, A., Keren, R., Nadkarni, V.: Does Simulation Improve Patient Safety?: Self-Efficacy, Competence, Operational Performance, and Patient Safety. Anesthesiology Clinics 25, 225–236 (2007)
19. Bleakley, A., Bligh, J., Browne, J.: Beyond Practical Reasoning. In: Medical Education for the Future: Identity, Power and Location, ch. 2. Springer, New York (2011)
20. Jensen, F.V.: An Introduction to Bayesian Networks, 188 p. UCL Press, London (1996)
21. Mossmann, J.B.: VR-MED: Domain-Specific Language for the Development of Virtual Environments Applied to Family Medicine. Technical report, Pontifícia Universidade Católica do Rio Grande do Sul (2011)
22. FIPA. SC00001L: Abstract Architecture Specification [S.l.] (2003), `http://www.fipa.org/specs/fipa00001/` (accessed in October 1, 2011)
23. Jade - Java Agent Development Framework, `http://jade.tilab.com/`
24. Brazilian Society of Family Medicine and Community (Sociedade Brasileira de Medicina de Família e Comunidade), `http://www.sbmfc.org.br/`

DSS for Winemaker: A Dynamic Modeling Approach

Hassan Ait Haddou[1,2], Guy Camilleri[1], and Pascale Zaraté[1]

[1] Toulouse University, Institut de Recherche en Informatique de Toulouse (IRIT)
118 Route de Narbonne 31062 Toulouse Cedex 9, France
[2] Toulouse University, Laboratoire de Génie Chimique (LGC)
{haddou,Guy.Camilleri,Pascale.Zarate}@irit.fr

Abstract. In this paper, we present a decision support system for the fermentation step in winemaking based on a mathematical model of kinetics of alcoholic fermentation. We used an optimization technique in order to predict the fermentation step. This optimization technique was carried out using the method of factorial analysis. The first interesting application of this system, rather than existing ones, comes from the fact that it can predict the evolution of pH during alcoholic fermentation. Recall that pH is used in oenology as an indicator of censorial properties, efficiency of sulfating and contamination risks. The second interesting application of this software is that it allows users "online" monitoring of the evolution of the constituents of grape musts.

Keywords: dynamic modeling, simulation, optimization, decision support systems, oenology.

1 Introduction

Decision support systems (DSSs) are generally designed for supporting decision makers in their decisional processes. Decision support systems are born in the 70's [1] and [2]. Their background has first of all to be presented.

Difference between Information and Decision must be shown. Decision-makers must take into account a lot of information coming from different entities and have sometimes a large amount of information to aggregate in order to reach the best solution. They need a personal and direct control on systems, which are designed for them. Decision and Information have to be classified referring to the level of management. We could distinguish three levels of management: operational level, control level and strategic management level. According to [3] at the operational level, information is numerous and very detailed. The same phenomenon could be observed for decision: there are a lot of decisions to make at the operational level and information usable for them is also in great proportion. At the control level, information is less numerous than in the previous case and decisions to make are more important. Information at this level is more aggregated. At the strategic management level, information is aggregated and not numerous and decisions to make have a very high impact in the management [4].

Decision-makers have to be supported in their task by systems like Decision Support Systems regardless of the level of management type.

J. Hernández et al. (Eds.): EWG-DSS 2011, LNBIP 121, pp. 74–87, 2012.

The decisional process handled by "winemakers" is generally not supported by software and it still remains a human process. Nevertheless, some systems have been developed in order to improve the production of wine and more specifically the organization of wine-makers cooperatives. For example [5] has developed a DSS in order to organize the production of wine.

Independently from the organization of the wine-maker cooperatives, the control and understanding of the alcoholic fermentation has been a subject of many investigations in the last few years. Indeed, several models of fermentation kinetics have been proposed and constitute the base of few existing decision support systems. [6] developed software named MEXTAR, which can be used to simulate alcoholic fermentations by combining kinetic and thermal models. [7] obtained good results on the prediction of the crystallization of tartaric salts in hydro-alcoholic solutions by using MEXTAR. However, the MEXTAR software did not take into account the evolution of pH. Recall that the optimization criteria of the quality of wine are generally accessible only by sensory analysis. This technique is very expensive and is not best suited to the control of alcoholic fermentation. Moreover, the pH is considered as an important decision criterion by winemakers and therefore, pH is an interesting indicator for the quality of wine which can at least replace the sensory analysis[1].

In this sense, [8] has developed a model to predict accurately pH evolution during alcoholic fermentation of must. We first extend this model to take into account amino acids and then use in the software that we developed. In this context, our main objective is to develop a modeling tool able to simulate the evolution of pH during fermentation and it is designed to assist winemakers to optimize tank management and to act upstream, if necessary, in the process.

Our approach is based on a mathematical model to predict the evolution of pH over time during fermentation. To develop this mathematical model, we use the data obtained by [8] from the fermentation in synthetic and natural grape. We have introduced into the mathematical model for predicting pH from the initial composition of the medium species of positively charged amino acids, neutral charge and negative charge and the dissociation equilibrium constraints. To establish a dynamic model of the alcoholic fermentation, it must first control the parameters that influence the evolution of pH throughout the fermentation. To do this, we conduct a sensitivity study on the constituents of the must to remove any component that does not have a great influence on the evolution of pH during fermentation. With this sensitivity analysis we have identified six principal constituents namely, the sugar, ethanol, biomass, amino acids, carbon dioxide and nitrogen.

This work is divided into four parts. The first part is introductory, and it contains the construction of the mathematical model and gives a preliminary analysis needed for the rest of this work. In particular, we give and test the validity of the mathematical model for predicting the evolution of pH during the alcoholic fermentation. We also describe the kinetic model and give dynamic characteristics of the process.

The purpose of the second part is to develop a decision support system for fermentation in winemaking by using the mathematical model of kinetics of alcoholic

[1] Sensory analysis consists in using human sensory to define the quality of the product.

fermentation developed in the first part. We first give a complete database that lists all components required for the inputs of the mathematical model developed before. The rest of this section is devoted to the decision support system and its functionalities.

Finally, in the last part, we validate the software by using four different mediums whose composition is well known.

2 Models and Simulation

The purpose of this section is to develop a mathematical model for predicting the evolution of pH during the alcoholic fermentation. This model is required to construct the decision support system and is part of the Model Base of the global system.

2.1 pH Simulation

[8] proposed a model to predict pH evolution during alcoholic fermentation of specific must by the microorganism QA-23 [9]. To do this, [8] used two kinds of models. The first one is used to calculate pH knowing the composition of the medium and the second model represents the dynamic of fermentation to find the evolution of the composition of the medium.

pH as a Mathematical Function
As shown in the introduction, the pH value is an important decision criterion for winemaker and it is necessary to give a mathematical model able to predict its evolution. To do this, we first establish the mathematical function modeling the evolution of pH.

pH is a measure of the acidity of a solution and it expresses the activity of hydrogen ions. The mathematical formula of pH, using a logarithmic scale, is given by:

$$pH = -\log(aH+) = -\log_{10}(\gamma H + mH+)$$

where γH+ is the ion activity coefficient and mH+ is the molality of hydrogen ions. The activity coefficient H^+ ($_{H+}$) is calculated using the method of [10].

By writing a mass balance on each species in solution, one can easily formulate the reactor model and then get a model including as many variables as the number of reactions in the medium. Otherwise, we will show in the next section that the number of reactions in the medium is reduced to three reactions.

The initial model developed in [8] takes into account: the temperature, the concentrations in sugar, ethanol, nitrogen compounds, mineral elements and some organic acids. We extend this model by adding mainly amino acids.

The initial difficulty can be overcome by reducing the numerical problem which is easy by writing the mass balance on an invariant of the reactive system. Then, the pH value is determined by solving a non-linear algebraic equations system consisted of mass balances, chemical equilibrium equations and the principle of electro-neutrality. Model implementation and simulations were carried out using fortran90 language. This enabled the application of different numerical methods and the Runge-Kutta fourth was used in all simulations.

Model Validation

In order to test the validity of the model, the synthetic medium was used and its constituents composed the inputs of the model. This medium was chosen because its composition is perfectly known. Experimental and simulated pH values are in a well agreement as shown in Figure 1.

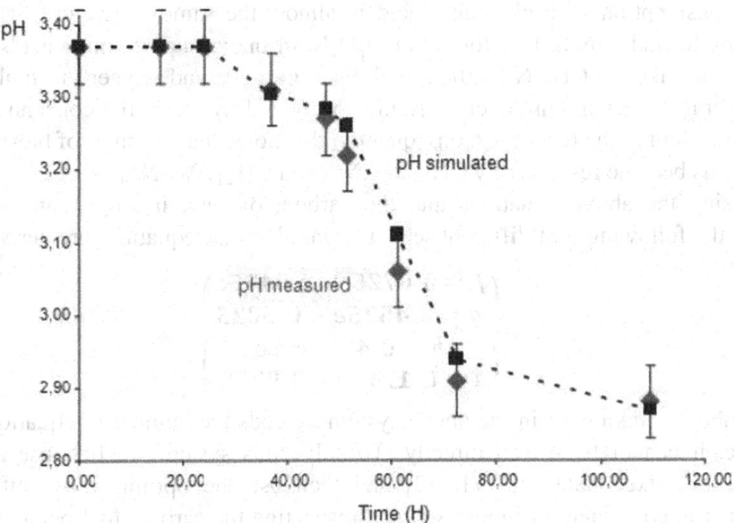

Fig. 1. pH evolution

2.2 Kinetic Model

Decision support criterion to be developed here requires modeling the evolution of each component that significantly influences the pH during the alcoholic fermentation. To do this, it is necessary to study the kinetic of the reaction scheme obtained by the study of sensitivity. According to the study of sensitivity, the compounds of the fermentation to be modeled are sugars, ethanol, biomass, amino acids, carbon dioxide and nitrogen. These constituents were specifically determined for alcoholic fermentation in winemaking conditions and based on the initial conditions. Taking into account the results of the study of sensitivity, the reaction scheme we have adopted is:

- Production of ethanol from glucose
- Biomass production from amino acids and sugars.

Therefore, this reaction scheme can be schematically represented as:

(R1): $C_6H_{12}O_6 \rightarrow 2CH_3 - CH_2 - OH + 2CO_2$

(R2): $C_6H_{12}O_6 + aNH_3 \rightarrow bCH_xO_yN_z + cCO_2 + dH_2O$

(R3): $CH_pO_qN_r + iC_6H_{12}O_6 \rightarrow ebCH_xO_yN_z + fCO_2 + gH_2O + hNH_3$

where *a,b,c,d,e,f,g,h* and *i* are the stochiometric coefficients to be found by the carbon balance, $CH_xO_yN_z$ and $CH_pO_qN_r$ are respectively the molecular formula of biomass and amino acids.

The constants *x,y* and *z* are calculated from elemental analysis of biomass. However, the molecular formula of the amino acids cannot be calculated directly. The experimental data used in this study takes into account 23 types of amino acids. The rate of consumption of each amino acid is almost the same. Therefore, it is very interesting to find a molecular formula $CH_pO_qN_r$ of one group of amino acids. To do this, we will take the CHON (carbon, hydrogen, nitrogen and oxygen) formula equal to the average of each amino acid formulas, weighted by the initial concentration of each amino acid in the reaction. Consequently, the molecular formulas of biomass and amino acids become respectively $CH_{1.79}O_{0.5}N_{0.2}$ and $CH_{2.14}O_{0.47}N_{0.43}$.

By using the above equations and the carbon, oxygen, hydrogen and nitrogen balance, the following four different sets of linear algebraic equations are derived:

$$(1): \begin{Bmatrix} f = 0.0725 + 0.0475e \\ g = 0.4525e - 0.6025 \\ h = 0.43 - 0.2e \\ i = 0.1746e - 0.9275 \end{Bmatrix}$$

The number of unknowns in the above system exceeds the number of equations and, therefore, it cannot be solved directly. To solve this system we first use a factor analysis for mixed data see [11, 12] and then use the optimizer by setting the stochiometric coefficient of biomass *e*, and respecting the carbon, hydrogen, nitrogen and oxygen balance for the stochiometric coefficients. According to our experiments data, the optimal value of *e* is equal to 10.60.

2.3 Mathematical Model

The purpose of this part is to model the evolution of compounds that significantly influence the pH during the alcoholic fermentation. The components included in this

Table 1. Mathematical models representing the kinetics of microbial growth

Model	Maximum specific cellular growth rate
Moser(1958)	$\mu = \mu_{max}\ S^n / S^n + K_s$
Hanson and Tsao(1972)	$\mu = \mu_{max}\ S^n / S^n - K_s$
Andrews (1968)	$\mu = \mu_{max}\ S / (K_s - S)(1 + SK_I)$
Han and Levenspiel(1988)	$\mu = \mu_{max}\ (1 - SS_n)^n\ S / S + K_s\ (1 - SS_n)^m$
Aiba et coll.(by Han and Levenspiel)	$\mu = \mu_{max}\ \exp(-SK_I)\ S / K_s + S$
Teissier. (by Han and Levenspiel)	$\mu = \mu_{max}\ \{\exp(-SK_I) - \exp(-SK_s)\}$
Luong(1987)	$\mu = \mu_{max}\ (1 + SS_c)^n\ S / S + K_s$
Aiba et coll. (1968)	$\mu = \mu_{max}\ K_pP\ S / K_s + S + K_p$
Kishimoto et coll. (1983)	$\mu = \mu_{max}\ S / (K_p + S)(1 + P^2)$
Han and Levenspiel(1988)	$\mu = \mu_{max}\ S(1 - PP_c)^n / S + K_s(1 - PP_c)^m$
Luong(1987)	$\mu = \mu_{max}\ (1 - KP)\ S / K_s + S$
Aiba et coll. (1968)	$\mu = \mu_{max}\ \exp(-KP)\ S / K_s + S$

study, are the following: sugar, ethanol, nitrogen, CO2, biomass and amino acids. Models representing the dynamics of these compounds in wine are not available in the literature. They should be developed to obtain a final model that could predict the development of lead compounds, to calculate the duration of fermentation and give at any time the pH of must. The various mathematical models most frequently used to represent the kinetics of microbial growth are summarized in Table 1. These models are all based on establishing a mass balance on one or more components.

2.4 Dynamic Characteristics of the Process

It was observed in [13, 14, 15, 16] that the evolution of pH depends only on the kinetic of the considered reactions. Therefore, let r_1, r_2 and r_3 be the speeds of the three previous reactions *R*1, *R*2 and *R*3 respectively. The following equations describe the time course of biomass, ethanol, sugar, amino acids and nitrogen:

$$(2):\left\{\begin{array}{c} \frac{dX}{dt} = 5.73r2 + e.r3 \\ \frac{dS}{dt} = -r1 - r2 - i.r3 \\ \frac{dEth}{dt} = 2r1 \\ \frac{dCO2}{dt} = 2r1 + 0.27.r2 + g.r3 \\ \frac{dNH3}{dt} = -1.15r2 + h.r3 \\ \frac{dAA}{dt} = -r3 \end{array}\right.$$

where *X*, *Eth*, NH_3, CO_2, *AA* and *S* correspond respectively to biomass, nitrogen, carbonic anhydride, amino acids and sugar.

We have a system of six differential equations of first order. To solve it we must give explicit expressions of r_1, r_2 and r_3.

According to [17], [18], the production of biomass from sugar is given by the following equation:

$$\frac{dX}{dt} = r2 = \mu max \frac{S}{S+k2} \quad (1)$$

where μ_{max} is the maximal specific growth rate and the saturation parameter to be found.

However, according to our experimental data, the production of biomass depends also on nitrogen concentration. It is therefore necessary to take into account this concentration in the last equation. Therefore, the equation (1) can be formulated as bellow:

$$\frac{dX}{dt} = r2 = \mu max \frac{S}{S+k2} \frac{[NH3]}{[NH3]+k4} \quad (2)$$

For the first reaction, we use the generalized logistic model, which serves conveniently for mathematical fitting. Consequently, the rate at which the concentrations of ethanol and sugar change is given by the following equation:

$$r_1 = k_1 [X] [S] \quad (3)$$

By the experimental data used to develop this model, we remark that the speed of the last reaction is proportional to the concentration of amino acids, namely:

$$r_3 = k_3\,[AA] \quad (4)$$

With respect to the expression of *r*1, *r*2 and *r*3, the dynamic model is described by the following differential equations:

$$(3):\left\{\begin{array}{c} \frac{dX}{dt} = 5.73\,k1\,[X]\,[S] + e.\,k3\,[AA] \\ \frac{dS}{dt} = -k1\,[X]\,[S] - \mu max\,\frac{S}{S+k2}\frac{[NH3]}{[NH3]+k4} - i.\,k3\,[AA] \\ \frac{dEth}{dt} = 2k1\,[X]\,[S] \\ \frac{dCO2}{dt} = 2k1\,[X]\,[S] + 0.27.\,\mu max\,\frac{S}{S+k2}\frac{[NH3]}{[NH3]+k4} + g.\,k3\,[AA] \\ \frac{dNH3}{dt} = -1.15\mu max\,\frac{S}{S+k2}\frac{[NH3]}{[NH3]+k4} + h.\,k3\,[AA] \\ \frac{dAA}{dt} = -k3\,[AA] \end{array}\right.$$

Parameters Determination

The purpose of this part is to describe how to find optimal parameters which make agreed simulated results from the equations system and experimental data. To do this, we used the system of differential equations to recalculate the concentrations of each component of the each environment studied.

The following partial criterion

$$Crit = \frac{([Concentration]exp - [Concentration]simulated)2}{[Concentration]exp}$$

is chosen for each component and then a global criterion which is equal to the sum of all criteria. For each fermentation medium, we then used an optimizer to find the best values of system parameters.

3 Oenodecision: The Decision Support System

The second part of this work is to develop the decision support software for fermentation in winemaking by using the mathematical model of kinetics of alcoholic fermentation developed in the first part of this paper. As mentioned previously, the proposed system is composed by a data base, a model base and a user friendly interface. The model base is described in the previous section and the data base is developed in the next section. The conceptual model of the data is built on specifications in Entities-Relationship model as shown in Figure 2.

This software is designed to allow the user to easily set up a system to monitor up to six variables (the concentrations in sugars, biomass, ethanol, amino acids and nitrogen) but it can be easily extended for other inputs.

Our objective was to develop a system available in a Web platform; it is implemented thanks to MySQL for the database and PHP for the interface. FORTRAN90 was used to solve the dynamics models and the model base is usable by the system through a DLL routines.

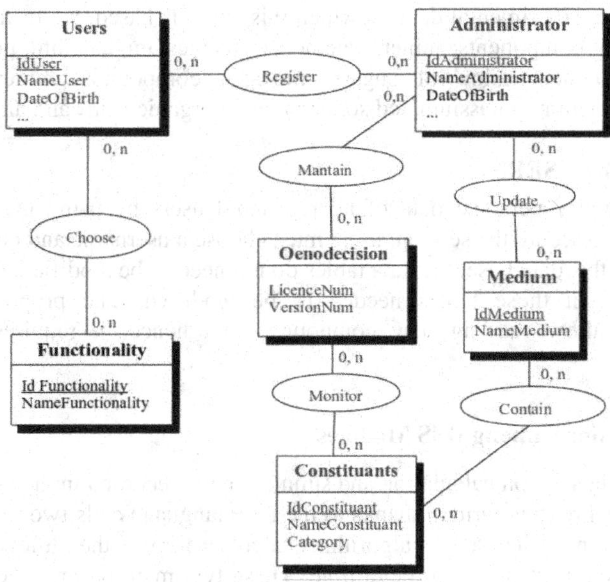

Fig. 2. Conceptual model of data

3.1 The Database

The Database is composed by 12 tables. Some tables are very simple and are not described in this study. We only describe the tables Constituents and the table Users.

Based on the figure 2, the relational schema is the following:

CONSTITUANTS (IdConstituant , NameConstituant , Category)
USERS (IdUser , NameUser , DateOfBirth,…)
ADMINISTRATOR (IdAdministrator , NameAdministratot , DateOfBirth,…)
MEDIUM (IdMedium , NameMedium)
FUNCTIONALITY (Id_Functionality , NameFunctionality)
OENODECISION (LicenceNum , VersionNum)
REGISTER (IdUser* , IdAdministrator*)
MAINTAIN (IdAdministrator* , LicenceNum*)
CHOOSE (IdUser* , Id_Functionality*)
UPDATE (IdAdministrator* , IdMedium*)
CONTAIN (IdMedium* , IdConstituant*)
MONITOR (LicenceNum* , IdConstituant*)

Database Table: CONSTITUANTS

Developing software monitoring the evolution of constituents of grape must, according to the evolution of pH, requires a database that lists all chemical components that influence the kinetics of alcoholic fermentation. In this study, we create a database including all inputs of the above model. This database can be upgraded easily by other entries according to the evolution of the mathematical model.

According to experimental data on which this study is based, we restrict ourselves to the following components: mineral elements (magnesium, calcium, potassium and sodium), the concentration of sugars, nitrogen compounds, mineral elements (magnesium, calcium, potassium and sodium), main organic acids and amino acids.

Database Table: USERS

This table contains personal data of all registered users by using the Registration form. In order to secure the session, users must choose a username and password.

To upgrade this data base, the data tables do not need to be modified. Only the type of data stored in those tables needed to be modified. The proposed interface automatically allows adding new compounds and hence, it requires a minimal maintenance.

3.2 Interactions among DSS Modules

All necessary data for ph calculation and simulation are recorded in the Database.

One principal routine written thanks to the PHP language calls two main programs written in Fortran 90. These two algorithms calculate for one the ph level and for the other the evolution of the ph at delta time. These two main programs constitute the models base of the DSS. The date exchanges between the database and the calculation routines are written directly in the PHP code thanks to call functions the database.

The human/machine interface is coded in PHP language.

3.3 Software Interface and Functionalities

The functionalities of the software developed here are described through a user-friendly interface and provide support for the design and implementation of application facilities as shown in Figure 3.

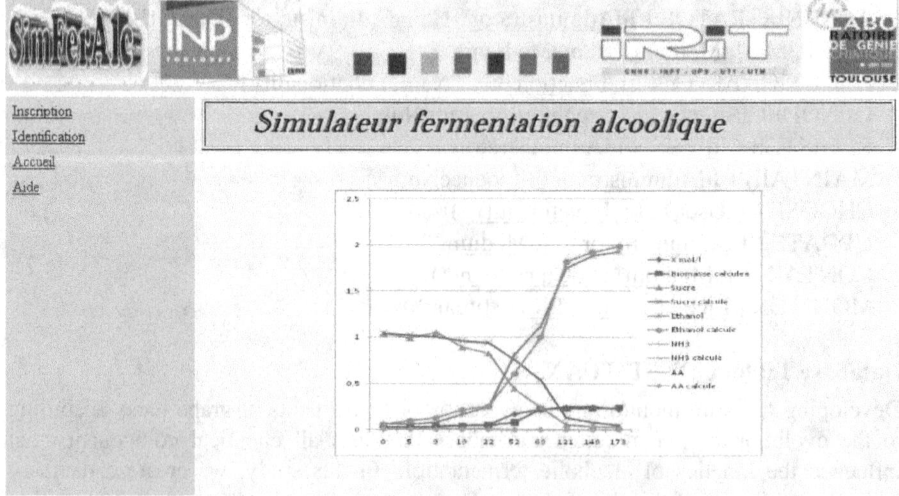

Fig. 3. Software interface

First Step: Registration and Identification
To use this software, a user must first register using the "Registration" form and choose a username and password. The information entered on this form is stored in the local database. The need for a secure session ensures that only the manager of the winery has the privilege to act in the process of fermentation.

Second Step: Identification and Functionalities
Once the new user is registered in the database and has chosen the appropriate login and password, he can now log in and choose between the two essential functionalities of the software described below.

pH Simulation:
The first feature of this interface consists on the computation of pH of the fermentation. To predict the final pH value of the fermentation, user completes the initial data from the must of grapes needed for this issue. These data are: temperature, mineral elements (magnesium, calcium, potassium and sodium) and the concentration of sugars, nitrogen compounds, mineral elements (magnesium, calcium, potassium and sodium), main organic acids and amino acids.

The entered data will constitute the inputs of the mathematical model developed in the first part of this paper. Once all required inputs are entered, the user validates by clicking on the button "submit" in the bottom of data form.

After validation, the program written in FORTRAN90 runs automatically in order to integrate the system of differential equations and then returns respectively, the pH value of the end of fermentation and the graphic of the evolution of the pH. The response times are very satisfactory and it is almost instantaneous.

Online Kinetic Monitoring:
The second feature of this software consists on the online monitoring of fermentation. As shown in the development of the kinetic model and according to the absolute sensitivity analysis that was carried out, the compounds of the fermentation to be monitored in this software are sugars, ethanol, biomass, amino acids, carbon dioxide and nitrogen.

The user selects the feature that allows monitoring the evolution of each component of the medium; a form appears containing boxes to be filled by respectively, the suitable time interval and the initial concentrations of each component of the chosen medium. When the form is filled out, the data from the form is added automatically to the database associated with this software. The user can then choose between three settings:

• View data table with respect to the given time interval;
• View of the graphical display of the results, namely, the evolution curve of each component from the start time to the end of each fermentation (figure 4);
• View the data table and curves simultaneously.

The user has the possibility here to see how the medium will evolve. The winemakers generally know when the fermentation is critical. Thanks to this expertise the system offers them the possibility to check if the fermentation will be critical or not. In that sense the wine-makers judgment is used in order to control the evolution of the fermentation. By this control the quality of the decision will necessarily be improved and by consequence the wine also will be improved.

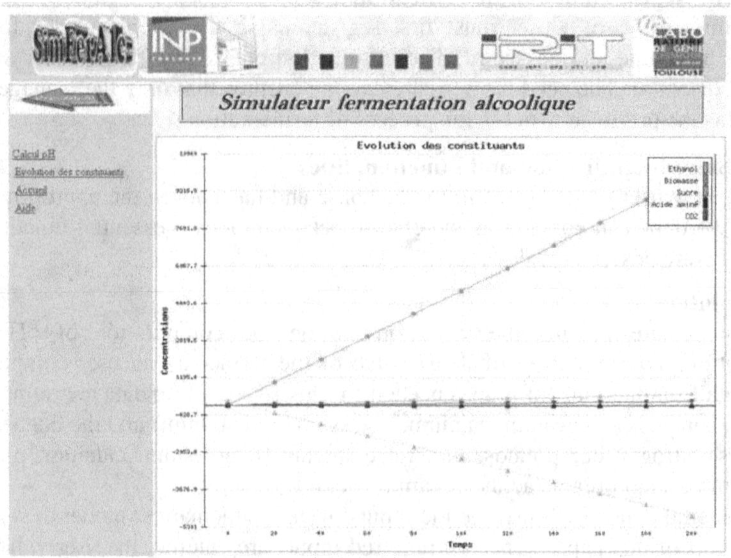

Fig. 4. Curves of simulated compounds

The effect of temperature has been studied by many authors [18, 20, 6], and has a significant effect on the duration of the fermentation and also for the maximum rate of sugar consumption. However, it is important to mention that the temperature is not taken into account in the model and in this software and we assumed that it is kept constant during fermentation. That is not necessarily the case in real life.

4 Models Validation

In order to test this software, we worked on four different mediums whose composition is well known. The initial concentrations of sugars, ethanol, biomass, amino acids, carbon dioxide and nitrogen of each medium are injected into the soft and the output results are compared with experimental results.

The experimental data (table 2) used here was those used by Akin, [8] that were obtained during the fermentation of a synthetic grape medium by *S.cerevisae* [20, 21, 22, 23]. The figure 5 below shows the comparison of the evolution of the pH simulated and the pHmeasured during the alcoholic fermentation of the white grape by *Saccharomycescerevisae*.

In the figure 5, experimental and simulated values of each compound are plotted. As can be seen, the predicted curves and experimental results are in excellent approximation.

Table 2. Table of experimental data of synthetic medium

Time (h)	pH	Biomass cel/mL	ethanol (g/L)	amino-acids (mg N/L)	co2 (g/L)
0	3,23	1000000	0,642832	305	0
15,7	3,23	2115340	0,771872	256	1,83
24	3,23	9249600	1,639648	243	2,474
36,937	3,16	46245000	7,435832	163	8,874
42,63	3,13	75845000	14,433968	93	20,09
47,53	3,13	133555000	22,346624	0	26,683
51,58	3,13	171865000	45,51024	0	41,551
61,16	3,15	204050000	59,769808	0	55,251
72,55	3,17	217035000	94,008568	0	85,953
109,54	3,25	22129000	0	0	0

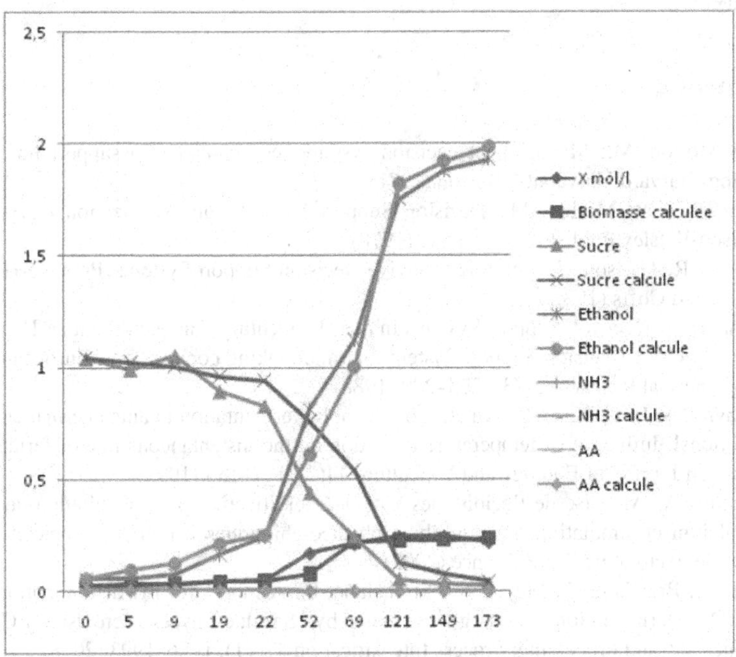

Fig. 5. Evolution of experimental and simulated compounds of grape

5 Conclusion

The presented software is the first software based on the model of prediction of pH. This is contrary to the concept what exists in the literature based on measurements of released during fermentation which is usually difficult and very expensive.

We also presented another functionality of the system for fermentation in winemaking based on a mathematical model of kinetics of alcoholic fermentation.

The optimization was carried out using the method of factorial analysis. The software developed here can simulate both the evolution of different compounds and predict pH from measurement of the main compounds of the medium.

In order to test different control structures, a parametric sensitivity analysis was carried out. The proposed software has been tested and validated on four different mediums. The system has also been proposed to real winemakers and was really successfully. One way to improve the system usability would be to connect the software to pH sensors.

One limit must be drawn, the model presented here does not take in account variation temperature and we assumed that it is constant equal to 20°c. Therefore, in the long term, the model must be extended to take in account this phenomenon.

Acknowledgments. This work has been conducted in collaboration with the Chemical Engineering Laboratory (LGC: http://lgc.inp-toulouse.fr/) at Toulouse University.

References

1. Scott Morton, M.: Management decision systems, computer based support for decision making. Harvard University, Boston (1971)
2. Keen, P., Scott Morton, M.: Decision Support Systems: an organizational perspective. Addison-Wesley Publishing Company (1978)
3. Sprague, R., Carlson, E.: Building Effective Decision Support Systems. Prentice-Hall, Inc., Englewood Cliffs (1982)
4. Marakas, G.: Decision Support Systems In the 21st Century, 2nd edn. Prentice-Hall (2003)
5. Gertosio, C.: A Decision Support System for wine-making cooperatives. European Journal of Operational Research 33(3), 273–279 (1988)
6. Sablayrolles, J.M., Barre, P.: Kinetics of alcoholic fermentation in anisothermal enological conditionsI. Influence of temperature evolution on the instantaneous rate of fermentation. American Journal of Enology and Viticulture 44(2), 127–133 (1993)
7. Devatine, A.: Maîtrise de l'acidité des vins. Désacidification par précipitation de malates de calcium et simulation des équilibres physico-chimiques à l'aide du logiciel Mextar. Thèse de doctorat de l'INP, France (2002)
8. Akin, H., Brandam, C., Meyer, M., Strehaiano, P.: A model for pH determination during alcoholic fermentation of a grape must by Saccharomyces cerevisiae. Chemical Engineering and Processing: Process Intensification 47(11), 1986–1993 (2008)
9. Nicolini, G., Larcher, R., Versini, G.: Status of yeast assimilable nitrogen in Italian grape musts and effects of variety, ripening and vintage. Vitis 43(2), 89–96 (2004)
10. Carnahan, B., Luther, H.A., Wilkes, J.O.: Applied Numerical Methods. John Wiley&Sons (1969)
11. Fillon, M.: Développement d'une méthodologie pour la modélisation et la simulation des réacteurs discontinus. Application à la fermentation brassicole. Thèse de doctorat de l'Institut National Polytechnique de Toulouse, France (1996)
12. Moreau, A.: Contribution au contrôle de la culture de Brevibacterium linens en réacteur batch. Modélisation et optimisation des cinétiques de croissance sur substrat mixte. Thèse de doctorat de l'Institut National Polytechnique de Toulouse, France (2000)

13. Taillandier, P., Bonnet, J.S.: Le vin: composition et transformations chimiques. Edition Lavoisier (2005)
14. Butzke, C.E.: Study of yeast assimilable N status in musts from California, Oregon and Washington. American Journal of Enology and Viticulture 49(2), 220–224 (1998)
15. Charnomordic, B., Glorennec, P.-Y., Guillaume, S.: An open source portable software for fuzzy inference systems. XI congresso espanol sobre tecnologias y logica fuzzy, ESIA-Université de Savoie, Leon, Spain, pp. 349-351 (2002)
16. Colombié, S., Malherbe, S., Sablayrolles, J.M.: Modeling alcoholic fermentation in enological conditions: feasibility and interest. American Journal of Enology and Viticulture 56(3), 238–245 (2005)
17. Balbi, N., Balbi, J.H., Chiaramonti, N., Khoumeri, B.: Modélisation de la dynamique de fermentation alcoolique. Journal of Thermal Analysis 44, 571–581 (1995)
18. Ramon-Portugal, F.: Interaction de type killer entre levures: analyse cinétique, co-culture et modélisation. Thèse de doctorat de l'Institut National Polytechnique de Toulouse, France (1995)
19. Malherbe, S., Fromion, V., Hilgert, N., Sablayrolles, J.M.: Modeling the effects of assimilable nitrogen and temperature on fermentation kinetics in enological conditions. Biotechnology and Bioengineering 86, 261–272 (2004)
20. Remedios-Marin, M.: Alcoholic fermentation modelling: Current state and perspectives. American Journal of Enology and Viticulture 50(2), 166–178 (1999)
21. Cramer, A.C., Vlassides, S., Block, D.E.: Kinetic model for nitrogen-limited wine fermentations. Biotechnology and Bioengineering 77(1), 49–60 (2002)
22. Dubois, D., Yager, R., Prade, H.: Fuzzy information engineering: A guided tour of applications. John Wiley (1997)
23. El-Haloui, N., Picque, D., Corrieu, G.: Alcoholic fermentation in winemaking: On-line measurement of density and carbon dioxide evolution. Journal of Food Engineering 8(1), 17–30 (1988)

Collaborative Dynamic Decision Making: A Case Study from B2B Supplier Selection

G. Campanella[1], A. Pereira[1], Rita A. Ribeiro[1,*], and Maria Leonilde R. Varela[2]

[1] UNINOVA–CA3, Campus FCT–UNL, 2829-516 Caparica, Portugal
gianluca@campanella.org, {ap,rar}@uninova.pt
[2] Departamento de Produção e Sistemas, Universidade do Minho, Portugal
leonilde@dps.uminho.pt

Abstract. The problem of supplier selection can be easily modeled as a multiple-criteria decision making (MCDM) problem: businesses express their preferences with respect to suppliers, which can then be ranked and selected. This approach has two major pitfalls: first, it does not consider a dynamic scenario, in which suppliers and their ratings are constantly changing; second, it only addressed the problem from the point of view of a single business, and cannot be easily applied when considering more than one business. To overcome these problems, we introduce a method for supplier selection that builds upon the dynamic MCDM framework of Campanella and Ribeiro [1] and, by means of a linear programming model, can be used in the case of multiple collaborating businesses planning their next batch of orders together.

1 Introduction

Complex decision making is a process extended in time: real-world decision problems are dynamic in the sense that they are the outcome of a sequence of decisions or of an exploratory process, during which both alternatives and criteria may vary. Dynamic decision making problems are characterized by three key properties:

1. the temporal profile of an alternative matters for comparison with other alternatives;
2. alternatives are not fixed, since they might be deemed nonviable and discarded, and likewise new options might be taken into consideration and added;
3. criteria are not fixed, not only because corresponding values might change over time, but also because new criteria might be considered, or existing ones removed.

Multiple-criteria decision making (MCDM) methods deal with selection of alternatives from evaluations over criteria. They model two fundamental aspects of decision problems:

* This work has been partially funded by Fundação para a Ciência e a Tecnologia, Portugal, under contract CONT_DOUT/49/UNINOVA/0/5902/1/2006.

J.E. Hernández et al. (Eds.): EWG-DSS 2011, LNBIP 121, pp. 88–102, 2012.

1. they capture the relevant quantitative and qualitative criteria – such as cost, efficiency, and performance – for a specific decision problem;
2. they support the intricate trade-off process when considering different alternatives.

They are, in general, methods for eliciting evaluations and aggregating criteria measurements in order to compose a ranked list of alternatives. However, they are unable to deal with dynamic situations: they usually assume a fixed set of alternatives and criteria, and thus cannot be used to adequately model the characteristics of a dynamic decision making process in a changeable environment.

Recently, Campanella and Ribeiro proposed a framework for *dynamic* MCDM [1] to address this gap in the decision making literature [2]. This framework was developed in the context of a specific spatial-temporal decision problem [3, 4]; it is, however, domain-independent and thus useful for any domain that includes dynamic decision making. In the present paper, we extend the dynamic MCDM framework of Campanella and Ribeiro [1] to the problem of supplier selection. This problem cuts across many different industries for which suppliers play a key role in the supply chain [5], and in its standard form can be easily stated as a MCDM problem.

This chapter is organized as follows. In Section 2, we describe the basic MCDM operations and the dynamic MCDM framework. In Section 3, we discuss how the problem of supplier selection can be tackled using the proposed framework, in the case of a single business as well as in the case of multiple collaborating businesses served by the same set of suppliers. In Section 4, we work through an illustrative example to facilitate the understanding and demonstrate the effectiveness of the proposed method. Finally, in Section 5, we conclude by suggesting other possible application areas, and by proposing directions for future research.

2 Dynamic Multiple-Criteria Decision Making

In general, the aim of MCDM methods is to identify the best compromise solution from a set of feasible alternatives assessed with respect to a predefined set of (usually conflicting) criteria.

The decision making literature contains many approaches to the *static* version of this problem [6, 7]. It makes sense that current techniques are geared towards a one-shot decision; complex decision problems – the kind that benefits from decision support systems – are often about making one important decision. These methods, however, are not easily adapted to *dynamic* decision making, which, quoting Brehmer [8], can be defined as

> ...decision making under conditions which require a series of decisions, where the decisions are not independent, where the state of the world changes, both autonomously and as a consequence of the decision maker's actions.

Dynamic decision making methods must thus be able to support interdependent decisions in an evolving environment, in which both criteria and alternatives may change, and later decisions need to take into account *feedback* from previous ones.

2.1 Structure of Static MCDM Methods

Before we introduce the dynamic MCDM framework of Campanella and Ribeiro [1], it is important to briefly describe the high-level structure of most static MCDM methods, since it constitutes the foundation upon which the framework is built. Broadly speaking, we can identify two phases in the decision making process, namely preference elicitation and aggregation.

Preference Elicitation. The first step of static MCDM methods is known as *preference elicitation* and consists in identifying the available alternatives, fixing the criteria that will be used in the evaluation, and deriving the preference structure, which may be expressed using different types of scales [9]. As noted by Aloysius et al. [10], this process is of paramount importance and may even directly affect user acceptance of MCDM methods; many different techniques have thus been proposed in the literature (see, for example, [11] and references therein).

Once the preference structure is obtained, it is necessary to translate it into numerical values that express the relative performance of each alternative with respect to each criterion; these values are usually assumed to belong to the unit interval $\mathbb{I} = [0, 1]$. Mathematically, a typical MCDM problem with m alternatives and n criteria is modeled by the matrix

$$\begin{array}{c} \\ a_1 \\ a_2 \\ \vdots \\ a_m \end{array} \begin{array}{c} \begin{array}{cccc} c_1 & c_2 & \cdots & c_n \end{array} \\ \begin{bmatrix} x_{11} & x_{12} & \cdots & x_{1n} \\ x_{21} & x_{22} & \cdots & x_{2n} \\ \vdots & \vdots & \ddots & \vdots \\ x_{m1} & x_{m2} & \cdots & x_{mn} \end{bmatrix} \end{array} = \begin{bmatrix} \boldsymbol{x}_1 \\ \boldsymbol{x}_2 \\ \vdots \\ \boldsymbol{x}_m \end{bmatrix}, \tag{1}$$

where $x_{ij} \in \mathbb{I}$ represents the level of achievement of alternative a_i, $i = 1, \ldots, m$ with respect to criterion c_j, $j = 1, \ldots, n$, with 0 interpreted as "no satisfaction" and 1 corresponding to "complete satisfaction".

In the case of imprecise or uncertain data, fuzzy logic can be used to guarantee normalization and comparability of input variables, which would be represented by means of fuzzy membership functions [12].

Aggregation. After numerical values for each alternative have been elicited, they can aggregated into another numerical value, also belonging to the unit interval, that is understood to represent the preferableness of that alternative relative to all others. Given these values, alternatives may then be ordered, thus producing a ranking, and the best one can be selected.

Aggregation is achieved by means of an *aggregation function* (sometimes improperly called aggregation operator), formally defined as follows [13].

Definition 1 (Aggregation Function). *An* aggregation function $f : \mathbb{I}^n \to \mathbb{I}$ *is a function of* $n > 1$ *variables that maps points* $\boldsymbol{x} = (x_1, \ldots, x_n)$ *in the unit* *hypercube* $\mathbb{I}^n$ *to single values in the unit interval* $\mathbb{I}$ *and that satisfies, for all* $\boldsymbol{x}, \boldsymbol{y} \in \mathbb{I}^n$,

$$\begin{cases} f(\underbrace{0, 0, \ldots, 0}_{n \text{ times}}) = 0 \\ f(\underbrace{1, 1, \ldots, 1}_{n \text{ times}}) = 1 \end{cases} \qquad \textit{(preservation of bounds)}, \tag{2}$$

$$\boldsymbol{x} \leq \boldsymbol{y} \Rightarrow f(\boldsymbol{x}) \leq f(\boldsymbol{y}) \qquad \textit{(monotonicity)}. \tag{3}$$

Remark 1 (Weight vector). In this context, it is common to introduce a weight vector $\boldsymbol{w} \in [0, 1]^n$ whose generic element $w_j, j = 1, \ldots, m$ is the weight associated to criterion c_j expressing its importance relative to all others. These weights must satisfy the normalization condition $\sum_j w_j = 1$.

Intuitively, mathematical properties of the function chosen for aggregation will directly affect output values and, therefore, the final ranking of alternatives. An important property that can be required of aggregation functions is *associativity*, defined as follows.

Definition 2 (Associativity). *A bivariate aggregation function* $f : \mathbb{I}^2 \to \mathbb{I}$ *is said to be* associative *if, for all* $x_1, x_2, x_3 \in \mathbb{I}$, *it holds that*

$$f(f(x_1, x_2), x_3) = f(x_1, f(x_2, x_3)). \tag{4}$$

Remark 2. By iterative application, any bivariate aggregation function unambiguously defines a family of n-ary aggregation functions for $n \geq 2$.

It is also common to classify aggregation functions according to their behavior; we have the following definitions [13].

Definition 3 (Conjunctive Aggregation Function). *An aggregation function is said to be conjunctive if, for every* $\boldsymbol{x} \in \mathbb{I}^n$, *it holds that* $f(\boldsymbol{x}) \leq \min(\boldsymbol{x})$.

Definition 4 (Averaging Aggregation Function). *An aggregation function is said to be averaging if, for every* $\boldsymbol{x} \in \mathbb{I}^n$, *it holds that* $\min(\boldsymbol{x}) \leq f(\boldsymbol{x}) \leq \max(\boldsymbol{x})$.

Definition 5 (Disjunctive Aggregation Function). *An aggregation function is said to be disjunctive if, for every* $\boldsymbol{x} \in \mathbb{I}^n$, *it holds that* $f(\boldsymbol{x}) \geq \max(\boldsymbol{x})$.

Definition 6 (Mixed Aggregation Function). *An aggregation function is said to be mixed if it behaves differently on different parts of its domain, and thus does not belong to any of the classes hitherto presented.*

The literature on aggregation functions is extremely rich, and entire books have been written on the subject. As a general introduction, we suggest the books by Beliakov et al. [13] and Torra and Narukawa [14]; other important references can be found in the paper by Campanella and Ribeiro [1].

2.2 Dynamic MCDM Framework

Having briefly presented the structure of static MCDM methods, we shall now introduce the dynamic MCDM framework proposed by Campanella and Ribeiro [1]. Its most prominent feature is the addition of *feedback* to the decision process, a critical aspect of how humans reach a decision, even in situation where the problem is fully specified [15]. The operations performed at each decision moment are schematically depicted in Figure 1, and will be fully described in the rest of this section.

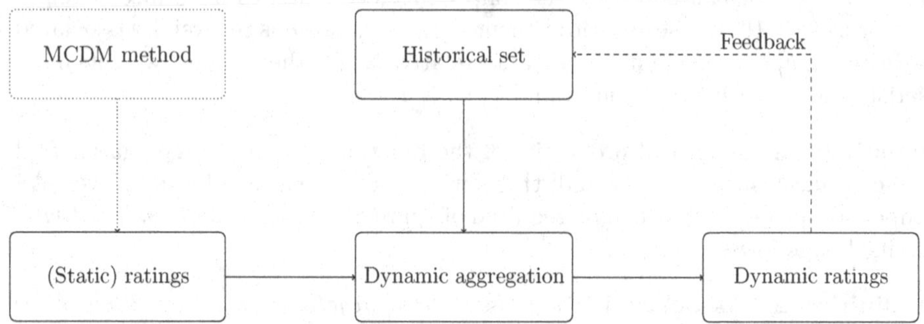

Fig. 1. Operations performed at each decision moment $t \in \mathcal{T}$ in the dynamic MCDM framework of Campanella and Ribeiro [1]: (static) ratings, computed using some MCDM method, are aggregated with information stored in the historical set to produce dynamic ratings, which are then used to update the historical set

To present the framework, let us introduce the following notation. We shall denote by $\mathcal{T} = \{1, 2, \ldots\}$ the (possibly infinite) set of discrete decision moments, and by $\mathcal{A}_t$ the set of alternatives that are available at each decision moment $t \in \mathcal{T}$. Furthermore, we assume that a static MCDM method is being used at each decision moment $t \in \mathcal{T}$ to compute ratings for each available alternative in $\mathcal{A}_t$, and that these (static) ratings are represented by the function $r_t : \mathcal{A}_t \to \mathbb{I}$. Note that we are only interested in the final aggregated value associated to each available alternative, meaning that criteria and, possibly, weights may vary among decision moments. Moreover, since we are dealing with a constantly changing set of alternatives, we have replaced the more common matrix notation presented earlier in the text with an appropriate set notation; when convenient, it is of course possible to carry out computations for a single decision moment in matrix form.

The dynamic nature of the decision process is dealt with by means of a feedback mechanism, controlled by an aggregation function f that makes use of an *historical set* of alternatives – its "memory" – defined as follows.

Definition 7 (Historical Set). *The* historical set *of alternatives at decision moment $t \in \mathcal{T}$ is a subset of all alternatives that have ever been available up to and including that decision moment,*

$$\mathcal{H}_t \subseteq \bigcup_{s \leq t} \mathcal{A}_s, \quad s, t \in \mathcal{T}. \tag{5}$$

Remark 3 (Retention policy). In practical applications, the historical set is updated incrementally. Let us define $\mathcal{H}_0 = \emptyset$ by convention; at each decision moment $t \in \mathcal{T}$, the historical set can thus be defined as follows,

$$\mathcal{H}_t \subseteq \mathcal{A}_t \cup \mathcal{H}_{t-1}, \quad t \in \mathcal{T}. \tag{6}$$

It is therefore necessary to define a *retention policy* that can be used to select alternatives that will be included in the historical set and carried over to the next decision moment.

Let us now define the dynamic rating function $\tilde{r}_t : \mathcal{A}_t \cup \mathcal{H}_{t-1} \to \mathbb{I}$ that, for each decision moment $t \in \mathcal{T}$, gives the rating of alternatives that belong to the current set of alternatives, or that have been carried over from a previous decision moment. We can distinguish three cases:

1. if the alternative belongs only to the current set of alternatives, meaning that no historical information is available, its dynamic rating corresponds to its (static) rating;
2. if the alternative belongs to both the current and historical set of alternatives, its dynamic rating is obtained by aggregating its (static) rating with its dynamic rating at the previous decision moment;
3. finally, if the alternative belongs only to the historical set of alternatives, meaning that no updated information is available, its dynamic rating corresponds to the one it had at the previous decision moment.

More formally, we have the following definition.

Definition 8 (Dynamic Rating Function). *For any alternative $a \in \mathcal{A}_t \cup \mathcal{H}_{t-1}$, the dynamic rating function is defined as follows,*

$$\tilde{r}_t(a) = \begin{cases} r_t(a) & a \in \mathcal{A}_t \setminus \mathcal{H}_{t-1} \\ f(r_t(a), \tilde{r}_{t-1}(a)) & a \in \mathcal{A}_t \cap \mathcal{H}_{t-1} \\ \tilde{r}_{t-1}(a) & a \in \mathcal{H}_{t-1} \setminus \mathcal{A}_t \end{cases}, \tag{7}$$

where f is some associative *aggregation function.*

Remark 4. The associativity requirement ensures that repeated pairwise application of the aggregation function f will yield, at decision moment $t \in \mathcal{T}$, the same result as application over the whole set of past (static) ratings $\{r_s(a),\ s = 1, \ldots, t\}$; this also means that this computation can be performed incrementally.

Apart from the associativity requirement, any aggregation function can be used for dynamic aggregation, which in this way takes into account satisfaction of criteria not only at the time of decision, but also at previous decision moments.

The dynamic MCDM framework, in fact, provides a way of capturing an intrinsic part of dynamic decision making problems – the *temporal profile* of ratings. Choosing appropriate aggregation functions, it is thus possible to reward alternatives that were consistently rated highly in the past, even if their most recent rating is somewhat lower than average, or conversely to favor large and recent increases in rating, ignoring poorer past performance. We will present an example of this mixed behavior in Section 4.

3 Dynamic MCDM for Supplier Selection

Supplier selection is a typical decision problem that goes beyond simple optimization. Due to its criticality, many authors have focused on the problem of identifying and analyzing supplier selection criteria. Already in 1966, Dickson [16] examined different supplier selection strategies by means of questionnaires that were distributed among selected managers from the United States and Canada. Clearly, as companies become more and more dependent on suppliers, outcomes of wrong decisions become more and more severe: for example, on-time delivery and material costs are both affected by careful selection of suppliers, especially in industries where raw material accounts for a significant part of the total cost [17].

The problem of supplier selection can be naturally modeled as a multiple-criteria decision making problem: businesses express their preferences on suppliers, which are then ranked and selected. In fact, numerous (static) MCDM methods, ranging from simple weighted averaging to complex mathematical programming models, have been applied to the supplier selection problem; among them, we note the work of Chan [18] (see also [19]), which is based on the well-known Analytic Hierarchy Process (AHP) of Saaty [20, 21], and the Data Envelopment Analysis (DEA) method that was originally developed by Charnes et al. [22] and that is now widely used. Regarding the collaborative aspect of supplier selection, however, as noted by Shi et al. [23],

> ...only a few studies have explored the multiple-participant characteristic of the supplier selecting process.

Many authors have also considered integrated approaches that combine two or more techniques, usually in a multiple-step process (for a detailed overview, see [24]).

While these methods are able to deal with criteria as diverse and competing as quality, service, reliability, organization, and other technical issues, they are not as effective in coping with varying supplier performances, and also do not take into account the possibility that the set of available suppliers might be altered, for example because some of them went out of business, while others emerged in the market. Moreover, they do not consider the possibility of a network of collaborating businesses planning their next batch of orders together. The first limitation can be easily addressed by understanding that the problem at hand is a prime example of a dynamic MCDM problem, since businesses *periodically* interact with suppliers and express their preferences. As regards the possibility of planning for more than one business, in the rest of this section we shall present a further extension to the dynamic MCDM framework of Campanella and Ribeiro [1] that, by means of a linear programming model, makes it possible to handle situations in which a number of collaborating businesses face several suppliers. As before, we shall begin by first considering the simpler case of a single business, and then extend it to more complex one of multiple businesses.

3.1 Single Business

Let us first consider the case in which a single business has to periodically select one or more suppliers to fulfill its needs for a certain period of time.

As in Section 2, we consider a discrete set of decision moments $\mathcal{T} = \{1, 2, \ldots\}$, and denote by $\mathcal{A}_t$ the set of n alternatives – i.e., suppliers – that are being considered at decision moment $t \in \mathcal{T}$. Note that the number of suppliers needs not be constant along time, as they can be both removed (for example, because they went out of business) and added (for example, because new business opportunities opened up). At each decision moment $t \in \mathcal{T}$, each supplier is also assumed to be assessed by the business according to some set of criteria (such as reliability, speed, and cost) that may also change over time; these assessments are then distilled down to single (static) ratings using some MCDM method, and further aggregated with information stored in the historical set to produce dynamic ratings from which a final ranking can be produced.

The dynamic MCDM framework of Campanella and Ribeiro [1] can thus be applied straightforwardly to the problem of supplier selection, bringing about the improvements over static MCDM methods that were discussed in the previous section.

3.2 Multiple Businesses

Let us now consider the more complex case of m businesses that are *collaboratively* planning their orders to a set of n suppliers; the situation is depicted in Figure 2. Note that we require *complete collaboration* among businesses, but not among suppliers; weaker collaborations among businesses could be studied in the context of game theory, though we do not do so here.

At a fixed decision moment $t \in \mathcal{T}$, we assume that each business b_j, $j = 1, \ldots, m$, has rated each supplier s_i, $i = 1, \ldots, n$, using some MCDM method, and that these ratings have been aggregated with historical information into dynamic ratings, as described before; in order to avoid a cumbersome notation, these ratings will simply be denoted by $\tilde{r}_t(i, j)$. Furthermore, we assume that each business has a certain demand $d_t(j)$, $j = 1, \ldots, m$, and that each supplier has a maximum capacity $c_t(i)$, $i = 1, \ldots, n$. The variables of the problem are represented by the quantities $x_t(i, j)$ that business b_j, $j = 1, \ldots, m$, shall order from supplier s_i, $i = 1, \ldots, n$ at decision moment $t \in \mathcal{T}$, as summarized in Figure 3. Clearly, the allocation of orders to suppliers (encoded by the variables $x_t(i, j)$) will change over time as a result of varying ratings, demands and capacities.

Before proceeding, let us introduce the following definitions.

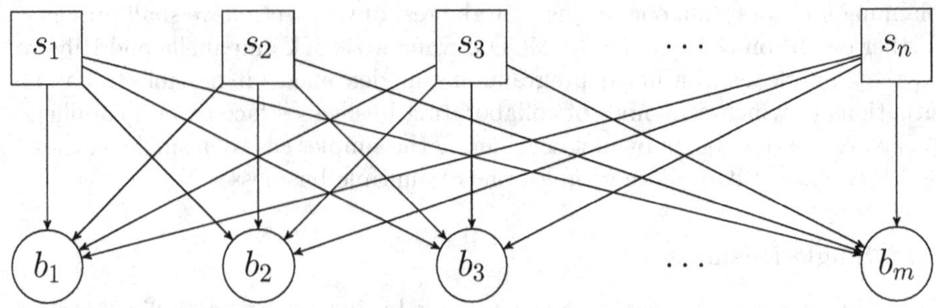

Fig. 2. Network of businesses and suppliers: at decision moment $t \in \mathcal{T}$, each business b_j, $j = 1, \ldots, m$, depicted here as a circle, orders a certain quantity $x_t(i, j)$ from supplier s_i, $i = 1, \ldots, n$, depicted here as a square

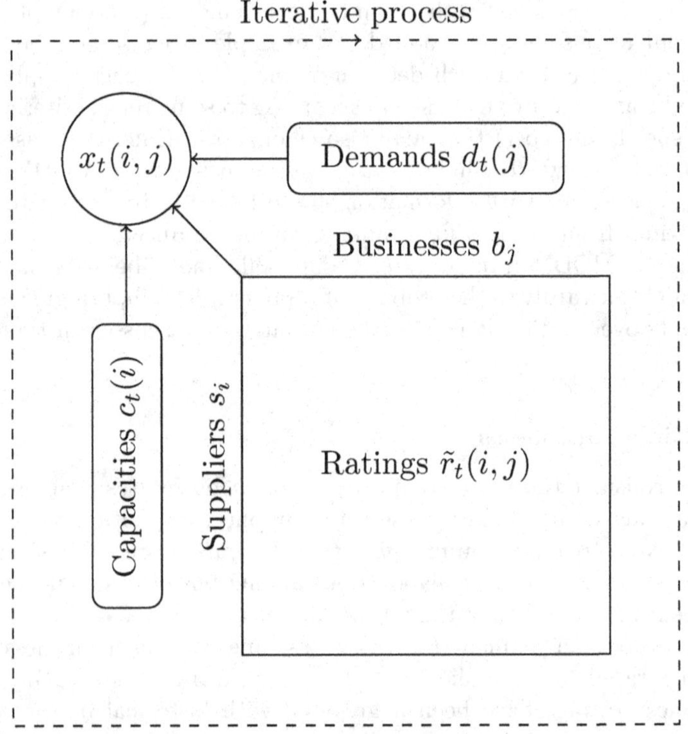

Fig. 3. Collaborative model: different variables enter into the construction of the optimal order quantities $x_t(i, j)$

Definition 9 (Satisfaction of a Business). *The* satisfaction of a business *b_j, $j = 1, \ldots, m$, at time $t \in \mathcal{T}$ with respect to a certain allocation of orders to suppliers is defined as follows,*

$$\sigma_t(j) = \sum_i \tilde{r}_t(i, j)\, x_t(i, j). \tag{8}$$

Definition 10 (Total satisfaction). *The* total satisfaction *of all businesses at time $t \in \mathcal{T}$ with respect to a certain allocation of orders to suppliers is defined as follows,*

$$\sigma_t = \sum_j \sigma_t(j). \tag{9}$$

We are now in a position to define the following linear program that maximizes the total satisfaction, making sure all demands are met and no capacity is exceeded,

$$\begin{aligned} \max\ \sigma_t &= \sum_j \sigma_t(j) \\ \text{s.t.}\ \sum_i x_t(i,j) &= d_t(j) \qquad j = 1,\ldots,m, \\ \sum_j x_t(i,j) &\leq c_t\,(i) \qquad i = 1,\ldots,n. \end{aligned} \tag{10}$$

This linear program would then be solved at each decision moment $t \in \mathcal{T}$ to determine the optimal order quantities. Note that similar linear programming models usually consider costs instead of satisfactions, and consequently seek to minimize the objective function. Using the proposed approach, on the other hand, each business can consider many more criteria that are then condensed into a single (static) rating; this rating is then further aggregated with historical information to yield a dynamic rating that is finally used in the linear program presented above.

4 Illustrative Example

To better understand how the dynamic MCDM framework of Campanella and Ribeiro [1] can be applied to the supplier selection problem with multiple businesses, we now work through a small illustrative example.

For simplicity, we consider a fixed set of four suppliers, named s_1 through s_4, and three businesses, named b_1 through b_3. Moreover, we also fix values for capacities and demands as follows,

$$\begin{aligned} c_1 &= 20, & d_1 &= 30, \\ c_2 &= 20, & d_2 &= 20, \\ c_3 &= 15, & d_3 &= 25, \\ c_4 &= 25. \end{aligned}$$

It is easy to verify that the total capacity exceeds the total demand, so that the linear program of Equation (10) will always have a solution. To keep the example small, we consider only three decision moments (which could correspond to monthly supplier evaluations, for example), and present three matrices each time, as shown in Figure 4:

1. the first matrix shows the (static) ratings for each pair of business and supplier;
2. the second matrix gives the dynamic ratings obtained using the dynamic MCDM framework;
3. finally, the third matrix represents the solution to the linear program of Equation (10).

Fig. 4. Layout of matrices presented for each decision moment

Changes in these matrices are highlighted in bold and indicated by a small arrow; for example, a value that rose from 0.5 to 0.6 would be written as $\mathbf{0.6}^{\uparrow}$, whereas a change in the opposite direction (i.e., from 0.6 to 0.5) would be written as $\mathbf{0.5}^{\downarrow}$.

The aggregation function used for dynamic aggregation is as follows,

$$f(x, y) = \frac{x\,y\,(1 - e)}{x\,y + e\,(1 - x - y)}, \quad x, y \in \mathbb{I}, \tag{11}$$

where $e \in (0, 1)$ is the so-called *neutral element* that was chosen here equal to 1/2. This aggregation function belongs to the class of *uninorms* [25, 26], which are associative aggregation function that exhibit an interesting kind of mixed behavior known as full reinforcement [27]: they are conjunctive when presented with input values below a given neutral element $e \in (0, 1)$), disjunctive for input values above e, and averaging otherwise (i.e., when one input value is below e and the other one is above it). This particular behavior is exemplified in Figure 5 for different values of e.

At the first decision moment, we have the following situation,

$$\begin{array}{c} \\ s_1 \\ s_2 \\ s_3 \\ s_4 \end{array}\begin{array}{c} \begin{array}{ccc} b_1 & b_2 & b_3 \end{array} \\ \begin{bmatrix} 0.40 & 0.50 & 0.70 \\ 0.60 & 0.20 & 0.60 \\ 0.70 & 0.90 & 0.80 \\ 0.90 & 0.70 & 0.90 \end{bmatrix} \end{array} \quad \begin{array}{c} \\ s_1 \\ s_2 \\ s_3 \\ s_4 \end{array}\begin{array}{c} \begin{array}{ccc} b_1 & b_2 & b_3 \end{array} \\ \begin{bmatrix} 0.40 & 0.50 & 0.70 \\ 0.60 & 0.20 & 0.60 \\ 0.70 & 0.90 & 0.80 \\ 0.90 & 0.70 & 0.90 \end{bmatrix} \end{array} \quad \begin{array}{c} \\ s_1 \\ s_2 \\ s_3 \\ s_4 \end{array}\begin{array}{c} \begin{array}{ccc} b_1 & b_2 & b_3 \end{array} \\ \begin{bmatrix} 0 & 5 & 15 \\ 5 & 0 & 10 \\ 0 & 15 & 0 \\ 25 & 0 & 0 \end{bmatrix} \end{array}$$

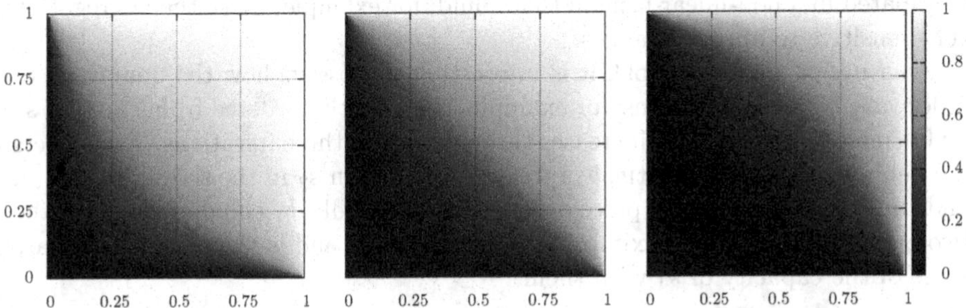

Fig. 5. Contour map of the aggregation function of Equation (11) for three different values of the neutral element e: from left to right, we have $e = 1/4$, $e = 1/2$ and $e = 3/4$

Since no historical information is available, the first and second matrices are of course equal.

At the second decision moment, we have the following situation,

$$\begin{array}{cc} & \begin{matrix} b_1 & b_2 & b_3 \end{matrix} \\ \begin{matrix} s_1 \\ s_2 \\ s_3 \\ s_4 \end{matrix} & \begin{bmatrix} 0.40 & 0.60^{\uparrow} & 0.70 \\ 0.60 & 0.20 & 0.50^{\downarrow} \\ 0.80^{\uparrow} & 0.90 & 0.80 \\ 0.80^{\downarrow} & 0.60^{\downarrow} & 0.80^{\downarrow} \end{bmatrix} \end{array} \quad \begin{array}{cc} & \begin{matrix} b_1 & b_2 & b_3 \end{matrix} \\ \begin{matrix} s_1 \\ s_2 \\ s_3 \\ s_4 \end{matrix} & \begin{bmatrix} 0.31^{\downarrow} & 0.60^{\uparrow} & 0.84^{\uparrow} \\ 0.69^{\uparrow} & 0.06^{\downarrow} & 0.60 \\ 0.90^{\uparrow} & 0.99^{\uparrow} & 0.94^{\uparrow} \\ 0.97^{\uparrow} & 0.78^{\uparrow} & 0.97^{\uparrow} \end{bmatrix} \end{array} \quad \begin{array}{cc} & \begin{matrix} b_1 & b_2 & b_3 \end{matrix} \\ \begin{matrix} s_1 \\ s_2 \\ s_3 \\ s_4 \end{matrix} & \begin{bmatrix} 0 & 0^{\downarrow} & 20^{\uparrow} \\ 15^{\uparrow} & 0 & 0^{\downarrow} \\ 0 & 15 & 0 \\ 15^{\downarrow} & 5^{\uparrow} & 5^{\uparrow} \end{bmatrix} \end{array}$$

We can clearly recognize the mixed behavior of the dynamic aggregation function in the dynamic ratings it produces: for example, since the value associated with the pair (s_1, b_1) was consistently lower than the neutral element, the corresponding dynamic rating was brought down; conversely, since the value associated with the pair (s_2, b_1) was consistently higher than the neutral element, the corresponding dynamic rating was pushed up. This was also reflected in the amount that business b_1 should order from supplier s_2, which tripled from the previous iteration.

Finally, at the third decision moment, we have the following situation,

$$\begin{array}{cc} & \begin{matrix} b_1 & b_2 & b_3 \end{matrix} \\ \begin{matrix} s_1 \\ s_2 \\ s_3 \\ s_4 \end{matrix} & \begin{bmatrix} 0.50^{\uparrow} & 0.60 & 0.70 \\ 0.70^{\uparrow} & 0.10^{\downarrow} & 0.40^{\downarrow} \\ 0.90^{\uparrow} & 0.90 & 0.80 \\ 0.80 & 0.40^{\downarrow} & 0.70^{\downarrow} \end{bmatrix} \end{array} \quad \begin{array}{cc} & \begin{matrix} b_1 & b_2 & b_3 \end{matrix} \\ \begin{matrix} s_1 \\ s_2 \\ s_3 \\ s_4 \end{matrix} & \begin{bmatrix} 0.31 & 0.69^{\uparrow} & 0.93^{\uparrow} \\ 0.84^{\uparrow} & 0.01^{\downarrow} & 0.50^{\downarrow} \\ 0.99^{\uparrow} & 1.00^{\uparrow} & 0.98^{\uparrow} \\ 0.99^{\uparrow} & 0.70^{\uparrow} & 0.99^{\uparrow} \end{bmatrix} \end{array} \quad \begin{array}{cc} & \begin{matrix} b_1 & b_2 & b_3 \end{matrix} \\ \begin{matrix} s_1 \\ s_2 \\ s_3 \\ s_4 \end{matrix} & \begin{bmatrix} 0 & 5^{\uparrow} & 15^{\downarrow} \\ 15 & 0 & 0 \\ 0 & 15 & 0 \\ 15 & 0^{\downarrow} & 10^{\uparrow} \end{bmatrix} \end{array}$$

The mixed behavior of the chosen dynamic aggregation function is again evident, even though it is now also being smoothed by the availability of more data: understandably, as more information becomes available, dynamically aggregated values tend to reflect the underlying trend in (static) ratings, though modulated in a non-linear fashion that could, for example, make the aggregation very sensitive to abrupt changes.

Even in our small example, it is interesting to observe how the quantities to order vary between iterations: for example, the quantity ordered from supplier s_4 by business b_3 consistently increases throughout the three iterations. Two effects are behind this change: firstly, b_3 rates s_4 better than s_2 in the second iteration, and thus is more willing to place orders there; secondly, b_1 collaborates with the two other businesses to maximize total satisfaction, and is thus willing to share some of the capacity of s_4 with them.

5 Conclusions

In this paper we have proposed an extension of the dynamic MCDM framework of Campanella and Ribeiro [1] to the problem of supplier selection for multiple collaborating businesses. The proposed method uses the dynamic MCDM framework as the dynamic component for individual decision makers, and a linear programming model for the collaborative component. It provides a unified method to assess supplier performances in a context in which businesses share information about suppliers among themselves, suppliers can appear and disappear, and supplier performances change over time.

As directions for future research, it would be important to understand the effect of missing or imprecise data and how it could be handled effectively. Regarding the supplier selection problem, the linear program could be reformulated to include more constraints, such as thresholds that would veto suppliers with consistently low ratings. It would also be interesting to relax the assumption of complete collaboration among businesses, as well as to apply the dynamic MCDM framework to the situation in which a number of businesses must jointly select some suppliers. This problem can actually be restated more broadly as a consensus problem, which was already identified as closely related to the dynamic MCDM framework [1].

References

1. Campanella, G., Ribeiro, R.A.: A framework for dynamic multiple-criteria decision making. Decision Support Systems 52(1), 52–60 (2011)
2. Townsend, J.T., Busemeyer, J.: Dynamic representation of decision-making. In: Port, R.F., van Gelder, T. (eds.) Mind as Motion: Explorations in the Dynamics of Cognition, pp. 101–120. MIT Press (1995)
3. Pais, T.C., Ribeiro, R.A., Devouassoux, Y., Reynaud, S.: Dynamic ranking algorithm for landing site selection. In: Magdalena, L., Ojeda-Aciego, M., Verdegay, J.L. (eds.) Proceedings of the Twelfth International Conference on Information Processing and Management of Uncertainty in Knowledge-Base Systems (IPMU), pp. 608–613 (2008)
4. Ribeiro, R.A., Pais, T.C., Simões, L.F.: Benefits of Full-Reinforcement Operators for Spacecraft Target Landing. In: Greco, S., Pereira, R.A.M., Squillante, M., Yager, R.R., Kacprzyk, J. (eds.) Preferences and Decisions. STUDFUZZ, vol. 257, pp. 353–367. Springer, Heidelberg (2010)

5. Kumar, M., Vrat, P., Shankar, R.: A fuzzy goal programming approach for vendor selection problem in a supply chain. Computers & Industrial Engineering 46(1), 69–85 (2004)
6. Chen, S.-J., Hwang, C.L., Hwang, F.P.: Fuzzy Multiple Attribute Decision Making: Methods and Applications. Lecture Notes in Economics and Mathematical Systems, vol. 375. Springer (1992)
7. Triantaphyllou, E.: Multi-Criteria Decision Making Methods: A Comparative Study. Applied Optimization, vol. 44. Springer (2000)
8. Brehmer, B.: Dynamic decision making: Human control of complex systems. Acta Psychologica 81(3), 211–241 (1992)
9. Stevens, S.S.: On the Theory of Scales of Measurement. Science 103(2684), 677–680 (1946)
10. Aloysius, J.A., Davis, F.D., Wilson, D.D., Taylor, A.R., Kottemann, J.E.: User acceptance of multi-criteria decision support systems: The impact of preference elicitation techniques. European Journal of Operational Research 169(1), 273–285 (2006)
11. Breivik, E., Supphellen, M.: Elicitation of product attributes in an evaluation context: A comparison of three elicitation techniques. Journal of Economic Psychology 24(1), 77–98 (2003)
12. Ribeiro, R.A.: Fuzzy multiple attribute decision making: A review and new preference elicitation techniques. Fuzzy Sets and Systems 78(2), 155–181 (1996)
13. Beliakov, G., Pradera, A., Calvo, T.: Aggregation Functions: A Guide for Practitioners. STUDFUZZ, vol. 221. Springer, Heidelberg (2008)
14. Torra, V., Narukawa, Y.: Modeling Decisions: Information Fusion and Aggregation Operators. In: Cognitive Technologies, Springer (2007) ISBN 978-3540687894
15. Jessup, R.K., Bishara, A.J., Busemeyer, J.R.: Feedback Produces Divergence From Prospect Theory in Descriptive Choice. Psychological Science 19(10), 1015–1022 (2008)
16. Dickson, G.W.: An Analysis of Vendor Selection Systems and Decisions. Journal of Purchasing 2(1), 5–17 (1966)
17. Çebi, F., Bayraktar, D.: An integrated approach for supplier selection. Logistics Information Management 16(6), 395–400 (2003)
18. Chan, F.T.S.: Interactive selection model for supplier selection process: an analytical hierarchy process approach. International Journal of Production Research 41(15), 3549–3579 (2004)
19. Chan, F.T.S., Kumar, N.: Global supplier development considering risk factors using fuzzy extended AHP-based approach. Omega 35(4), 417–431 (2007)
20. Saaty, T.L.: Decision Making for Leaders: The Analytic Hierarchy Process for Decisions in a Complex World, 3rd edn. Analytic Hierarchy Process Series, vol. 2. RWS Publications (1999) ISBN 978-0962031786
21. Saaty, T.L.: Fundamentals of Decision Making and Priority Theory With the Analytic Hierarchy Process, 1st edn. Analytic Hierarchy Process Series, vol. 6. RWS Publications (2000) ISBN 978-0962031762
22. Charnes, A., Cooper, W.W., Rhodes, E.: Measuring the efficiency of decision making units. European Journal of Operational Research 2(6), 429–444 (1978)
23. Shi, J., Huani, W., Zhang, L., Huang, G.Q., Mak, K.L.: Collaborative supplier selection on the Web. In: Proceedings of the 2000 IEEE International Conference on Management of Innovation and Technology (ICMIT), Singapore, vol. 2, pp. 827–831 (2000)

24. Ho, W., Xu, X., Dey, P.K.: Multi-criteria decision making approaches for supplier evaluation and selection: A literature review. European Journal of Operational Research 202(1), 16–24 (2010)
25. Yager, R.R., Rybalov, A.: Uninorm aggregation operators. Fuzzy Sets and Systems 80(1), 111–120 (1996)
26. Fodor, J.C., Yager, R.R., Rybalov, A.: Structure of Uninorms. International Journal of Uncertainty, Fuzziness and Knowledge-Based Systems 5(4), 411–427 (1997)
27. Yager, R.R., Rybalov, A.: Full reinforcement operators in aggregation techniques. IEEE Transactions on Systems, Man, and Cybernetics, Part B: Cybernetics 28(6), 757–769 (1998)

New Belief Function Based Methods for Multi-Criteria Decision-Making

Jean-Marc Tacnet[1] and Jean Dezert[2]

[1] Irstea, UR ETGR Erosion Torrentielle Neige Avalanches,
2 rue de la Papeterie - BP 76, F-38402 St-Martin-d'Heres, France
[2] The French Aerospace Lab, F-91761 Palaiseau, France
jean-marc.tacnet@irstea.fr
jean.dezert@onera.fr

Abstract. Any decision is closely linked to the quality and availability of information. Innovative methodologies dealing with imperfect information provided by more or less reliable and conflicting sources are proposed to help decision-makers. Our methods combine new uncertainty theories within Multi-Criteria Decision-Making methods. In our evidential reasoning based approach for multi-criteria decision analysis, we use the fuzzy sets, the possibility and belief function theories as conceptual analytical frameworks. In DSmT-AHP, we replace the initial AHP aggregation principles by a fusion process with the introduction of discounting factors able to discriminate importance and reliability of criteria. In our COWA-ER, we propose a cautious Ordered Weighted Averaging method for multi-criteria decision making under uncertainty. All these methods fit well in the domain of expert assessment for the context of natural hazards in mountains. We present a synthesis of the three aforementioned methods which are detailed in papers listed in the bibliography.

Keywords: MCDA, belief functions, DST, DSmT, Risk assessment.

1 Introduction

Rapid mass movement hazards such as snow avalanches put humans and property at risk with dramatic consequences, and decisions are needed to protect people and assets in mountains. In a context of insufficient knowledge on natural phenomena, expert assessments are required for multiple decisions and risk management purposes using multidisciplinary quantitative or qualitative approaches, see Fig. 1 explained in details in [18,19].

Those expert assessments are considered as collaborative decision processes. They depend on the availability, quality and uncertainty of available information resulting from measurements, historical analysis, numerical modeling, eye witness accounts as well as subjective, possibly conflicting, assessments made by the experts themselves. As an example, the definition of risks zones is often based on the extrapolation of historical information known on particular points using morphology based analysis as summarized in Fig. 2.

J.E. Hernández et al. (Eds.): EWG-DSS 2011, LNBIP 121, pp. 103–120, 2012.

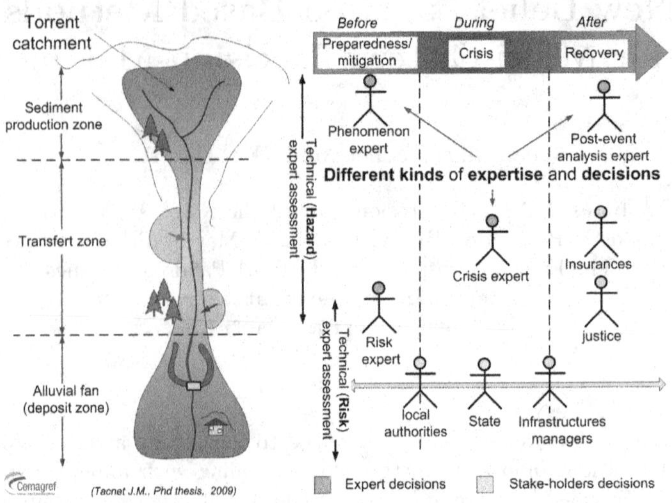

Fig. 1. Managing risk implies a complex and collaborative decision context

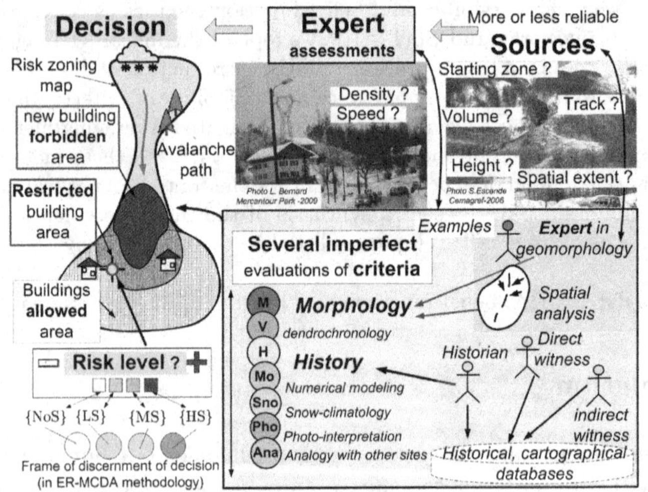

Fig. 2. A multi-source context

Also, phenomenon scenarios and decisions may rely on very uncertain and conflicting information without being able to fully determine what actually occurred, with imprecise, conflicting, or simply unknown information used in the hypotheses attempting to explain the result. Shared decision-aid tools are expected to produce, use expert assessments in an integrated risk management system able to consider the technical, environmental and social aspects of a decision [18].

MCDM methods aim to choose, rank or sort alternatives on the basis of quantitative or qualitative criteria and preferences expressed by the DM. Specific decision making methods are expected to help DM based on imperfect information provided by heterogeneous more or less reliable and conflicting sources. Considering uncertainty in MCDM remains an important issue in many fields of applications [6,11,17]. Here we describe three new methodologies that mix uncertainty theories, with a special interest in belief function theory and MCDM. Next section describes the ER-MCDA approach followed by the DSmT-AHP which proposes an evolution of AHP but also a very new discounting technique for importance. We present also the COWA-ER which is an interesting evolution of existing OWA method in the context of decision under uncertainty. The conclusion proposes a synthesis and cross-comparison of these methods and perspectives.

2 ER-MCDA: MCDA Mixed with Evidential Reasoning

2.1 Types of Information Imperfection and Related Theories

A decision is closely related to information quality. Uncertainty, as often used in common language, is indeed only one of all the various types of information imperfection which include inconsistency (related to conflict between sources), imprecision (e.g. interval of numerical values), incompleteness (lack of information, missing but existing data) and aleatory or epistemic uncertainty (resp. corresponding to aleatory events or lack of knowledge) [18]. In addition to the classical framework of probability, new uncertainty theories have been proposed to handle those different types of imperfect information such as evaluations provided through natural hazards expert assessment: fuzzy sets theory for vague information [25], possibility theory for uncertain and imprecise information [10,26]. Evidence or belief function theory allows one to represent and fuse information evaluation provided by more or less reliable and conflicting sources on the same hypotheses of a set called the frame of discernment. Each source (e.g., an expert) defines bba's. In the classical DST [13], all the hypotheses are exhaustive and exclusive. A new theory called DSmT [14] provides a more versatile framework to represent uncertain, imprecise but also vague concepts. Information fusion consists in conjoining or merging information that stems from several sources and exploits that conjoined or merged information in various tasks such as answering questions, making decisions, numerical estimation [5]. Sources can be discounted with regard to their reliability [16].

2.2 Principles of ER-MCDA Methodology

ER-MCDA [18,19,20] is a methodology that combines Saaty's AHP [12], a multi-criteria decision analysis method, and information fusion using belief function theory to represent, fuse and propagate information imperfections. Experts, considered more or less reliable, provide imprecise and uncertain evaluations of quantitative and qualitative criteria that are combined through information fusion. Fuzzy Sets and Possibility theories are used to transform quantitative and qualitative criteria into a common frame of discernment for decision in DST and DSmT contexts. A simplified version of an existing method, developed to assess the sensitivity of a snow avalanche site [18,19,20,21] is used as an example in Fig. 3. The principle is to evaluate the sensitivity of an avalanche site according to the main criteria denoted as hazard (morphology, history, and snow climatology) and vulnerability (permanent winter occupants, dwellings, and infrastructures).

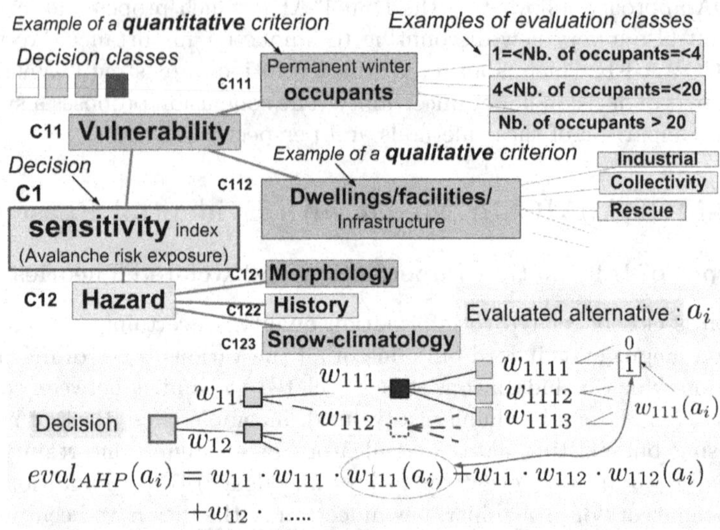

Fig. 3. Principle of AHP for the analysis of the sensitivity of a snow avalanche site

2.3 Management of Imprecision, Reliability and Importance of Sources

The ER-MCDA process consists in four separate steps: 1) problem analysis, 2) imperfect evaluation of criteria, 3) mapping of imperfect evaluation into basic belief assignments, and 4) the fusion of criteria to produce the decision as depicted in Fig. 4. Step 1 describes the DM problem, identifies qualitative and quantitative decision criteria and assesses the dimensions of the event. The decision hypotheses (e.g., site sensitivity levels) are used to define the common frame of discernment that will be used for information fusion: low (LS), medium (MS) and high sensitivity (HS). Quantitative criteria are evaluated through possibility distributions representing both imprecision and uncertainty (step 1 in Fig. 5). A mapping model, defined as a set of fuzzy intervals L-R, links a criterion evaluation and the decision classes: it plays more or less a similar role to the utility function in a MCDM based on total aggregation. For each evaluation of a criterion by one source, each interval of the possibility distribution is mapped to the common frame of discernment of decision according to surface ratios. At the end, all the criteria evaluations are transformed in bba's according the common frame of discernment of decision (steps 2, 3 and 4 in Fig. 5).

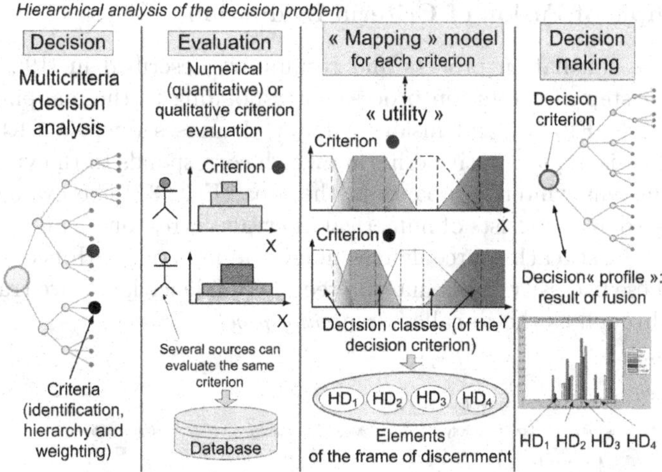

Fig. 4. The four steps of the ER-MCDA methodology

These bba's are then fused in a two-step process (Fig. 5). The first step consists in the fusion of bba's corresponding, for each criterion, to the different evaluations provided by different sources, see step 5, in Fig. 5. The second step consists in the fusion of the bba's corresponding to each criterion and resulting from the first step of fusion. In this second step, each criterion is considered as a source which is discounted according to its importance in the decision process with a specific discounting method, see step 6 in Fig. 5 and the section 3 devoted to DSmT-AHP and also detailed in [8,15].

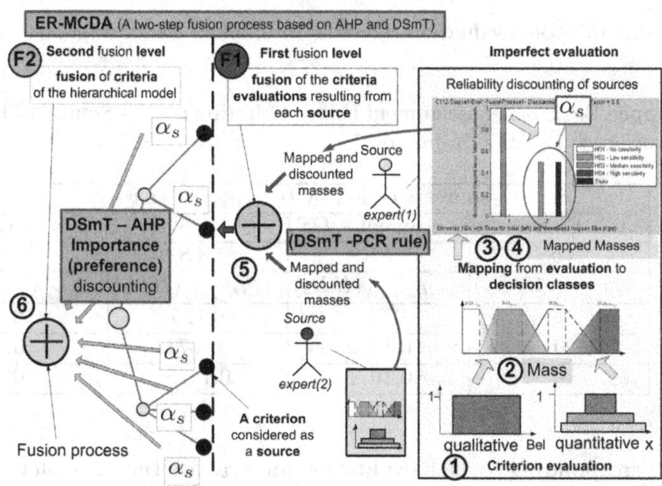

Fig. 5. The classical AHP principle is replaced by a two-step fusion process considering both evaluation imperfection, reliability and importance of criteria and sources

2.4 Example of Fusion of Criteria Evaluation

The complete calculation process and results are described in [19]. We show here the first step of the fusion process corresponding to the mapping of evaluations (step 2, FIG. 5) and fusion of mapped masses (step 5, FIG. 5). The criterion $C_{[111]}$ is a quantitative criterion which corresponds to the vulnerability due to permanent winter occupants in the area (FIG. 3). The evaluation provided by the sources consists of numerical intervals corresponding to the number of occupants. First, each source defines numerical intervals with necessity levels (FIG. 6). These necessity levels, interpreted as confidence levels are transformed into bba's through as the so-called *"mapping process"*.

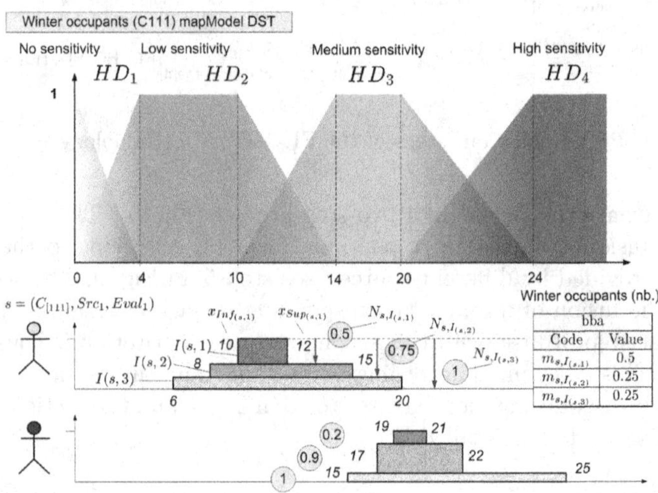

Fig. 6. From evaluation intervals to mapped *bba* of intervals

Table 1. Mapped Basic belief assignment (bba)- Criterion $C_{[111]}$ - Source 1 - Evaluation 1 - Fusion process # 1 - *DST* framework

		source s coded by $(C_{[111]}, Src_1, Eval_1)$			
		Frame of discernment - DST - $\Theta = \{NoS, LS, MS, HS\}$			
		NoS	LS	MS	HS
Int.	Code	$m_{s,I_{(s,Int)}}(HD_1)$	$m_{s,I_{(s,Int)}}(HD_2)$	$m_{s,I_{(s,Int)}}(HD_3)$	$m_{s,I_{(s,Int)}}(HD_4)$
1	$I(s,1)$	0	0.375	0.125	0
2	$I(s,2)$	0	0.1429	0.1071	0
3	$I(s,3)$	0	0.1071	0.1429	0

The *bba* corresponding to each evaluation interval are then transferred to each element of the frame of discernment corresponding to the chosen mapping model (*DST* or *DSmT* mapping model) according to their areas. The mapped *bba*

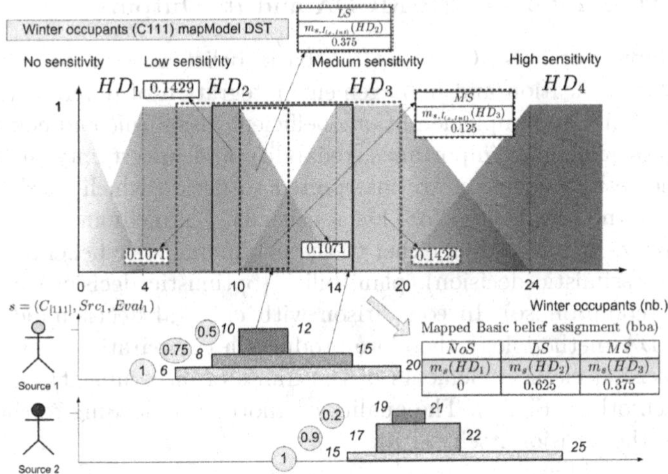

Fig. 7. From mapped *bba* of evaluation to mapped *bba* of criterion $C_{[111]}$

for the first evaluation (including 3 intervals) of the source 1 is compiled in TAB. 1 (where NoS, LS, MS and HS mean respectively No, Low, Medium and High Sensitivity) and described in a graphical way in FIG. 7.

A comparison of different combination rules (*Dempster-Shafer*, *Smets* and *PCR6* rules) in a *DST mapping* framework can be done using the same input data taking into account un-discounted or discounted evaluation sources (e.g. TAB. 2) according to the user choice (e.g. source 1 is 50% reliable, its discounting factor is 0.5). In TAB. 2, $m_1 = m_{(C_{[111]},Src_1,Eval_1)}$, $m_2 = m_{(C_{[111]},Src_2,Eval_1)}$.

Table 2. Basic belief assignment (bba)- Criterion $C_{[111]}$ - Discounted evaluation sources - *DST* Framework - Fusion order ($\oplus Criterion(\oplus Source - Evaluation)$)

	Frame of discernment - *DST* - $Card(\Theta) = 4$						
	α	$\emptyset$	HD_1	HD_2	HD_3	HD_4	Θ
	Discounting factor	empty set	NoS	LS	MS	HS	Θ
$m_1(.)$	0.5	0	0	0.3125	0.1875	0	0.5
$m_2(.)$	0.7	0	0	0	0.621	0.079	0.3
Fusion process # 1 - Dempster-Shafer rule							
$m_{(C_{[111]})} = m_1 \oplus m_2$		0	0	0.1223	0.6306	0.0514	0.1957
Fusion process # 2 - Smets' rule							
$m_{(C_{[111]})} = m_1 \oplus m_2$		0.2335	0	0.0937	0.4834	0.0394	0.15
Fusion process # 3 - PCR6 rule							
$m_{(C_{[111]})} = m_1 \oplus m_2$		0	0	0.1784	0.6229	0.0487	0.15

2.5 The Main Inputs of ER-MCDA and Its Outputs

The main inputs of ER-MCDA are the basic belief assignments elicitations, the conflict identification and management, integration of different theoretical frameworks, choice and implementation of efficient fusion rule and new discounting techniques managing importance, reliability and uncertainty in the fusion process. The results of fusion are interpreted to decide which sensitivity level will be chosen (no sensitivity, NoS; low sensitivity, LS; medium sensitivity, MS; high sensitivity; HS) according either to the maximum basic belief assignments, credibility (pessimistic decision), plausibility (optimistic decision) or pignistic probability (compromise). In comparison with classical decision-aid methods, the ER-MCDA methodology therefore produces a comparative decision profile in which decision classes (elements of the frame of discernment) can be compared to each other (Fig. 8). The quality of information leading to the decision is related to the decision itself.

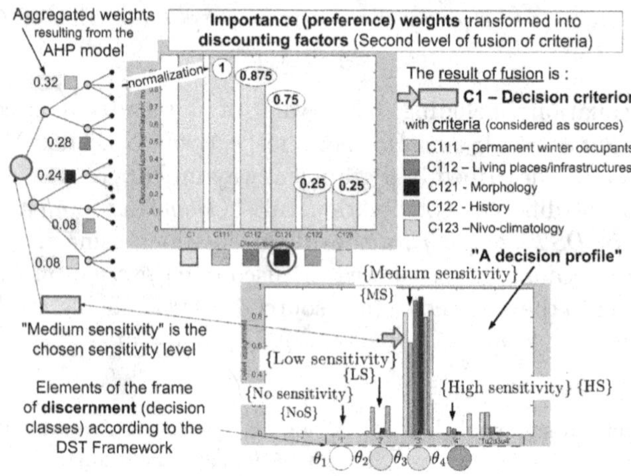

Fig. 8. ER-MCDA produces a decision profile showing the best decision but also the confidence in the result due the quality of information, heterogeneity and reliability of sources

3 The DSmT-AHP Approach

Dempster-Shafer-based AHP (DS-AHP) proposed by Beynon [1,2] has introduced a merging of Evidential Reasoning (ER) with Saaty's Analytic Hierarchy Process (AHP) [12] to consider the imprecision and the uncertainty in evaluation of several alternatives. The idea is to consider criteria as sources and derive weights as discounting factors in the fusion process [4]. To overcome the limitations and drawbacks of Dempster's rule of combination (its counter-intuitive results when conflict is high, and the possible veto power of a source), a new efficient rule of combination called PCR5 and based on the proportional conflict redistribution principle has been developed in the framework DSmT [7]. DSmT-AHP [8] is an improvement of DS-AHP approach because it uses a more efficient[1] rule of combination and makes a clear difference between importance and reliability of sources [15]. Basically, DSmT-AHP aims to perform a similar purpose as AHP or DS/AHP that is to find the preferences rankings of the decision alternatives (DA), or groups of DA. DSmT-AHP approach consists in three steps:

- Step 1: we extend the construction of the matrix for taking into account the partial uncertainty (disjunctions) between possible alternatives. If no comparison is available between elements, then the corresponding elements in the matrix is zero. Each bba related to each (sub-) criterion is the normalized eigenvector associated with the largest eigenvalue of the "uncertain" knowledge matrix (as done in standard AHP approach);
- Step 2: we use the DSmT fusion rules, typically the PCR5 rule, to combine bba's drawn from step 1 to get a final MCDM priority ranking. This fusion step must take into account the different importances (if any) of criteria as it will be explained in the sequel;
- Step 3: decision-making can be based either on the maximum of belief, or on the maximum of the plausibility of DA, as well as on the maximum of the approximate subjective probability of DA obtained by different probabilistic transformations.

The MCDM problem deals with several criteria having different importances and the classical fusion rules cannot be applied directly as in step 2. In AHP, the fusion is done from the product of the bba's matrix with the weighting vector of criteria. Such AHP fusion is nothing but a simple componentwise weighted average of bba's and it doesn't actually process efficiently the conflicting information between the sources. It doesn't preserve the neutrality of a full ignorant source in the fusion. To palliate these problems, we have proposed a new solution for combining sources of different importances in [15]. Briefly, Shafer's discounting technique [13] for taking into account the reliability factor $\alpha \in [0,1]$ of a given source with a bba $m(.)$ and a frame of discernment Θ is defined by:

$$\begin{cases} m_\alpha(X) = \alpha \cdot m(X), & \text{for } X \neq \Theta \\ m_\alpha(\Theta) = \alpha \cdot m(\Theta) + (1-\alpha) \end{cases} \tag{1}$$

The importance discounting of a source having the importance factor β and associated bba $m(.)$ is defined by [15]:

$$\begin{cases} m_\beta(X) = \beta \cdot m(X), & \text{for } X \neq \emptyset \\ m_\beta(\emptyset) = \beta \cdot m(\emptyset) + (1-\beta) \end{cases} \tag{2}$$

Note that with this importance discounting approach, we allow to deal with non-normal bba since $m_\beta(\emptyset) \geq 0$. The interest of this new discounting is to preserve

[1] Since it doesn't degrade the specificity of the resulting bba contrariwise to Dempster's rule [7].

the specificity of the primary information since all focal elements are discounted with same importance factor and no mass is committed back to partial or total ignorances. Working with positive mass of belief on the empty set is not new and has been introduced in nineties by Smets in his transferable belief model [16]. Here, we use the positive mass of the empty set as an intermediate/preliminary step of the fusion process. $\beta = 1$ is chosen if the source has a full importance, and $\beta = 0$ if one wants to grant no importance to the source. Other values of β allow to choose an intermediate importance one wants to grant to a given source in the fusion process.

The fusion of bba's in DSmT-AHP is done with PCR5 rule defined for two sources of evidence (it has been generalized in [15]) by $\forall A \in 2^{\Theta}$ (A may be the empty set too):

$$m_{PCR5_{\emptyset}}(A) = \sum_{\substack{X_1,X_2 \in 2^{\Theta} \\ X_1 \cap X_2 = A}} m_1(X_1)m_2(X_2) + \sum_{\substack{X \in 2^{\Theta} \\ X \cap A = \emptyset}} \left[\frac{m_1(A)^2 m_2(X)}{m_1(A)+m_2(X)} + \frac{m_2(A)^2 m_1(X)}{m_2(A)+m_1(X)}\right] \quad (3)$$

where 2^{Θ} is the power-set of Θ, $m_1(.)$ and $m_2(.)$ are the two bba's to combine. All fractions in (3) having zero denominators are discarded. A very detailed presentation with examples of DSmT-AHP and importance discounting technique can be found in [8,15].

4 The COWA-ER Approach

When decision is done under uncertainty, choosing alternatives can have different consequences depending on the external context (or states of the world). The new COWA-ER methodology is a cautious adaptation of Yager's OWA method [23] based on evidential reasoning [22]. COWA-ER has been proposed for decision making under uncertainty to take into account imperfect evaluations of the alternatives and unknown beliefs about groups of the possible states of the world (scenarios). The Fig. 9 shows the framework of the classical decision under risk where the states of the world are characterized by their probabilities of occurrence. In the COWA-ER, the states of the world are characterized by a bba rather than a mass of probability in order to better model the uncertainty one has on the problem under consideration.

COWA-ER mixes cautiously the principle of Yager's Ordered Weighted Averaging (OWA) [23,24] approach with the efficient fusion of belief functions proposed in DSmT [14]. The original OWA approach considers several alternatives A_i evaluated in the context of different uncertain scenarii S_i and includes several ways (pessimistic, optimistic, Hurwicz, normative) to interpret and aggregate the evaluations with respect to a given scenario. COWA-ER uses simultaneously the two extreme pessimistic and optimistic decision attitudes combined with the

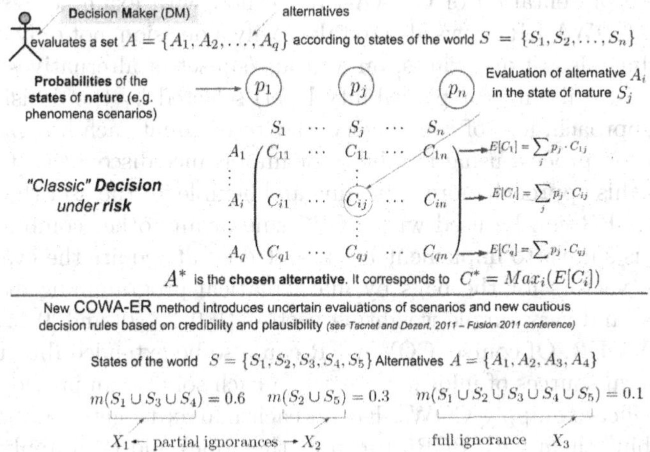

Fig. 9. Context of decision under uncertainty and basic belief assignments

PCR5 rule as shown on Fig. 10. The COWA-ER methodology is based on the following steps:

- Step 0: take the pessimistic and optimistic valuations of the expected payoffs as in OWA to get an imprecise expected payoff vector;
- Step 1: normalization of imprecise values of the payoff vector in $[0, 1]$;
- Step 2: conversion of each normalized imprecise value into bba $m_i(.)$;
- Step 3: fusion of bba $m_i(.)$ with PCR5 rule;
- Step 4: choice of the final decision based on the resulting combined bba.

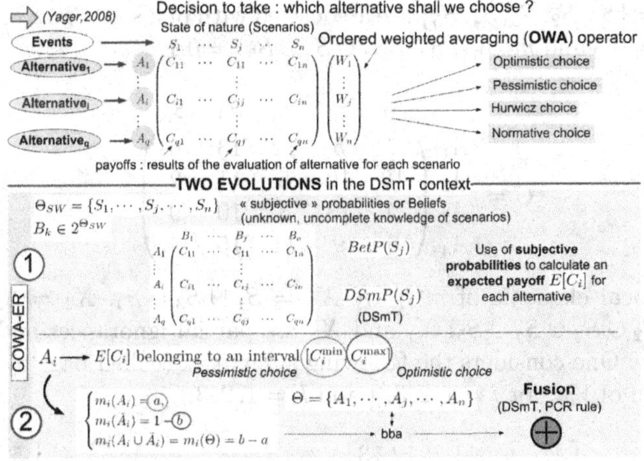

Fig. 10. COWA-ER proposes two evolutions of Yager's OWA method

A complete presentation of COWA-ER method with example has been detailed in [22]. COWA-ER allows also to take easily a decision, not only on a single alternative, but also, if one wants, on a group/subset of alternatives satisfying a minimum of credibility (or plausibility level) selected by the decision-maker. Using such approach, it is of course very easy to discount each bba $m_i(.)$ entering in the fusion process using reliability or importance discounting techniques, which makes this approach more appealing and flexible for the user than classical OWA. COWA-ER can be used with PCR5 rule or any other combination rule if needed. It is simple to implement because it doesn't require the evaluation of all weighting vectors for the bags by mathematical programming as in OWA. Only extreme and very simple weighting vectors $[1, 0, \ldots, 0]$ and $[0, \ldots, 0, 1]$ are used in COWA-ER. Of course, COWA-ER can also be extended directly for the fusion of several sources of informations when each source can provide a payoffs matrix. It suffices to apply COWA-ER on each matrix to get the bba's of step 3, then combine them with PCR5 (or any other rule) and then apply step 4 of COWA-ER. We can also discount each source easily if needed. All these advantages makes COWA-ER approach very flexible and appealing for MCDM under uncertainty.

4.1 A Numerical Example of COWA-ER

One considers a collection of q alternatives belonging to a set $A = \{A_1, A_2, \ldots, A_4\}$ and a finite set $S = \{S_1, S_2, \ldots, S_5\}$ of states of the nature. The payoff/gain C_{ij} of the decision maker in choosing A_i when S_j occurs are given by positive (or null) numbers in the $q \times n$ matrix defined by $C = [C_{ij}]$ where $i = 1, \ldots, 4$ and $j = 1, \ldots, 5$ (eq. (4)). The decision-making problem consists in choosing the alternative $A^* \in A$ which maximizes the payoff to the decision maker given the uncertain knowledge on the state of the nature and the payoffs matrix C. Uncertain states of nature $S = \{S_1, S_2, S_3, S_4, S_5\}$ are associated with bba's $m(S_1 \cup S_3 \cup S_4) = 0.6$, $m(S_2 \cup S_5) = 0.3$ and $m(S_1 \cup S_2 \cup S_3 \cup S_4 \cup S_5) = 0.1$.

$$C = \begin{array}{c} \\ A_1 \\ A_2 \\ A_3 \\ A_4 \end{array} \begin{array}{c} \begin{array}{ccccc} S_1 & S_2 & S_3 & S_4 & S_5 \end{array} \\ \begin{pmatrix} 7 & 5 & 12 & 13 & 6 \\ 12 & 10 & 5 & 11 & 2 \\ 9 & 13 & 3 & 10 & 9 \\ 6 & 9 & 11 & 15 & 4 \end{pmatrix} \end{array} \tag{4}$$

The $r = 3$ focal elements of $m(.)$ are $X_1 = S_1 \cup S_3 \cup S_4$, $X_2 = S_2 \cup S_5$ and $X_3 = S_1 \cup S_2 \cup S_3 \cup S_4 \cup S_5$. X_1 and X_2 are partial ignorances and X_3 is the full ignorance. One considers the following submatrix (called bags by Yager) for the derivation of V_{ik}, for $i = 1, 2, 3, 4$ and $k = 1, 2, 3$.

$$M(X_1) = \begin{bmatrix} M_{11} \\ M_{21} \\ M_{31} \\ M_{41} \end{bmatrix} = \begin{bmatrix} 7 & 12 & 13 \\ 12 & 5 & 11 \\ 9 & 3 & 10 \\ 6 & 11 & 15 \end{bmatrix} \qquad M(X_2) = \begin{bmatrix} M_{12} \\ M_{22} \\ M_{32} \\ M_{42} \end{bmatrix} = \begin{bmatrix} 5 & 6 \\ 10 & 2 \\ 13 & 9 \\ 9 & 4 \end{bmatrix}$$

$$M(X_3) = \begin{bmatrix} M_{13} \\ M_{23} \\ M_{33} \\ M_{43} \end{bmatrix} = \begin{bmatrix} 7 & 5 & 12 & 13 & 6 \\ 12 & 10 & 5 & 11 & 2 \\ 9 & 13 & 3 & 10 & 9 \\ 6 & 9 & 11 & 15 & 4 \end{bmatrix} = C$$

• Using pessimistic attitude, and applying the OWA operator on each row of $M(X_k)$ for $k = 1$ to r, one gets finally[2]: $V(X_1) = [V_{11}, V_{21}, V_{31}, V_{41}]^t = [7, 5, 3, 6]^t$, $V(X_2) = [V_{12}, V_{22}, V_{32}, V_{42}]^t = [5, 2, 9, 4]^t$ and $V(X_3) = [5, 2, 3, 4]^t$. For $i = 1, 2, 3, 4$ one gets the following generalized expected values using vectorial notation:

$$[C_1, C_2, C_3, C_4]^t = \sum_{k=1}^{r=3} m(X_k) \cdot V(X_k) = [6.2, 3.8, 4.8, 5.2]^t$$

According to these values, the best alternative to take is A_1 since it has the highest generalized expected payoff.

• Using optimistic attitude, one takes the max value of each row, and applying OWA on each row of $M(X_k)$ for $k = 1$ to r, one gets: $V(X_1) = [V_{11}, V_{21}, V_{31}, V_{41}]^t = [13, 12, 10, 15]^t$, $V(X_2) = [V_{12}, V_{22}, V_{32}, V_{42}]^t = [6, 10, 13, 9]^t$, and $V(X_3) = [13, 12, 13, 15]^t$. Finally, $[C_1, C_2, C_3, C_4]^t = [10.9, 11.4, 11.2, 13.2]^t$ and the best alternative to take with optimistic attitude is A_4 since it has the highest generalized expected payoff.

We consider now the pessimistic and optimistic valuations of the expected payoffs. The expected payoffs $E[C_i]$ are imprecise since they belong to interval $[C_i^{\min}, C_i^{\max}]$ where bounds are computed with extreme pessimistic and optimistic attitudes, and one has:

$$E[C] = \begin{bmatrix} E[C_1] \\ E[C_2] \\ E[C_3] \\ E[C_4] \end{bmatrix} \subset \begin{bmatrix} [6.2; 10.9] \\ [3.8; 11.4] \\ [4.8; 11.2] \\ [5.2; 13.2] \end{bmatrix}$$

Therefore, one has 4 sources of information about the parameter associated with the best alternative to choose. For decision making under imprecision, we use the belief functions framework and to adopt the COWA-ER methodology.

In **step 1**, we divide each bound of intervals by the max of the bounds to get a new normalized imprecise expected payoff vector $E^{Imp}[C]$. In our example, one gets:

$$E^{Imp}[C] = \begin{bmatrix} [6.2/13.2; 10.9/13.2] \\ [3.8/13.2; 11.4/13.2] \\ [4.8/13.2; 11.2/13.2] \\ [5.2/13.2; 13.2/13.2] \end{bmatrix} \approx \begin{bmatrix} [0.47; 0.82] \\ [0.29; 0.86] \\ [0.36; 0.85] \\ [0.39; 1.00] \end{bmatrix}$$

In **step 2**, we convert each imprecise value into its bba considering as frame of discernment, the finite set of alternatives $\Theta = \{A_1, A_2, A_3, A_4\}$ and the sources of belief associated with them obtained from the normalized imprecise expected

[2] Where X^t denotes the transpose of X.

payoff vector $E^{Imp}[C]$. The modeling for computing a bba associated to the hypothesis A_i from any imprecise value $[a;b] \subseteq [0;1]$ is done by $m_i(A_i) = a$, $m_i(\bar{A}_i) = 1 - b$, and $m_i(A_i \cup \bar{A}_i) = m_i(\Theta) = b - a$, where $\bar{A}_i$ is the complement of A_i in Θ. With such simple conversion, one sees that $Bel(A_i) = a$, $Pl(A_i) = b$. The uncertainty is represented by the length of the interval $[a;b]$ and it corresponds to the imprecision of the variable (here the expected payoff) on which is defined the belief function for A_i. In the example, one gets:

Table 3. Basic belief assignments of the alternatives

Alternatives A_i	$m_i(A_i)$	$m_i(\bar{A}_i)$	$m_i(A_i \cup \bar{A}_i)$
A_1	0.47	0.18	0.35
A_2	0.29	0.14	0.57
A_3	0.36	0.15	0.49
A_4	0.39	0	0.61

In **step 3**, we combine bba's $m_i(.)$ by an efficient rule of combination called PCR5 [14] (other rules such as Dempster-Shafer, Dubois & Prade, Yager's rule) could be used as variants of COWA-ER PCR5. The result of the combination of bba's with PCR5 for our example is given in Table 4.

Table 4. Fusion of the four elementary bba's with PCR5

Focal Element	$m_{PCR5}(.)$
A_1	0.2488
A_2	0.1142
A_3	0.1600
A_4	0.1865
$A_1 \cup A_4$	0.0045
$A_2 \cup A_4$	0.0094
$A_1 \cup A_2 \cup A_4$	0.0236
$A_3 \cup A_4$	0.0075
$A_1 \cup A_3 \cup A_4$	0.0198
$A_2 \cup A_3 \cup A_4$	0.0374
$A_1 \cup A_2 \cup A_3 \cup A_4$	0.1883

The last **step 4** is the decision-making from the resulting bba of the fusion step 3. This problem is recurrent in the theory of belief functions and several attitudes are also possible. Table 5 shows what are the values of credibilities (Bel), plausibilities (Pl), pignistic probabilities ($BetP$) and $DSmP_{\epsilon=0}$ for each alternative in our example.

Based on the results of Table 5, we note, in this example, that there is no ambiguity in the decision making. Whatever the attitude is taken by the decision-maker (the max. of Bel, the max. of Pl, the max. of BetP or the max. of DSmP), the decision to take will always be A_1. Such behavior is probably not general in

Table 5. Credibility (Bel), plausibility (Pl), pignistic probability ($BetP$) and $DSmP$ of A_i

A_i	$Bel(A_i)$	$BetP(A_i)$	$DSmP(A_i)$	$Pl(A_i)$
A_1	0.2488	0.3126	0.3364	0.4850
A_2	0.1142	0.1863	0.1623	0.3729
A_3	0.1600	0.2299	0.2242	0.4130
A_4	0.1865	0.2712	0.2771	0.4521

all problems, but at least, it shows that in some cases like in Yager's example, the ambiguity in decision can be removed when using COWA-PCR5 instead of OWA which is an advantage of our approach.

4.2 Expected Utility Theory Approach

A simpler (but less efficient) method for MCDM under uncertainty can be used if one has only very limited computational resources. This method consists to use the classical concept of expected utility based on BetP (or DSmP) probabilistic transformation of bba's associated with the states of the world [14]. BetP and DSmP are numerical methods for transforming (approximating) any general bba into a probability measure. Due to space limitation constraint, we will not go here in the mathematical details of these transformations because they can be easily and freely found with many examples in [14], Vol.2. Only a simple example is given in Fig. 11 for convenience.

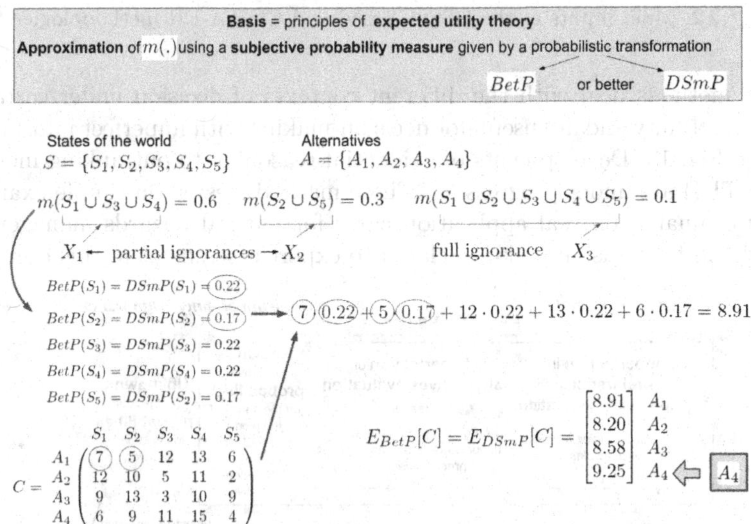

Fig. 11. Probabilistic transformation of bba for expected utility method

5 Synthesis and Conclusion

A new framework, composed of ER-MCDA, DSmT-AHP and COWA-ER, has been proposed based on the belief functions theory and MCDA methods for decision making. It considers both information imprecision, uncertainty, inconsistency and also reliability of heterogeneous sources. It uses recent and efficient fusion rules and discounting techniques. DSmT-AHP introduces imprecise evaluations of subsets and new discounting techniques. COWA-ER uses a decision method based on expected DSmP and a framework for multi-criteria decision in an uncertain context as shown in Fig. 12. ER-MCDA integrated approach uses multiple heterogeneous sources providing imperfect evaluations of criteria.

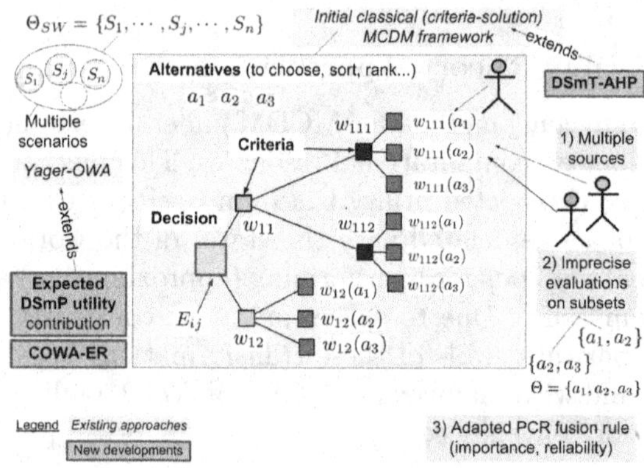

Fig. 12. Main inputs of the DSmT-based and COWA-ER methodologies

These methods deal with the different contexts of decision under certainty, risk or uncertainty and are useful for decision-making with imperfect information [22] – see Fig. 13. Developments of evidential reasoning to outranking methods (Electre TRI) are under progress [9]. These methods tested on simple examples are now evaluated on real application cases for natural hazards management. They fit well for decision making related to expert assessment in this domain.

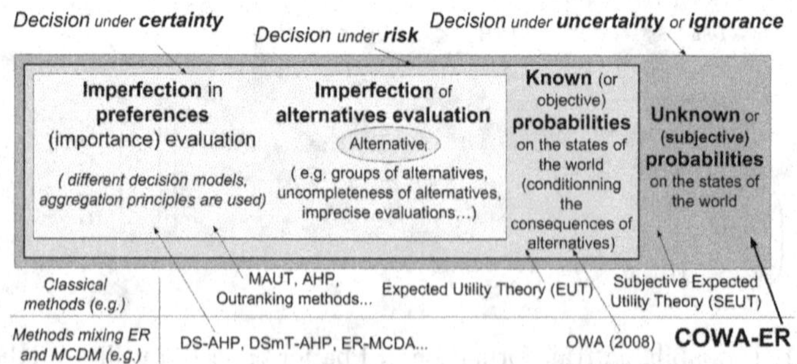

Fig. 13. Synthesis of the new methods for MCDM under imperfection and uncertainty

Acknowledgments. These works are partially founded by the PARAmount Project of the European InterReg Alpine Space program and the ANR GESTRANS project.

References

1. Beynon, M., Curry, B., Morgan, P.: The Dempster-Shafer theory of evidence:an alternative approach to multicriteria decision modelling. Omega 28(1), 37–50 (2000)
2. Beynon, M.: DS/AHP method: A mathematical analysis, including an understanding of uncertainty. Eur. J. of Oper. Research 140, 148–164 (2002)
3. Beynon, M.: Understanding local ignorance and non-specificity within the DS/AHP method of multi-criteria decision making. Eur. J. of Oper. Research 163, 403–417 (2005)
4. Beynon, M.: A method of aggregation in DS/AHP for group decision-making with non-equivalent importance of individuals in the group. Comp. and Oper. Research (32), 1881–1896 (2005)
5. Bloch, I., Hunter, A., Appriou, A., Ayoun, A., Benferhat, S., Besnard, P., Cholvy, L., Cooke, R., Cuppens, F., Dubois, D., Fargier, H., Grabisch, M., Kruse, R., Lang, J., Moral, S., Prade, H., Saffiotti, A., Smets, P., Sossai, C.: Fusion: General concepts and characteristics. International Journal of Intelligent Systems 16(10), 1107–1134 (2001)
6. Bouyssou, D.: Modelling inaccurate determination, uncertainty, imprecision using multiple criteria. LNEMS vol. 335, pp. 78–87 (1989)
7. Dezert, J., Smarandache, F.: Proportional Conflict Redistribution Rules for Information Fusion. In: Dezert, J., Smarandache, F. (eds.) Advances and Applications of DSmT for Information Fusion- Collected Works, vol. 2, pp. 3–68. American Research Press, Rehoboth (2006)
8. Dezert, J., Tacnet, J.-M., Batton-Hubert, M., Smarandache, F.: Multi-criteria decision making based on DSmT-AHP. In: Proc. of Belief 2010 Int. Workshop, Brest, France, April 1-2 (2010)
9. Dezert, J., Tacnet, J.-M.: Soft ELECTRE TRI outranking method based on belief functions. In: 14th International Conference on Information Fusion Proceedings, Singapore, July 9-12 (2012)
10. Dubois, D., Prade, H.: Possibility Theory:an approach to Computerized Processing of Uncertainty. Plenum Press, New York (1988)
11. Roy, B.: Main sources of inaccurate determination, uncertainty and imprecision in decision models. Mathematical and Computer Modelling 12(10-11), 1245–1254 (1989)
12. Saaty, T.L.: The analytic hierarchy process. McGraw Hill, New York (1980)
13. Shafer, G.: A mathematical theory of evidence. Princeton University Press (1976)
14. Smarandache, F., Dezert, J. (eds.): Advances and Applications of DSmT for Information Fusion, pp. 1–3. American Research Press, Rehoboth (2004-2009), `http://fs.gallup.unm.edu//DSmT.htm`
15. Smarandache, F., Dezert, J., Tacnet, J.-M.: Fusion of sources of evidence with different importances and reliabilities. In: 13th International Conference on Information Fusion Proceedings, Edinburgh, UK, July 26-29 (2010)
16. Smets, P.: The Combination of Evidence in the Transferable Belief Model. IEEE Trans. PAMI 12, 447–458 (1990)

17. Stewart, T.J.: Dealing with Uncertainties in MCDA. In: Figueira, J., Greco, S., Ehrgott, M. (eds.) Multiple Criteria Decision Analysis:state of the Art Surveys. International Series in Operations Research and Management Science, vol. 78, pp. 445–470. Springer, Heidelberg (2005)
18. Tacnet, J.-M.: Prise en compte de l'incertitude dans l'expertise des risques naturels en montagne par analyse multicritéres et fusion d'information. PhD thesis in Environmental Engineering Sciences, Ecole Nationale Supérieure des Mines, Saint-Etienne, France (2009)
19. Tacnet, J.-M., Batton-Hubert, M., Dezert, J.: Information fusion for natural hazards in mountains. In: Dezert, J., Smarandache, F. (eds.) Advances and Applications of DSmT for Information Fusion- Collected Works, vol. 3, pp. 565–659. American Research Press, Rehoboth (2009)
20. Tacnet, J.-M., Batton-Hubert, M., Dezert, J.: A two-step fusion process for multicriteria decision applied to natural hazards in mountains. In: 1st International Worshop on Belief functions (Belief 2010) Proceedings, Brest, France (2010)
21. Tacnet, J.-M., Batton-Hubert, M., Dezert, J., Richard, D.: Applying new uncertainty related theories and multicriteria decision analysis methods to snow avalanche risk management. In: International Snow Science Workshop (ISSW) Proceedings, Squaw Valley, Colorado, USA, October 17-22 (2010)
22. Tacnet, J.-M., Dezert, J.: Cautious OWA and evidential reasoning for decision under uncertainty. In: 14th International Conference on Information Fusion Proceedings, Chicago, Illinois, USA, July 5-8, pp. 2074–2081 (2011)
23. Yager, R.: On ordered weighted averaging operators in multi-criteria decision making. EEE Trans. on SMC 18, 183–190 (1988)
24. Yager, R.: Decision making under Dempster-Shafer uncertainties. STUDFUZZ, vol. 219, pp. 619–632 (2008)
25. Zadeh, L.: Fuzzy sets. Information and Control 8, 338–353 (1965)
26. Zadeh, L.: Fuzzy sets as a basis for a theory of possibility. Fuzzy Sets and Systems 1, 3–28 (1978)

Acronyms

For conciseness, the following acronyms have been used in this paper:
AHP=Analytic Hierarchy Process; DST=Dempster-Shafer Theory;
DSmT=Dezert-Smarandache Theory; BF=Belief function;
DM=Decision-Making (or Decision-Maker); bba=basic belief assignment;
OWA=Ordered Weighted Averaging; COWA=Cautious OWA;
ER=Evidential reasoning; MCDM=Multi-Criteria Decision-Making;
MCDA=Multi-Criteria Decision Analysis.

Support to Collaboration for Wealth and Estate Planning Using the SEPlanS Platform

Isabelle Linden[1], Jean-Marie Jacquet[2], Gustavo Ospina[2], and Mihail O. Staicu[2]

[1] University of Namur, Departement of Business Administration
Namur, Belgium
isabelle.linden@fundp.ac.be
www.fundp.ac.be/~ilinden

[2] University of Namur, Faculty of Computer Science
Namur, Belgium
{jmj,gos,msc}@info.fundp.ac.be
www.info.fundp.ac.be/~{jmj,gos,msc}

Abstract. When it comes to tax duties, Belgian fiscal authorities never forget a citizen. Not only that his revenues, whatever they are, are taxed along all his life but, when he dies, an important part of his assets is taken by the state as a death tax, to be paid by his heirs. Consequently, many Belgians are looking for strategies to minimize these taxes and are helped in this task by advisers who offer several forms of support, often consisting of investments or take actions being bought. However, wealth and estate planning is actually a very complicated and highly unstructured process. In this paper, we identify the profiles of the key players, present the SEPlanS platform and analyse how it can contribute to support collaboration among them.

Keywords: Decision Support, Collaboration Tool, Expert System, Wealth planning, Estate planning.

1 Introduction

When it comes to tax duties, Belgian fiscal authorities never forget a citizen. Not only that his revenues, whatever they are, are taxed along all his life but when he dies, an important part of his assets is taken by the state as a death tax. Consequently, many Belgians are looking for strategies to minimize this loss of wealth. The question is particularly relevant for owners of SMEs. Indeed, although they have the intuition of being heavily taxed, they are, in general, unaware of fiscal possibilities and, even worse, having little time to spend on matters other than their core business, have in general not taken the time to think of the end of their career. Yet, for demographic reasons induced by the 2nd world war, they are very numerous and form the majority of contractors in Belgium. Estate management must be regarded from a twofold perspective: on the one hand, from the point of view of civil law, which specifies the heirs and the shares for each of them, and, on the other hand, from the point of view

J.E. Hernández et al. (Eds.): EWG-DSS 2011, LNBIP 121, pp. 121–133, 2012.

of fiscal law, whose principles should be used in order to compute the amount of taxes to be paid by each heir. This general principle applies everywhere in Belgium. However, some rules and details vary according to the region where the deceased lived. In Belgium, management of estates is entrusted to the solicitors. However, very often, a solicitor only obtains an overview of a wealth after his owner has died. At that moment, he can only apply the law without having the possibility to take any measures that could decrease the amount of taxes. Nevertheless, during his lifetime, any owner may resort to a wealth administrator and/or an asset manager to support its asset management activities. Both the administrator and the manager provide advices in order to increase and reinforce the wealth position of their clients. Moreover, a tax advisor may also be in the position to suggest some forms of investment or asset reallocations in order to benefit from tax reductions under various forms. Recently, a new kind of advisers appeared, namely the "asset and estate planners". They try to integrate the two paths indicated above: estate management during lifetime and when death occurs. They mainly suggest to their clients actions in order to increase the proportion of the assets received by the heirs and limit the losses due to taxes and fees. Simultaneously, they take care of preserving a sufficient comfort to their clients whose needs could increase due to many reasons such as health problems. For instance, one possible strategy is to donate some assets to the heirs before the death of the person. However, this scenario must be handled with utmost care, especially since nobody may indicate with a sufficient degree of probability the time of his death, nor the precise amount of money required for guaranteeing a comfortable living during his lifetime. Usually, such planners are not solicitors and their activity is limited to the application of best practices.

Regarding the decision process, wealth and estate planning gives rise to an atypical collaboration. The leading actor is the client. He is in charge of taking the final decisions, and is the only one supporting their results. He is the less skilled actor of the domain and has in charge the orchestration of the consultation process, the selection and revocation of the other actors and the specification of their goals.

Given the above background, it is obvious that an automatic system that may offer guidance and efficiency in estate management activities is extremely useful for both estate management clients and their advisers. Such a help is aimed to be provided by the SEPlanS expert system. More precisely, the goal of the SEPlanS expert system is, on the one hand, implicit collaboration between owners, wealth administrators, assets managers, tax advisers and solicitors by integrating their point of views on a wealth position into such an expert system and, on the other hand, to facilitate information transfer between the contemplated actors. The tool, currently under development, supports the guidance of the evolution of wealth. In order to further enhance the attributes of the tool, an encyclopaedia has been developed and is being integrated with the tool in order to support the understanding of each specific domain languages. This tool is being developed during the SEPlanS project, funded by the Walloon Region of Belgium.

The rest of this paper is structured as follows. Section 2 describes existing related tools, how they inspired our work and why they were not sufficient to our purpose. In section 3, we describe briefly the development methodology and the architecture of the tool and, in section 4, we present at a high level the main features of the tool. Then the core of our purpose is reached in section 5 by describing the typical users profiles and developing the mechanisms for collaboration through knowledge and data sharing that SEPlanS makes possible. Finally, we draw some conclusions and proposals for extensions.

2 Related Work

The NaviPlan Software [1], by Emerging Information Systems Inc. (EISI), is presented as a financial planning software. It is available in several editions dedicated to different levels of wealth status for each client category and two versions, implementing US and Canadian contexts, respectively. On the basis of the description of the current wealth position of a couple, NaviPlan generates reports analysing the current financial position and compare its evolution with respect to predefined goals. Then it suggests some actions and evaluates their impact on the various goals under assessment. Even if it is more goal-oriented, NaviPlans main goals are highly similar to SEPlanS. However, it considers a very different context, as well at the domain practices level from the perspective of the applicable laws. Unfortunately, this is not an open source product, and there is no public information about its architecture and development methodology. Moreover, it has been developed to provide access to one advisor to clients folders, not as a collaboration tool.

Two softwares implementing the Belgian system are available. The first one, developed by Me Dons, solicitor, is called Successierekenaar [2], the Dutch word for estate calculator. It consists in a support tool for solicitors in estate management. The second software, commercialised by Kluwer, is accessible through the monKEY.be web platform [3] that provides many resources for accountants and tax specialists. Leaving out some minor differences between them, both provide support for the management of estate when the client dies. Of course, they can be of use for a simulation of a decease or on basis of virtual future position, but, in this case, the evaluation of this position has to be done out of the tool, without support. Moreover, these tools do not provide any comparison or advising mechanism. As NaviPlan, they do not offer collaboration mechanisms and no information is available about their architecture and development methodologies.

Apart from softwares, collaboration mechanisms for wealth and estate planning have been studied for example in [4]. This piece of work focuses on the involvement of stakeholders, in particular heirs, in the definition of the goals in order to avoid post-death conflicts. In the Belgian context, this aspect is of lower interest, indeed, laws involve definitions of protected heirs and many mechanisms to avoid grabbing.

Recommendations exist concerning financial planning, among which, the ISO 22222 norm on "personal financial planning". This norm "defines the personal financial planning process and specifies ethical behaviour, competences and experience requirements for personal financial planners" [5]. It is focussed on the behaviour of the individual advisor and does not consider collaboration mechanisms.

It seems to be an agreement on the importance of an holistic view in financial planning [4,6], in particular, [7] studies partnership among lawyers and accountant mainly focussing on legal issues. However, but of [8] concerning the collaboration of artificial agents, we are not aware of publication studying collaboration mechanisms in private financial context.

3 Methodology and Architecture

The development is the result of a collaboration of two teams, one, in the University of Namur (FUNDP), composed of computer scientists, and the other, in the Catholic University of Mons (FUCAM), composed of lawyers and finance experts. Figure 1 summarizes the development methodology and the architecture of the software.

At the first stage, focus groups and expert interviews where organised to obtain a birds-eye-view over the practice area. The presence in the team of both academic experts and practitioners gave the opportunity of a wide range of contacts which were managed according to standard interview methodologies. Moreover, two of the computer scientists attended a 30 hours course about estate management dedicated to financial experts. These activities resulted in a highly documented relational model describing the information necessary to be captured in order to describe the wealth position of a (couple of) customer(s). Among others, this description involves the family members, the precise description of their assets and revenues, as well as debts, expenses and fees. It also involves the description of the type of ownership (freehold, bare ownership, usufruct, etc.), insurances, revenues, common expenses and scheduled ones. Such schema provided the structure of the database aimed to storing the client directories. The data acquisition interface is a user-friendly graphic web interface allowing the client himself, or anyone to whom he gives this right, to introduce and/or modify any of the contemplated elements in the system.

Another important output of the analysis is the writing of an encyclopaedia, the wikiPlanSpedia. This tool has been developed as a wiki and can be read in a web browser. However, its most important feature is its integration with the user interface: tooltips are associated with domain specific words; each of them providing a short definition extracted from the WikiPlanSpedia and an hyperlink to the relevant page in it.

One of the core parts of the system, which is totally transparent to the user, is the knowledge base. It results from a close collaboration between domain experts and computer scientists. Following a well-structured formal process and using a specific knowledge acquisition tool [10], they translate together laws and expertise into logical rules expressed in the Prolog programming language [9].

Users do not need to be aware of this architecture. They connect to the system using a graphical interface reachable through a web browser. Given a clients

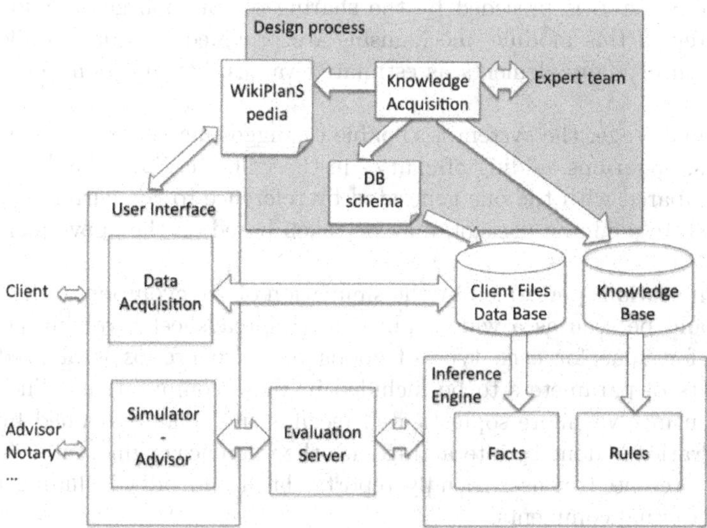

Fig. 1. Development methodology and software architecture

profile, introduced thanks to the data acquisition interface, the simulator and advisor interface provide access to various configurable reports that are described in the next section.

4 SEPlanS Tool

Given a customers wealth position, the system provides various analysis features. The first one is represented by the generation of a report on the current wealth position of the customer. It includes a comparison with the intentional financial profile evaluated by the means of a questionnaire (according to MiFID European Union law [11]). Subsequently to this point, the wealth position can be evaluated at any future date and a report can be generated regarding this estimated future position. The computation of the future wealth position is mainly based on the evolution of the value of goods and debts. It also integrates expected revenues and expenses and their evolutions. This default simulation can be interrupted by a check of the estimated values of goods and debts. The values can be modified and the structure of the report can be customised.

Related to this first set of functions, particular goals as the acquisition of a house, expenses related to childeren's studies, or wedding, or travels,... can be integrated through the definition of planned savings and expenses.

The second main set of functions concern estate computation. The estate value may be computed at the current date or simulated in any future date. In this second case, SEPlanS firstly computes the wealth position at the specified date, possibly evaluate the family composition according to the life expectancy, and finally, compute the required estate. For a married person, according to Belgian rights, this last step is preceded by the sharing of common goods and debts. At every step of this module, mechanisms are provided in order to allow the customisation of many elements as estimated values, life duration, and report structure.

At the final stage, the system is capable of suggesting some actions such as investments, donations, adding of clauses in the will, etc. Such simulations can then be compared with the one generated by reference to the current position. Thus, an estate planning decision may be taken based on the above mentioned data.

The computations performed by the simulation of the evolution of the wealth position could be seen as a wide sophisticated spreadsheet involving not only evaluation formulae for each type of goods but also proposals of predefined coherent sets of parameters to be included in these computations. The estate computation involves more sophisticated mechanisms, mainly defined by laws. Their integration is done by interacting with the inference engine. In both cases, results are presented in user-friendly reports (html and pdf) including tables, charts and textual comments.

At any stage, when the tool has to compute values, the computation itself can be customized or the values may be modified by the user according to its own expertise. According to the users knowledge level and his willingness of modifying the results of the system, four types of use can be considered. They are summarised in Figure 2.

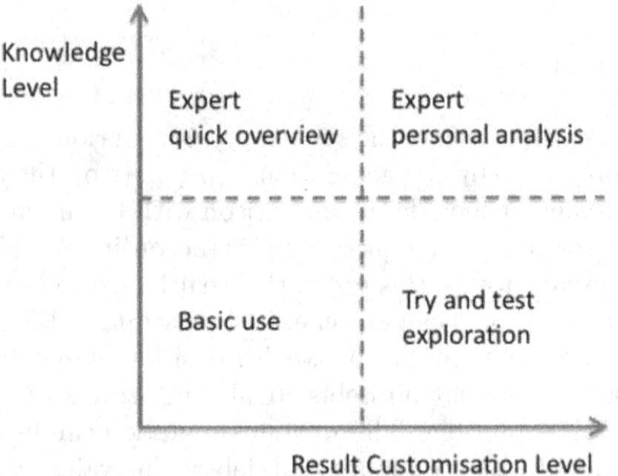

Fig. 2. Uses of the SEPlanS system

Any user having little knowledge on wealth and estate planning can use the SEPlanS results as such, without any customisation. We call such a use a basic use. An expert may choose the same basic use of the platform, obtaining thereby a quick overview of the situation, while the customisation of the results according to his own experience or the use of other personal simulation tools, will provide him the opportunity for detailed personal analyses. A fourth use of the tool consists in a customisation by a non-expert. This could be relevant for a learner in a try and test exploration methodology. However such usage feature falls outside the scope of this paper.

The evaluation and simulation algorithms involved in the tools' systems are one of the knowledge sharing mechanisms, discussed below.

5 Expert Users Profiles

It is worth noting that one user may be an expert in certain topics and a basic user in other topics. For example, a solicitor is an expert in estate management but may have little knowledge over insurance contracts, while a tax advisor is probably not experienced in estate management, but has extensive practice in fiscal optimisation. Excepted for the solicitors, having a well defined practice area, the abilities of the various advisers may be somewhat different according to their expertise background and the position names used in their company. As an example, an asset manager in a company can be called wealth administrator in another one. Therefore, in order to avoid confusion, we have identified five main skills related to asset and estate planning: finance, real estate, insurance, civil law and tax law. Subsequently, we specified typical user profiles as summarized in Figure 3. Such profile names are used according to these acceptances in the rest of the paper.

	Finance	Real Estate	Insurance	Civil Law	Tax Law
Solicitor		xxx		xxx	xxx
Asset manager	xxx		x		
Wealth administrator	xxx	xxx	xxx	x	x
Tax advisor	x	x	x	x	xx
Insurer			xxx	x	x
Asset and estate planner	x(x)	x(x)	x(x)	x(x)	x(x)

Fig. 3. Statement of Professional Skills

The solicitor has a master degree in law; he is well aware of civil and tax law and real estate (solicitors are in charge of writing bill of sale for real estate business). An asset manager is usually a bank employee who provides financial investment advices. His opinions concern mainly the characteristics of the products but his consideration for the clients global position is limited to the obligations arising from the Mifid Directive. His knowledge of insurances is limited to the mechanisms associated with some particular financial products. Conversely, the wealth administrator distinguishes himself from the asset manager mainly by the fact that his advices are not limited to financial products but he also considers real estate elements and other sophisticated insurance items. Usually, he has a (more) global view over his clients wealth position and also has some basic knowledge of civil and tax law. However, he does not manage all the products himself. Regarding real estate and some insurances, he is limited to an advice or need the collaboration of some other actor. Very often, this function, which requires many high level skills, is not played by a single person but by a multidisciplinary team. The tax advisor has basic knowledge in all the skills, being particularly specialised in taxes. Nevertheless he may be specialised to taxes for living people and being less aware of the principles applying to inheritance taxes. As expected, the insurer is highly specialised in insurances, and is aware of civil and tax aspects of his products. It follows from the above that it is difficult to characterise the asset and estate planner profile. Indeed, such a task would require a high level in all skills, but then it becomes a team profile. Therefore, for the purpose of this project, we considered the asset and estate planner as a single person, covering all the skills, at a higher or lower level. In addition to his personal skills profile, this person is mainly characterised by his ability to interact with all the other profiles.

6 Collaboration with SEPlanS : An Example

When considering only its main functionalities, the SEPlanS system could appear only as an old-fashion expert. Indeed, it can be used as such by a client managing his assets and accepting the systems computation results without any discussion with any other advisor or expert. However, the tool has been designed in the aim of considering more sophisticated scenarios. For readability purposes, let us present here a short one. The reader can easily imagine numerous variations around this typical basic scenario. Note that it is not the purpose in this paper to explore which are the best choices in particular cases, but to expose how the SEPlanS software can be a collaboration tool for individuals and their advisors.

Let us consider a baby boomer of the 2nd world war, John. He is now 66 years old. He has built and still owns a small apple juice factory. His wife is 63, they have three children who are all married and have children. Only the second son, Mark, is working in the small company. John would like to retire and transmit his company to Mark. However, he wants to preserve equity among his three children. Moreover, John and his wife are planning to make multiple travels all around the world as long as their health will allow it. It is to note that since the recent financial crises, John has little confidence in financial products.

Until now, John was supported by an accountant for his company management. But regarding his private management, he only met a tax advisor once a year in order to fill his tax return and occasionally a bank investment advisor for selecting an investment without worrying about his global wealth position. Today, he decides to investigate estate-planning opportunity. He first contacts a solicitor. On the basis of a rough description of Johns family and wealth position, the solicitor determines who are the heirs, how much each of them will receive and pay in case John dies today! The solicitor also offers some suggestions on actions that could decrease the actual amount of fees. Most of them consist in (partial) donation to his children and decrease Johns overall estate. This makes him somewhat afraid when thinking of the cost of the planned travels. Then, he meets a bank asset manager who suggests him some investments associated with insurances and that have some fiscal deduction associated. But what will append if John dies? Moreover, in his complete situation is the deduction applicable? The questions are too tricky for a quick answer. He would have similar problems with any other kind of advisor. If John decides to test SEPlanS, he first has to introduce into the system the data related to his family and his wealth situation. The SEPlanS platform provides a graphical user interface to support data introduction. It is designed to guide the user through an intuitive sequence of steps. However, each item can be reached directly, for well-aware users and to facilitate edition. Interfaces allow a very detailed description of all family relations, goods, insurances, debts and will. Links to the wikiSEPlanSpedia are associated with any term that could be unclear for non expert. When he introduces his data, the information is structured according to requirements of an expert and the help supports John as if he had an expert of all the domains behind his shoulder. As regards the family, a wizard suggests a sequence for introducing the useful part of the family. Moreover, any other concerned person, as friend involved in the will, can be introduced. This wizard has been conceived with respect to the knowledge of the civil law that specifies who are the heirs. Now, John can run all the reports and simulations. He can simulate the actions previously suggested by the solicitor and observe their impacts both on the evolution of his wealth position and on the total amount of taxes and fees considering different dates for his death. Using the same tool and the complete information introduced by John, the solicitor can refine his analyses and suggest actions taking into account various goals such as the scheduled travel expenses. A few months later, when completing his tax return, John meets his tax advisor. They seized the opportunity to discuss some investment strategy. Thanks to SEPlanS, they can run simulation and evaluate its impact on the estate planning objectives. According to the suggested actions, John takes an appointment with the assets manager. John is a bit suspicious about the level of risk of the proposed investment. Using SEPlanS, he can simulate them and compare his resulting profile with his expectations. And so on, and so forth, expert meeting, after expert meeting, each of them can reuse the data and analyses of the other advisers and, using the default version of the modules in SEPlanS, they can evaluate the impact of their own action according to others point of view. When finally, John will die, the solicitor will have of a complete file, containing the complete information about his past and present wealth position, the heirs, Johns will, and things will be easily managed exactly according to Johns plan.

7 Collaboration Characteristics and Mechanisms

The scenario considered above emphasizes that wealth and estate planning involve actors with different profiles, interests and motivations. The orchestration of their work is unstructured and, very likely, lead by the actor that has the less skills in the domain: the client himself. The client is in charge of selecting (and revoking) all the other actors. His sequence of request for advices and meeting can be guided by advice as well as opportunities or occasional concerns. Therefore, an important part of the collaboration is mainly implicit: actors never meet, there is no a priori orchestration rule, and there is no formal channel for message transfer or action negotiation. Moreover, the client is the only decision maker and all other actors are only advisors. However, a set of elements involved in the SEPlanS platform contribute to support their collaboration in wealth and estate planning for their common client. Three characteristics of the platform offer an efficient support to this collaboration: the knowledge embodied in the system, the support for information sharing, and the possibility of combining default and customized modules. Let us consider in turn each of them. After that, we will discuss advices integration.

7.1 Knowledge in the SEPlanS System

Probably the least visible knowledge included in the framework lies in the data structure. Indeed, the elaboration of the abstract schema of data and relationships among them was an impressive piece of work. Now, it is completely hidden behind the user interfaces and inside computation rules. However, the completeness of the information and the proper use of each piece of data are guaranteed by this invisible schema. Moreover, it provides an efficient transfer of a client's data avoiding many risk of ambiguity. This risk of misunderstanding and ambiguity is also limited by the wikiSEPlanSpedia. The encyclopedia can be browsed in order to obtain information on a given topic. It is also highly related with the platform through the tooltips associated with each domain specific word in the interface. The main goal of these tooltips is to support the user when he consults and/or manipulates information in the platform related to the domain for which he is not an expert. The most obvious expertise of the system lies in its default evaluation and simulation modules. Using them, an expert of one domain can obtain a first advice of an expert from another domain without requiring formal contacts. All the knowledge involved in the system does not provide collaboration support as such. However, these different elements provide a common language and platform to the various profiles of users and provide an efficient support to mutual understanding.

7.2 Information Sharing

Client files sharing is the most obvious collaboration mechanism provided by the system. The file of a customer can not only contain information on his current wealth position and way of life but the system also allows the recording of transactions scheduled in the future. With data, actors can also decide to share their analysis results. All the customized analyses are specific to the expert who has conducted them. When he decides to provide some of them to the customer, that can be done by adding them to the customers file and allowing communication to other actors.

7.3 Combination of Default and Customizable Modules

We mentioned that the existence of default and customizable versions of all the modules allows various scenarios of use of the platform: from the inexperienced user default simulations to the expert personalized analysis. The capability of combining default and proper behaviour for any module also contribute to collaboration in two ways. Firstly, as a single player, little related to other actors, an expert could be tempted of limiting his consideration to the ones strictly useful for his domain and use some homemade computation tool which supports all of his own expertise. The customizability of the modules guarantees to the expert that he will manipulate a module at least as efficient as his own. Moreover, the default version of the other modules will increase his analysis capabilities regarding related area of the domain. Secondly, receiving a report of an expert A in domain a, an expert B in domain b can observe the impact of modification in b, through the use of default modules.

7.4 Advices Integration

The decision process itself is not modified by using the SEPlanS platform. The client is still the only final decision maker and still responsible for the orchestration of the consultation process. However, we claim that the platform provide an efficient support both to the client and to each of the advisors. Previous subsections enhanced mainly the support to experts. Let us now consider the support provided to the client in particular for advices integration, in particular in the case of conflicting advices. At the client's level, one of the main benefits of using the SEPlanS platform is the standardisation of the information, and the language used in the analysis which highly facilitates integration and comparisons of results. Secondly, as the platform's simulation modules are available, a client that decided, for any reason, not to provide complete information to (one of) the expert(s) has the opportunity to check by himself the recommandations' impact on his global wealth postion. Regarding conflict resolution between possible actions, the platform provides to the client the capability to compare the expected results of these actions to his personal intended profile. Moreover, through the simulations, he can observe their impacts on his various goals, integrated or not in the system. The platform won't perform the choices but provides an efficient access to relevent comparisons.

8 Conclusions and Future Work

Wealth and estate planning is a highly unstructured process. In this paper, we identify the profiles of the key players. Furthermore, we illustrate and analyse how the SEPlanS platform can contribute to support collaboration among them in order to provide advice to the only decision maker: the client. The main mechanisms comprise the inclusion of knowledge in the platform architecture, data and analyses sharing and the capability of combination of default and customised modules for conducting analysis.

The SEPlanS prototype is currently under development. It is fully functional for single persons, some particular mechanisms concerning couple are specified and under implementation. Tests by experts have been conducted for singles. A second test phase, for singles and couples is scheduled in the next months. This prototype embodies the complete knowledge of experts required for estimations and simulations. However, the estimations modules could be improved with more sophisticated evolution models. In particular, we are planning to utilise knowledge present in web databases about financial values evolution [12], every day life Belgian families expenses [13], etc.

Finally, if the selection of the business model is out of the scope of the paper (and is not finalised until now), it is to note that it won't be without impact on the collaboration mechanisms. Without going into the details of business models and licences definition, let us discuss here two main architectures that are under consideration. The first one consists in local deployment of the tool and storage of the data. In this architecture, the client is the manager of his data, he can decide to hide some information before exporting his data to an expert (using a usb-key or dropbox for example). Conversely, the results and analyses provided by the experts can be imported locally. In the second model, the application is available through a web-platform. In this case, preserving the client's privilege on his data will require some improvement of the architecture presented in this paper. Indeed the solution should involve the capability for the client to define data access privilege and security mechanisms to ensure their respect. The convenience of this second solution is that it does not require transfer of information and consequently ensures the coherence of the integrated set of information.

Acknowledgment. We want to express acknowledgements to Wallonia that funded this work under the project SEPlanS as a Wist 2 project. Our thanks also go to our colleagues Prof. Dominique Helbois, Prof. Patrick Jaillot, Drs. Frédéric Gandibleux, Frédéric Rouleaux and Olivier Rouleaux from the Catholic University of Mons who are the financial, law and planning experts collaborating in this project.

References

1. NaviPlan, `http://www.eisi.com/en/products/default.shtml`
2. Spruyt, E., Ruysseveldt, J., Dons, P.: Successierekenaar Simulateur Succession, `http://www.successierecht.be/`
3. Kluwer, monKEY.be, `http://www.kluwer.be/monkey/Default.aspx`

4. David, G., John, G., Edward, K.: Holistic Estate Planning and Integrating Mediation in the Planning Process. Real Property, Probate and Trust Journal 39, 509–540 (2004)
5. ISO 22222:2005 - Personal Financial Planning, `http://www.iso.org/iso/iso_catalogue/catalogue_tc/catalogue_detail.htm?csnumber=43033`
6. Steven, S.G.: Multidisciplinary Bar and Financial Planners: The Recommendation of the District of Columbia Bar Special Committee on Multidisciplinary. Practice Capital University Law Review 32 (2003)
7. Michael, S.W., Holter Norma, C.: Multidisciplinary Practices: Reality Or Illusion. International Business & Economics Research Journal 1(5) (2002)
8. Gao, S., Wang, H., Xu, D., Wang, Y.: An Intelligent Agent-assisted Decision Support System for Family Financial Planning. Decision Support Systems 44(1), 60–78 (2007) ISSN 0167-9236, doi:10.1016/j.dss.2007.03.001
9. Shapiro Ehud, Y., Leon, S.: The Art of Prolog: Advanced Programming Techniques. MIT Press, Cambridge (1994)
10. Jacquet, J.-M., et al.: SEPlanS Technical Report: Knowledge Acquisition. University of Namur, Namur (2011)
11. Directive 2004/39/EC of the European Parliament and of the Council of 21 April 2004 on markets in financial instruments amending Council Directives 85/611/EEC and 93/6/EEC and Directive 2000/12/EC of the European Parliament and of the Council and repealing Council Directive 93/22/EEC
12. Center for Study of Financial Market Evolution, `http://www.csfme.org/`
13. Statiscis Belgium, `http://statbel.fgov.be/fr/binaries/PRX-2006-2011_tcm326-119953.xls`

A Knowledge System for Integrated Production Waste Elimination in Support of Organisational Decision Making

Shaofeng Liu[1], Fenio Annansingh[1], Jonathan Moizer[1], Li Liu[1], and Wei Sun[2]

[1] University of Plymouth, PL4 8AA, Plymouth, Devon, UK
{shaofeng.liu,fenio.annansigh,jonathan.moizer}@plymouth.ac.uk,
li.liu@postgrad.plymouth.ac.uk
[2] Beijing University of Technology, Beijing, China
swei303@emails.bjut.edu.cn

Abstract. This paper discusses a knowledge system for organisational decision making on waste elimination to achieve lean production. The system is named Production Waste Elimination Knowledge System (ProWEKS). An empirical study was undertaken to obtain production engineers and managers' empirical knowledge and expertise. A knowledge acquisition matrix has been designed for the knowledge elicitation activity. A waste elimination knowledge model is proposed which captures the inter-relationships between different knowledge components across four knowledge layers including know-what, know-how, know-why and know-with. A knowledge base has been developed based on the knowledge model through constructing a decision tree. The system is demonstrated and evaluated using a quality control decision case from the electronics industry. The main contribution of the paper is that it proposes a new knowledge architecture which comprehensively captures not only the know-what and know-how, but also the know-why and know-with of the waste elimination knowledge for lean production.

Keywords: Collaborative Decision Making, Integrated Waste Elimination, Multi-layer Knowledge Model, Rule-based Knowledge Systems, Lean Production Management.

1 Introduction

Production management has multiple performance objectives to meet, such as quality, cost, speed, flexibility and reliability [1]. To increase their competitiveness, companies are striving for innovative ways to balance different objectives for maximum overall performance. Waste elimination has been recognised as a key strategy to help achieve superior overall performance. In operations, waste is generally defined as the "non-value-adding activities", i.e. the activities which a customer is not willing to pay for [2]. Significant levels of waste could lay dormant in production operations, resulting in the inefficient use of resources and subsequent increases in costs.

J.E. Hernández et al. (Eds.): EWG-DSS 2011, LNBIP 121, pp. 134–150, 2012.

Waste elimination is one of the key ingredients of the lean production philosophy developed by Toyota from the 1950s through to the 1970s. The principles and components of a lean production system were described in detail by Womack, Jones and Roos [3]. Even though the lean production philosophy was originally developed for manufacturing automobiles, its principles and techniques have been applied to operations in many other industries, as varied as retail, healthcare and financial services [4]. Subsequently, experts in many industries have created and accumulated a rich knowledge base in waste elimination and applied it to improve resource utilisation, reduce costs, shorten lead time and increase quality, flexibility and dependability.

Because of the complex composition of production waste and the disparate nature of where this waste occurs in an organisation, production waste elimination has been traditionally managed in a rather fragmented manner. Typically, waste has been classified into seven types, and different types of waste have been dealt with separately [1]. It is common for large, knowledge-intensive companies to develop a rich body of waste elimination knowledge and store it in different silos (i.e. knowledge to eliminate different type of waste is generated and enclosed within different departments in an organisation. For example, inventory waste elimination knowledge is most likely developed in warehouses by inventory managers, whilst process waste elimination knowledge is developed on workshop floors by production engineers). Over time, these silos can start to function in a completely isolated manner, compromising an organisation's abilities and overall performance [5]. Some of the expert knowledge generated has never been properly captured, stored, transferred, shared or re-used. Operations managers and production engineers at one level of the organisation structure are struggling to seek the right knowledge for improved decision making; whilst on the other hand knowledge developed and accumulated by experienced managers, engineers and domain experts at a different organisational level is out of other people's reach. Those individual pockets of tacit knowledge could disappear easily when the experts leave the company or change their jobs. Therefore, there is an urgent need to investigate effective knowledge management approaches to capture and retain expert knowledge for long-term support in production operations collaborative decision making, so that inexperienced and novice decision makers at all organisational levels can efficiently share and re-use the expert knowledge to improve their judgement and reach better collective decisions [6].

This paper proposes a decision-focused knowledge framework and develops a knowledge-based decision support system, named Production Waste Elimination Knowledge System (ProWEKS), which can offer expert advice on waste elimination solutions in production operations through producing an holistic view of the problem. A knowledge model is defined and represented using visual logic programming tool VisiRule [7]. The ProWEKS system is developed using AI system shell Flex (http://www.lpa.co.uk/ind_pro.htm). Application of the knowledge system for decision support has been illustrated through an industrial case study. The ProWEKS has proven effective in enabling decision makers to achieve company-wide integrated management for lean production.

The paper is organised into seven sections. The next section reviews related literature followed by research methodology in Section 3. The ProWEKS architecture and development are then discussed in Sections 4 and 5, followed by its application in Section 6. Section 7 presents further discussion and draws conclusions.

2 Literature Review

Lean production objectives are often expressed as ideals, such as "to meet demand instantaneously with perfect quality and no waste" [2]. Three key issues define the lean production philosophy: the elimination of waste, the involvement of all staff in the operation, and the drive for continuous development [1]. All three issues have received wide research interest, and significant advancements have been achieved in each of the key area. For example, Total Quality Management (TQM) and total people involvement have been developed as exemplary methods to encourage a high degree of personal responsibility, engagement and "ownership" of operations [8,9]. Popular continuous improvement approaches include Business Process Re-engineering [10], Six Sigma [11], and improvement cycles such as PDCA (plan-do-check-act) and DMAIC (define-measure-analyse-improve-control) [12]. This paper focuses on company-wide waste elimination, which is arguably the most significant part of the lean production philosophy.

Identification of waste is the first step towards waste elimination. Seven types of waste have been identified by Toyota. They are over-production, waiting time, excessive transport, process, inventory and motion, and defectives [4]. Existing research has widely discussed the nature of each type of the waste. Significant amount of knowledge about how to eliminate the waste has been generated over the years. This includes streamlined flow (such as value-stream mapping and increase flow visibility), close matching of supply and demand (e.g. pull control, kanbans), flexible processes (such as customisation and deliver to order), and minimising variability (e.g. the 5-s technology and total productive maintenance) [1,2,4]. However, existing work has not adequately addressed the inter-relationships between the different types of waste [13]. In particular, there is little report on the use of integrated management approaches to support decision making in company-wide waste elimination.

A key reason behind the failure to achieve integrated waste elimination decisions has been identified as the lack of adequate support for developing effective knowledge management methods for collaborative decision making in organisations [14, 15]. Firstly, different waste types are often embedded within different areas of operations in companies, especially large corporations where complex organisation structure is evident. In such cases, the knowledge, either explicit or tacit, is generated and owned by different silos. Secondly, even though there is a culture of knowledge sharing in the company, people tend to find that significant technical barriers exist which hinders knowledge sharing and re-use [5,6]. Many key issues are yet to be adequately addressed, for example, from a knowledge providers perspective, there are issues of knowledge repository, classification and retrieval, while from knowledge re-users' viewpoint, key issues include decision situations where knowledge may be re-used, and how the knowledge can be best re-used by different decision makers [16]. In recent years, knowledge-based decision support systems have made great advances in theory and have been widely applied to production management areas [17, 18]. However, to the authors' best knowledge, there has not been such a system specifically designed and developed for lean production in support of its collaborative decision making. To fill this gap, this paper addresses the knowledge issue from the knowledge providers' view by defining a waste elimination knowledge model and developing an intelligent decision support system to facilitate knowledge capture, storage, sharing and re-use in lean production for collaborative decision making.

3 Research Methodology

This section discusses a research methodology related to both knowledge elicitation (empirical study) and knowledge system development. Acquiring knowledge from domain experts has always been a difficult, tedious and costly process [6]. There has been no pre-defined procedure to guarantee knowledge acquisition and representation. In addition, no lifecycle is available to help to specifically develop decision-focused knowledge systems. This section of the paper presents the methods explored for the acquisition and capture of production waste elimination knowledge. As illustrated in Figure 1, methods for knowledge elicitation included in-depth interview with domain experts alongside the use of a knowledge acquisition matrix. With respect to knowledge system development, two AI tools, VisiRule and Flex, are chosen for the design of knowledge base (visual modelling) and to assist with the rule-based programming. The main reasons for choosing the above methods are discussed in detail in the next two sub-sections.

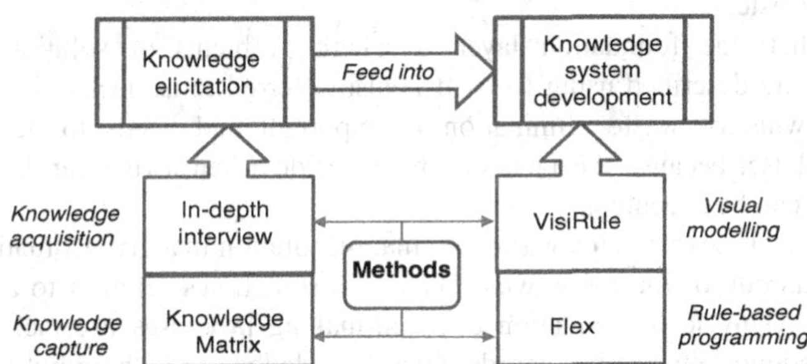

Fig. 1. Research methodology for knowledge elicitation and system development

3.1 Methods for the Elicitation of Production Waste Elimination Knowledge

An empirical study has been undertaken with respect to facilitating waste elimination, enhancing the lean production decision making process, and improving decision makers' behaviour in knowledge sharing and re-use. The main focus of this work is on the management practices of waste elimination including establishing what the main causes of wastes in the organisation are, how this waste is identified, measured and dealt with, and why particular solutions are employed to eliminate the waste. The study has also investigated operations managers' decision making behaviour, such as how they make decisions on waste elimination, what processes and models they use to govern their decision choices, and what has been done to improve the collective decision performance within their organisation. The research has further investigated decision makers' different roles in knowledge re-use (as knowledge producers, as shared work practitioners, as expertise-seeking novices or as secondary knowledge miners), their reasons for knowledge re-use, what they know, do not know and need to know when making decisions, how they locate knowledge and expertise, and how they select expertise and apply the knowledge in lean production decision making process. The main research method employed for the knowledge elicitation was in-depth one-to-one interviews carried out with domain experts to collect primary data in lean manufacturing [19]. The interviews were semi-structured in nature, with a predefined list of questions but allowing the interviewees to freely give answers and expand on the initial questions. In-depth interview was deemed to be an appropriate methodological vehicle given the goal of obtaining richness in data through engaging in insightful discussion with operations managers and production engineers regarding their waste elimination strategies and practices [20]. All interviews were audio recorded so that accurate information can be gained for transcription and to allow direct quotations to be used for later analysis.

In order to capture the empirical knowledge from multiple perspectives, the research developed a knowledge acquisition matrix based on a multi-layer knowledge model, so that a systematic body of knowledge could be obtained for the development of the knowledge base at a later stage in the research process. Figure 2 shows the key structure of the multi-layer knowledge model defined in this paper. The knowledge model consists of four knowledge layers for the elimination of the seven types of production waste.

Know-what: the foundation layer is where problems or solutions for waste elimination are described using facts. It is also referred to as declarative knowledge. The know-what of waste elimination is important and needs to be stored in a knowledge-base, because the facts can help decide when a rule can be fired and a programme can be executed.

Know-how: how to reach a waste elimination solution in a given situation based on the understanding of the know-what [17]. It is sometimes referred to as procedural knowledge. Many lean production decision-making processes use tacit knowledge, which is difficult to express in words. Such knowledge are nothing but the steps in a procedure. Examples of know-how are rules, strategies and models. In the ProWEKS knowledge base, the know-how in the format of rules are responsible for taking actions based on the facts, i.e. the know-what, in the knowledge-base.

Know-why: principles underlying know-how and know-what for decision justification in production waste elimination. The most valuable thing about having access to domain experts' knowledge for decision consultation is not only to improve the speed, accuracy and consistency of decisions, but also the ability to back the decisions up. Experts in lean manufacturing can provide justifications for a conclusion, hypothesis, a test or a recommendation with regard to waste elimination.

In addition, experts can also question the validity of existing facts and bring hypotheticals into the picture of integrated lean production management. Investigating know-why for waste elimination decisions will have two main advantages: explanations and hypothetical reasoning. The ProWEKS built upon the know-why will be able to help decision makers reason about how changes affect an existing solution and allow explanations for decisions to be provided, which can add significant comfort value for the system users, i.e. production engineers and operations managers as decision makers in the organisation.

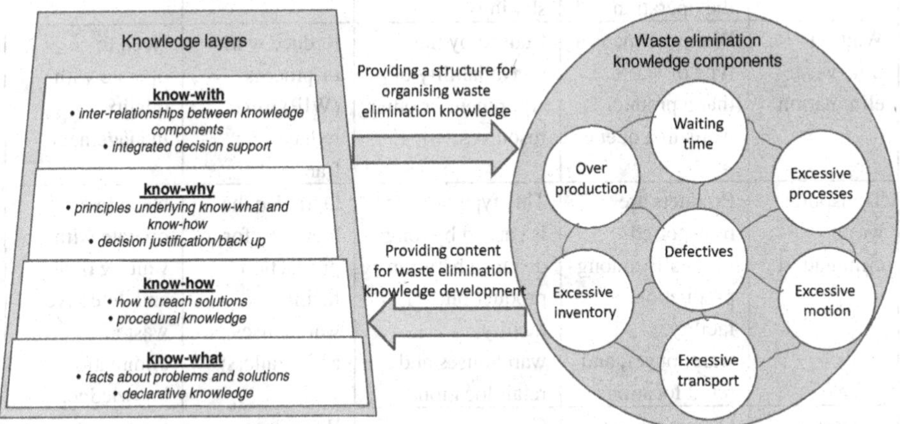

Fig. 2. Waste elimination knowledge model

Know-with: top layer, interrelationships among knowledge components for integrated decision support. Defining the relational knowledge will help address how to reduce one type of waste without negatively affecting other types of waste. Furthermore, exploring the know-with facet of knowledge will equip decision makers with the knowledge in an organisational decision network to understand the multi-directional impacts and effects of solutions to different types of waste, to resolve conflicting interests and decision preferences, and to better support orchestrated organisational decision making.

Using the above four-layer knowledge model, a knowledge acquisition matrix has been populated, based on both the theoretical and empirical study of the electronics manufacturing industry. Knowledge was collected from computer factories responsible for laptop manufacturing and assembly. Apart from the domain experts, other sources used for data collection included textbooks, articles, multimedia documents, databases, special research reports and the information available on the company websites [1, 2, 21]. It should be noted that Table 1 only shows the top level structure of the knowledge acquisition matrix by using some examples. A large collection of knowledge rules can be substantiated for each cell of the Table. The actual size of the knowledge base of the ProWEKS is much larger than the knowledge acquisition matrix itself. To date, over five hundred pieces of rules have been populated for lean production decision support in the ProWEKS demonstration system.

Table 1. Waste elimination knowledge acquisition matrix populated with electronics manufacturing

	Know-what	Know-why	Know-how	Know-with
Over-production elimination	Produces more than is immediately needed by the next process in the operation	Caused by inaccurate forecast of demand and by lack of information sharing	Implement information integration systems such as ERP	Co-operate with process and inventory waste elimination knowledge
Waiting time waste elimination	Waiting time is a type of waste that a product waits in a queue	Caused by the unavailability of equipment or other resources,	Reduce work-in-process (WIP) time; reduce transport	Need to co-operate with quality management
Transport waste elimination	Products are transported internally among production facility, warehouses, and retail locations	This type of waste is caused by long distance between production facility, warehouses and retail locations	Optimise the locations for production facility, warehouses and retailers;	Need to co-operate with waiting time and defectives waste elimination knowledge,
Process waste elimination	Occurs when nonessential operations happen	Caused by poor product design (such as components)	Reducing process steps and the times associated with them	Co-operate with motion and defectives elimination
Inventory waste elimination	Extra inventory is a type of waste	Causes extra storage and handling requirements	Implement JIT	Co-operate with over-production and defectives waste elimination
Motion waste elimination	Unnecessary movement of raw materials and components	Motion waste is caused by poor layout, work and process design	Improve layout design, work design and process design	Co-operate with process waste elimination
Defectives waste elimination	Occurs when any product or component is not produced according to specifications.	Is caused by poor process and product design, incompetent resources, and poor quality materials	Implement quality approaches (such as SPC, TQM, Six Sigma	Co-operate with process and inventory waste elimination

This section not only discussed the nature of each type of waste, but also the knowledge about why particular types of waste occur and what the consequences are, is considered. Besides the know-what and know-how of production waste elimination, the "know-how" about waste elimination provides solutions that can be used by non-experts as well as inexperienced operations managers and production engineers. Equally important, the "know-with" reveals the inter-relationships between the knowledge elements on the elimination of different types of waste. It is evident that reducing the impact of the various types of production waste requires careful systems thinking, i.e. an integrated management approach [4].

3.2 Methods for the Development of a Knowledge-Based Decision Support System

Development of a high quality knowledge-based DSS needs two important mechanisms: a process that provides disciplines (well-defined, structured guides that developers can follow), and an integrated Artificial Intelligence (AI) environment which can provide developers with a platform to readily develop their own applications. Knowledge-based DSS may be developed using many different tools, including algorithmic programming languages (e.g. Basic, C, C++), AI languages (such as Prolog and Lisp), and expert system shells (Dhar and Stein, 1997). Methods for the development of the ProWEKS are LPA Prolog system tools, specifically VisiRule and Flex [7]. There are three main reasons for choosing the LPA Prolog system tools: (1) LPA Prolog system is a fully integrated logic programming environment; (2) the embedded toolkit VisiRule allows the creation of visual knowledge models using flowcharts and backward chaining inference engine; (3) the embedded toolkit Flex supports rule-based programming, frame-based reasoning with inheritance and contains its own knowledge specification language. The combination of VisiRule and Flex provides a powerful development platform with logic programming function and visual presentation.

Other decision methods such as multi-criteria decision making (MCDM) tools were also initially considered as an option for the production waste elimination decision case. The research investigated an MCDM system, Super Decisions (http://www.superdecisions.com/), for its feasibility for the integrated management decision support. It was found that MCDM tools such as Super Decisions are competent in developing decision models that help with understanding the complex decision situations such as with various decision variables and clusters of criteria. MCDM tools also allow decision makers to incorporate their preferences and priorities in the decision analysis. However, most MCDM tools such as Super Decisions are developed based on the Analytic Hierarchical Process (AHP) and Analytic Network Process (ANP) methods. An important consideration in AHP and ANP is the consistency of the pairwise judgements provided by the decision makers. With numerous pairwise comparisons, perfect consistency is difficult to achieve [22]. In fact, some degree of inconsistency can be expected to exist in almost any set of pairwise comparisons. In reality, if the consistency ratio is 0.01 or less, the consistency of the pairwise comparisons is considered reasonable. In integrated waste elimination decision making, consistency is extremely important otherwise it would be impossible for decision makers at different organisational levels and in different departments to synchronise their decisions in order to achieve the organisation's overall goal [23]. Knowledge-based decision support systems can provide the crucial knowledge base that all decision makers could access, share and re-use so that decision consistency can be improved. A key benefit of having chosen an existing AI system shell, LPA Prolog systems tools VisiRule and Flex, as a platform to develop ProWEKS is that developers can focus on the system core capabilities, i.e. the design of rules for the lean production knowledge base, thus saving significant time from writing codes for preliminary functions such as creation of user interface menus and window panels. Flex is an easy to customise platform which offers users with the flexibility to re-develop and address the end user's requirements. Integrated with the graphical knowledge capture tool VisiRule, Flex allows the generation and execution of programming codes without leaving the design environment [7].

4 The Architecture of the Knowledge System ProWEKS

This section proposes an architecture for the knowledge system ProWEKS which comprises five key software components: an Organisational Decision Network Manager, a Waste Elimination Knowledge Base, a Knowledge Refinement module, an Inference Engine, and a Decision Justifier. Figure 3 illustrates the architecture designed for the ProWEKS. The user interface of the ProWEKS is provided by the adopted AI system shell and therefore is not considered as a key component for the system architecture design. The main functions of each module are discussed below.

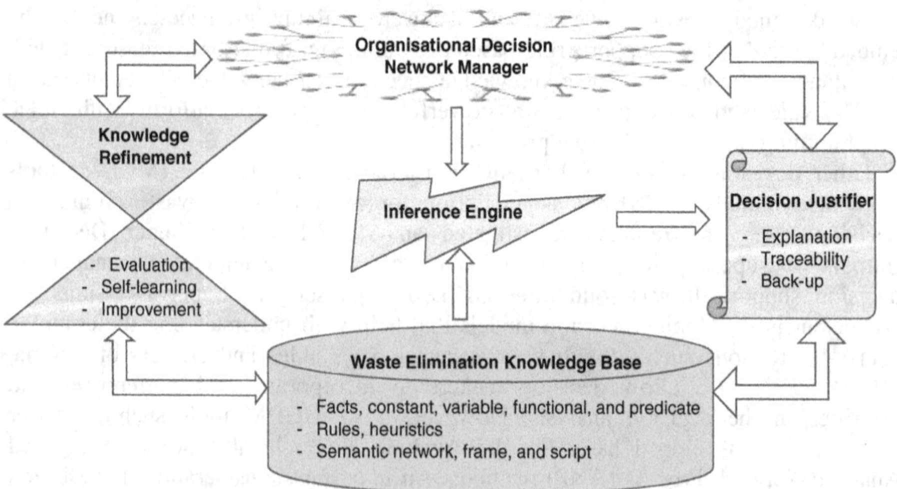

Fig. 3. Architecture of the software system ProWEKS

Organisational Decision Network Manager: This component is designed to manage network configuration of decision nodes (representing different decision makers) in the organisation [24], decision propagation paths, and decision settling policy in case of conflicting preferences and interests existing between different decision makers.

Waste Elimination Knowledge Base: One of the most important components in a knowledge –based system is probably the knowledge base. It is a mechanism for referring to existing knowledge and generating new knowledge, i.e. inference, reasoning and explanation. The knowledge base will include domain experts' knowledge of production waste elimination with four sets of rules to represent the know-what, know-how, know-why and know-with. A fifth set of rules, namely meta-rules (rules concerned with how to process the relationships across the other four rule sets), has also been defined.

Knowledge Refinement module: This module imitates human experts so as to analyse their knowledge and its effectiveness, learn from it, and improve on it for future decision consultations. The knowledge refinement module is implemented through a self-learning mechanism that allows it to adjust its knowledge base and its processing of knowledge based on the evaluation of its recent past performance. From this viewpoint, the Knowledge Refinement module is an intelligent component of ProWEKS.

Inference Engine: The Inference Engine is the "brain" of the ProWEKS. Specifically, the Inference Engine has the control structure governing how the knowledge rules should be interpreted and fired (activated) to reach appropriate waste elimination decisions.

Decision Justifier: The Decision Justifier provides clear explanations of waste elimination knowledge re-use and decision making through its ability to trace responsibility for conclusions to their sources. It can trace such responsibility and explain the ProWEKS behaviour by interactively answering questions such as: How was a certain conclusion reached? Why was a certain alternative rejected? And what is the complete plan of decisions to be made in reaching the conclusions?

The software modules designed within the architecture allows the ProWEKS system to have unique features which distinguish it from other knowledge-based systems, namely:

(1) ProWEKS can support collaborative decision making in an organisational context by using the functions of the Organisational Decision Network Manager.

(2) It can provide intelligent decision support based on the self-learning mechanism provided by the Knowledge Refinement module.

(3) It can provide comfort for decision makers with explanation, traceability and back-up functions from the Decision Justifier.

5 Development of the Knowledge System ProWEKS

Knowledge management has been perceived as an optional sub-system for a decision support system. Typically, Decision Support Systems (DSS) are comprised of three sub-systems: a data management sub-system, a model management sub-system, and a dialogue sub-system (or called user interface) [5]. However, modern complex DSS may require an additional component that provides expertise to the decision makers. DSS including such a component becomes a knowledge-based DSS [6]. A knowledge-based DSS acts as a consultant, as it advises and guides non-experts. The ProWEKS for integrated waste elimination proposed in this paper is a knowledge-based DSS in nature, which provides operations managers and production engineers with both suggestions of solutions to production waste elimination (through the "know-how" and "know-with" built in the system) and explanations about the solutions (through the "know-what" and "know-why").

Three main approaches to the development of modern DSS that can provide interpretation of knowledge include rule-based reasoning, case-based reasoning and hybrid approach (combination of both). The ProWEKS utilises rule-based reasoning for the knowledge capture and interpretation. As the methods and the architecture for ProWEKS development have been discussed in detail in Sections 3 and 4, respectively, this section focuses on the system development process and the design of the knowledge base.

5.1 ProWEKS Development Process

The iterative process for the ProWEKS development consists of three key steps: the design of the knowledge base, implementation of the system, and evaluation of the system. Figure 4 illustrates the process with support of the chosen AI tools.

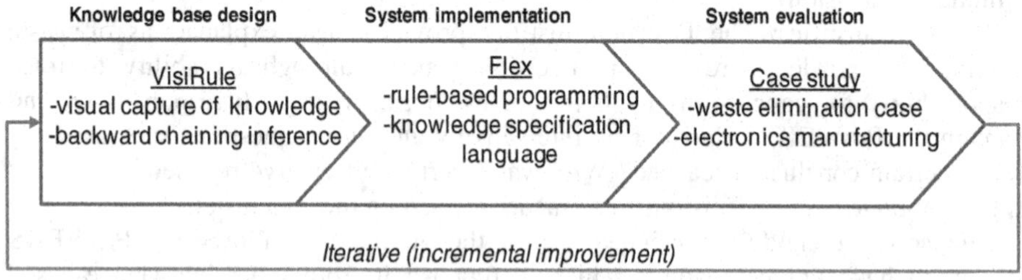

Fig. 4. ProWEKS development process

Step 2 of the process – system implementation, employs the AI tool, Flex, to facilitate the rule-based programming where the knowledge specification language embedded within Flex is used. System evaluation with case studies will be discussed in detail in Section 6. The following Section 5.2 will discuss Step 1 of the process – knowledge base design.

5.2 The Design of the ProWEKS Knowledge Base

The key element of a knowledge-based system like ProWEKS is its knowledge base. For many decades rules have served as a fundamental knowledge representation scheme in AI. A rule-based approach is advantageous when experts are available and able to specify with a high degree of confidence what and why they do in specific situations [5]. The task for the model and system developer is to extract as much knowledge as possible and turn this knowledge into rules. However, these rules must cover the problem area comprehensively so that there are no inappropriate "holes" in its knowledge base [6].

Based on the above consideration, the ProWEKS knowledge base must construct rule sets which comprehensively cover knowledge on the elimination of all identified main types of waste in the production operations. The overall design of the logic and flow in the knowledge base is shown in the decision tree as illustrated in Figure 5. A decision tree is preferred to an inference net for the design of ProWEKS because the experts interviewed could articulate clearly (without much trial and error) the sequence of steps involved in reaching a conclusion for waste elimination [25].

As can be seen from the Figure 5, the production waste elimination decision tree has seven parallel branches corresponding to the seven different types of waste. Within each branch, four knowledge layers are systematically structured from the "know-what" through "know-how" and "know-why" to "know-with". The seven branches merge at the end of the process, i.e. a step to check the inter-operability of the different knowledge components. If any conflicts arise, then further actions need to be taken to resolve the conflicting situations. New rules can be added at this stage to reflect the knowledge about how a conflict is reconciled.

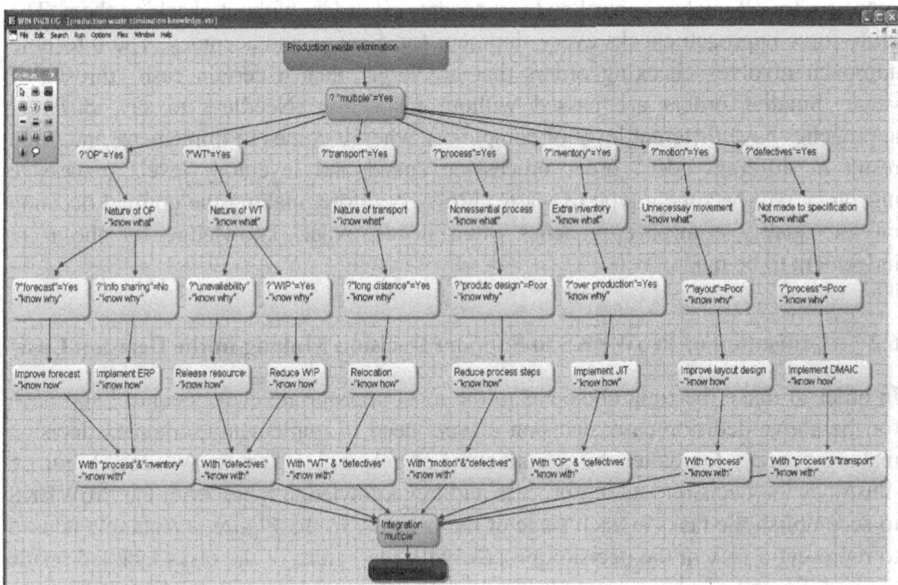

Fig. 5. Decision tree for the production waste elimination knowledge base

6 ProWEKS Application

This section explores the ProWEKS demonstration system with a case study to test the decision-focused knowledge framework proposed in this paper. The decision case is presented first, and then some results are shown in the Section 6.2.

6.1 Case Example

For evaluation purpose, the ProWEKS demonstration system utilises information from an industrial case. In the case example, operations managers need to consider elimination of defectives through quality control of suppliers. In the electronics industry, many companies such as Dell use hundreds of suppliers in their global supply networks [8]. Due to the sheer number and disparate nature of the suppliers, quality standards and internal quality control process used by the suppliers can vary significantly. Many defects within final products such as laptops result from the poor quality of the sub-assemblies and components (such as microprocessors, memory, graphics cards etc.) provided by their suppliers. Therefore, undertaking strict quality control is essential in eliminating defects to ensure the final product quality.

Many quality control approaches have been developed and adopted in operations management, most notably SPC (Statistical Process Control), TQM and Six Sigma for quality management, and PDCA and DMAIC for continuous improvement [1, 8]. Specifically in relation to the quality control of suppliers, there are three main approaches widely in use: no-inspection, the brute-force approach and the threshold approach [1, 6]. The no-inspection approach is the simplest which depends on the suppliers for all quality control and just accepts all orders without checking them. The brute-force approach checks every shipment for damage and accuracy. The threshold approach involves checking orders that are larger than a certain cash "threshold" value. Smaller orders are passed without inspection. Needless to say, different approaches have different level of complexity when it comes to implement, and often result in different costs, order processing speed and inventory levels (excessive inventory will become a type of waste) [26]. Therefore, making the optimal decision on the quality control approaches often needs expert knowledge for the right judgement to be made.

6.2 Utilisation of ProWEKS to Support Decision Making in the Decision Case

In order to make the right choice as to the most appropriate quality control approach for the above decision case, decision makers need to implement a complex decision making process facilitated by a collection of relevant expert knowledge. Figure 6 illustrates the decision making process and key knowledge types from the ProWEKS to accomplish the tasks at each stage of the process. In the Figure, a rectangle is used to represent a task in the decision process with the nature of the tasks labelled inside the box. Some tasks have a note (represented by a curved shape) attached to the tasks to provide further information. The types of the knowledge required to perform the tasks are indicated using an oval shape joined with the tasks. The decision point is represented by a diamond symbol.

Within Figure 7 is a collection of screenshots of the ProWEKS demonstration system. In the ProWEKS demonstration system, the knowledge is represented by the logic rules shown in the decision tree. The rules designed within VisiRule are then transformed into programming codes in Flex, as shown in Window (a) in the Figure 7. These coded rules are then compiled within the AI environment, as illustrated in Window (b). ProWEKS users can interact with the system through the Graphical User Interface (as in Window (c)) answering prompts by simply performing a "point and click" action following the defined logic. Final solutions suggested by the system (i.e. the threshold approach in this case example) are displayed to users in easy-to-understand messages, as illustrated in the Window (d).

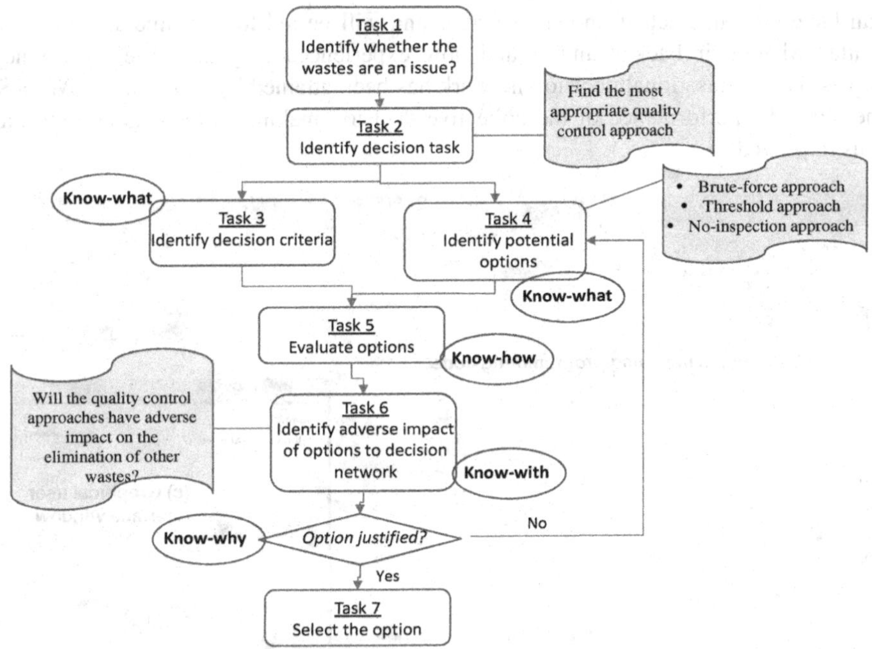

Fig. 6. ProWEKS support for the decision making process

The "Explanation" button in the GUI window as seen in the Figure 7(c) is important to the ProWEKS because the most valuable things about having access to expert knowledge are not only the accuracy of decisions but also the ability to back them up. The "Explanation" function (based on the know-why in the knowledge base) allows the ProWEKS users to seek for justification of waste elimination solutions. The ability to provide explanations for decisions can add significant comfort value for the decision makers. However, the provision of explanations to underpin decision making in the ProWEKS also comes at a cost. Firstly, system developers have to understand the waste elimination problem area much better than where a black box approach like a neural network is employed. Firstly, they have to extract all types of waste elimination knowledge for knowledge components in the demonstration system, which takes a significant amount of time and effort. Secondly, from a computational point of view, extra overhead is incurred in terms of memory and reasoning machinery, which is sometimes referred to as "reason maintenance" [6].

Based on the evaluation report from the ProWEKS users, it is clear that the users can efficiently access the expert knowledge, using the system inference engine to help reach the decision choices effectively. The speed of the system firing and retrieving solutions for specific decision problems is sufficient. The types of the knowledge inside the knowledge base are transparent to the system users. Hence, novice decision makers who do not have much domain knowledge in production waste elimination will have little difficulty in using the system and reaching the right decisions. All decision makers on the organisation decision network who have access to the system can have the same set of knowledge rules and will be led to the same solutions, no matter what their background is and how experienced they are. The consistency across the organisational decision network has been attained by using the ProWEKS, therefore the performance of the collective decision making in the organisation has thus improved.

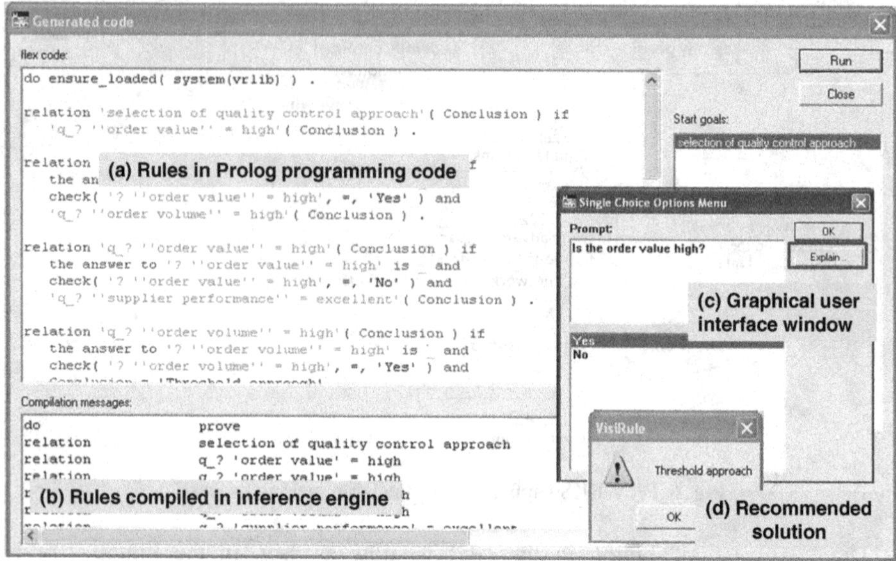

Fig. 7. A screenshot of the ProWEKS system and experimental results

7 Discussion and Conclusions

This paper discussed a knowledge-based DSS called ProWEKS which can offer organisation-wide waste elimination guidance and recommendations to operations managers and production engineers involved in the decision making process to help them strive for operations excellence. The main contributions of the paper are as follows:

- it has proposed a new decision-focused knowledge architecture that can capture waste elimination knowledge in four inter-related layers for seven knowledge components with respect to the elimination of wastes from over-production, waiting time, excessive process, motion, inventory and transport, and defectives. Apart from the "know-what" and "know-how", the knowledge architecture defines two new layers: "know-why" and "know-with". The inclusion of the "know-why" in the knowledge architecture provides the means to back up decisions with justification and explanations. The "know-with" enables the consideration of inter-relationships between the different types of waste in decision making, and hence the adverse effect from the decision of eliminating one type of waste to another can be avoided.

- it has discussed the capture of waste elimination knowledge through using the AI toolkit VisiRule, allowing the knowledge objects and relationships to be visualised, thus enabling transparent design, update and maintenance of knowledge within the knowledge base.
- it integrates the waste elimination knowledge model into an AI system shell, Flex, which allows the inference results to be visualised and presented to all decision makers for better collaborative decision making.

Further research will be exploring two key issues:

(1) the consolidation of the knowledge-base to include a second layer meta rules, so that the priorities of the knowledge can be specified. For example, priorities could be given to the knowledge rules that match the most recent facts.

(2) the extension of the ProWEKS to a web-based system in order to promote knowledge sharing and reuse in the context of global supply chains [27].

References

1. Slack, N., Chambers, S., Johnston, R.: Operations Management, 6th edn. FT Prentice Hall (2010)
2. Boyer, V.: Operations and Supply Chain Management: World Class Theory and Practice. South-Western Cengage Learning, Australia (2010)
3. Womack, J.P., Jones, D.T., Roos, D.: The Machine That Changed the World: the Story of Lean Production. Harper Perennial, New York (1991)
4. Holweg, M.: The genealogy of lean production. Journal of Operations Management 25, 420–437 (2007)
5. Turban, E., Sharda, R., Delen, D.: Decision Support and Business Intelligence Systems. Prentice Hall, New Jersey (2011)
6. Akerkar, R.A., Sajja, P.S.: Knowledge-Based Systems. Jones and Bartlett Publishers, Sdbury (2010)
7. Spenser, C.: Drawing on your knowledge with VisiRule. IEEE Potentials, 20--25 (January/February issue, 2007)
8. Hafeez, K., Malak, N., Abdelmeguid, H.: A framework for TQM to achieve business excellence. Total Quality Management & Business Excellence 17(9), 1213–1229 (2006)
9. Mann, R.: Revisiting a TQM research project: the quality improvement activities of TQM 18(7-8), 751–761 (2008)
10. Shen, C.W., Chou, C.C.: Business process re-engineering in the logistics industry: a study of implementation, success factors and performance. Enterprise Information Systems 4(1), 61–78 (2010)
11. Zu, X., Fredendall, L.D., Douglas, T.J.: The evolving theory of quality management: the role of Six Sigma. Journal of Operations Management 26, 630–650 (2008)
12. Sokovic, M., Pavletic, D.: Quality improvement – PDCA vs. DMAIC and DFSS. Strojniski Vestnik – Journal of Mechanical Engineering 53(6), 369–378 (2007)
13. Rawabdeh, I.A.: A model for the assessment of waste in job shop environments. International Journal of Operations and Production Management 25(8), 800–822 (2005)
14. Moham, K., Ramesh, B.: Traceability-based knowledge integration in group decision and negotiation activities. Decision Support Systems 43, 968–989 (2007)

15. Riezebos, J., Klingenberg, W., Hicks, C.: Lean production and information technology: connection or contradiction? Computers in Industry 60, 237–247 (2009)
16. Markus, M.L.: Toward a theory of knowledge re-use: types of knowledge re-use situations and factors in re-use success. Journal of Management Information Systems 18(1), 57–91 (2001)
17. Chen, Y.J.: Development of a method for ontology-based empirical knowledge representation and reasoning. Decision Support Systems 50, 1–20 (2010)
18. Liu, S., Duffy, A.H.B., Whitfield, R.I., Boyle, I.M.: Integration of decision support systems to improve decision support performance. Knowledge and Information Systems - An International Journal 22(3), 261–286 (2010)
19. Saunders, M., Lewis, P., Thornhill, A.: Research methods for business students, 5th edn. FT Prentice Hall, Harlow (2009)
20. Quinlan, C.: Business Research Methods. Cengage Learning EMEA, Hampshire (2011)
21. Gebus, S., Leviska, K.: Knowledge acquisition for decision support systems on an electronic assembly line. Expert Systems with Applications 36(1), 93–101 (2009)
22. Saaty, T.L., Vargas, L.G.: Decision making with the analytic network process. Springer, New York (2006)
23. Kainuma, Y., Tawara, N.: A multiple attribute utility theory approach to lean and green supply chain management. International Journal of Production Economics 101, 99–108 (2006)
24. Liu, S., Duffy, A.H.B., Whitfield, R.I., Boyle, I.M., McKenna, I.: Towards the realisation of an integrated decision support environment for organisational decision making. International Journal of Decision Support Systems Technology 1(4), 38–58 (2009)
25. Siegel, J.G., Shim, K., Walker, J.P., et al.: The Artificial Intelligence Handbook: Business Applications in Accounting, Banking, Finance, Management and Marketing. Thomson South-western (2003)
26. Barnes, D.: Operations Management: an International Perspective. Thomson Learning, London (2008)
27. Hernández, J.E., Poler, R., Mula, J., Peidro, D.: A collaborative knowledge management framework for supply chains: a UML-based model approach. Journal of Industrial Engineering and Management 1(2), 77–103

Impact of and Interaction between Behavioral and Economic Decision Support in Electronic Negotiations

Johannes Gettinger[1], Alexander Dannenmann[2], Daniel Druckman[3], Michael Filzmoser[1], Ronny Mitterhofer[1], Andreas Reiser[2], Mareike Schoop[2], Rudolf Vetschera[4], Per van der Wijst[5], and Sabine Köszegi[1]

[1] Institute of Management Science, Vienna University of Technology, Austria
[2] Information Systems I, University of Hohenheim, Germany
[3] Department of Public and International Affairs, George Mason University, United States
[4] Department of Business Administration, University of Vienna, Austria
[5] Department of Communication and Information Science, Tilburg University, The Netherlands

Johannes.Gettinger@tuwien.ac.at

Abstract. In this study we compare the effects of two distinct approaches in negotiation support: negotiation analysis providing economic decision support, and mediation analysis offering behavioral decision support. Those negotiators with economic or behavioral decision support at their disposal were expected to reach better results. Furthermore, behavioral decision support would not only lead to more integrative behavior, but also to more satisfaction about process variables. The hypotheses were tested in a laboratory experiment with 224 undergraduate students from four European universities. Contrary to our expectations, economic decision support did not yield better results, but instead increased informal communication, whereas behavioral decision support led to fewer, but larger concessions. Satisfaction of subjects with the negotiation process and outcomes reflects the strength of the support approaches. The implications of these results and the impact of both types of decision support are discussed.

Keywords: Negotiation, mediation, behavioral support, economic support, empirical study.

1 Introduction

Negotiations are iterative communication and decision making processes between two or more agents (parties and their representatives) who (1) cannot achieve their objectives through unilateral actions; (2) exchange communicative acts comprising offers, counter-offers and arguments; (3) deal with interdependent tasks; and (4) search for a consensus which is a compromise decision [1]. Based on this definition, we can derive two main aspects of negotiations, decision making and communication.

J.E. Hernández et al. (Eds.): EWG-DSS 2011, LNBIP 121, pp. 151–165, 2012.

Negotiations are specific communication processes that can be divided into offer communication and non-offer communication (i.e. arguments explaining offer communication, greetings, addresses etc.). Communication is "at the heart" of negotiations; there can be negotiations about communication [2], but no negotiation proceeds without communication. In order to reach an agreement, various decisions have to be made. The negotiation issues have to be specified and rated, offers and counter-offers need to be evaluated and compared, and negotiators have to decide whether to accept or reject a deal.

One could assume that electronic negotiations merely transplant the characteristics of traditional negotiations into the digital realm. However, the medium itself adds benefits to the negotiations. Electronic negotiations are "restricted by at least one rule that affects the decision-making or communication process, if this rule is enforced by the electronic medium supporting the negotiation, and if this support covers the execution of at least one decision-making or communication task" [3, p. 147]. Therefore, support in negotiations refers to both decision-making and communication, as well as to the process and outcome. One goal is to support the negotiator in efforts to reach the best possible agreement with a particular negotiation partner based on preferences set at the beginning of the negotiation. The second objective is to enable good communication, e.g. by preventing misunderstandings, enabling discussions, offering explanations, and utilizing goal-oriented communication [4].

Even if communication problems can be solved and offers made by the negotiation partner are considered acceptable, negotiations can – and often do – terminate unsuccessfully. Conflicts occur during negotiations. A conflict is the source of the negotiation, as one would not negotiate if the other partner agreed immediately. In addition to this initial conflict, dynamic conflicts can arise during the negotiation process. These conflicts need to be resolved to prevent final rejections [5]. In general, conflicts can be a result of insufficient concessions, incompatible preferences, or inadequate communication. If the partners fail to solve these conflicts, the negotiation will terminate. Negotiation support in the business context does not yet include the help of an expert (system), which could offer possible solutions not previously envisioned by the negotiators. Such systems are called mediation systems.

At this point, the two paradigms of negotiation support and mediation support are primarily separated and form two distinct streams of support philosophy. No single system exists to integrate negotiation and mediation support. Therefore, we aim to analyze the separate impact of these two distinct, integrated support philosophies, as well as their interaction on several subjective and objective dimensions of the negotiation process and outcome.

In order to address these questions, an empirical study with international participants has been conducted using the negotiation support system *Negoisst* [4, 6] (providing communication and decision support) and the mediation system *vienNA* [7-9] (providing mediation support). Before discussing the results, the paper presents the theoretical and conceptual background of the study and the research method, including a brief introduction of the systems.

2 Theoretical Background

In this study, we compare the effects of two distinct support approaches in negotiation support: (i) negotiation analysis and (ii) mediation. Negotiation analysis applies formal models from other fields (e.g. economics, game theory, decision analysis) to provide advice on how to conduct and conclude negotiations efficiently. This approach highlights an economic perspective on negotiations, as it aims to avoid suboptimal trade-offs or lost opportunities that prevail in face-to-face negotiations [10, 11]. Electronic negotiation support systems (eNSS) that follow an economic decision support (EDS) approach such as *Inspire* [12] or *Smart Settle* [13] aim to improve the efficiency of negotiations by providing support during all phases: (i) preparation, (ii) conduct, and (iii) post-settlement. In the preparation phase, issues and options of the negotiation problem are identified; the negotiators' preferences for possible alternatives are elicited and formally represented in the form of a utility function. In the conduct phase, eNSS provide protocols for the exchange of offers and support negotiators through evaluation and graphical illustration of offers and counter-offers according to their preferences. Another common support function of eNSS for the post-settlement phase of negotiations is the generation and recommendation of Pareto-improvements to a tentative agreement reached by the negotiating parties. This ensures Pareto-efficiency for the outcome so that no value is left on the bargaining table. Most eNSS not only support decision making of the individual negotiators, but also joint communication between the negotiation parties [14].

In contrast to negotiation analysis, which focuses on decision support, communication research perceives a negotiation as a particular form of communication. It emphasizes the communication support components of eNSS. The possibility for negotiators to communicate via the eNSS can be further extended through pragmatic and semantic enrichment as implemented in *Negoisst* [4]. The majority of empirical studies compare eNSS with implemented economic support to face-to-face negotiations and confirm its positive effects on the outcomes of negotiations. Compared with face-to-face negotiations, economic support leads to better joint outcomes, more equity and enhanced fairness [15, 16, 12, 13]. Galin et al. [17] analyze electronic negotiation processes with regard to behavioral aspects and find more hard tactics in e-negotiations when measured against face-to-face negotiations. In their comparison of the effect of economic decision and communication support on negotiation behavior with communication support only, Koeszegi et al. [18] find substantial differences in the communication processes between different support levels.

This research on eNSS suggests the following hypotheses:

H1: More agreements will be reached by negotiators provided with EDS implemented in the eNSS *Negoisst* than by negotiators for whom this type of support is not available.

H2: Better joint agreements will be reached by negotiators provided with EDS implemented in the eNSS *Negoisst* than by negotiators for whom this type of support is not available.

H3: More fair agreements will be reached by negotiators provided with EDS implemented in the eNSS *Negoisst* than by negotiators for whom this type of support is not available.

Mediation is the second support approach considered in this study. It is based largely on research in behavioral social psychology. Mediation is an approach to overcome impasse situations in negotiations by increasing the negotiating parties' flexibility, i.e. their willingness to move away from initial positions or the discovery of new solutions to dividing issues [7-9]. Systems providing such a behavioral decision support (BDS) emphasize the benefits of conducting mediation tasks by means of information technology and electronic communication. E-mediation allows for a timely monitoring and diagnosis of the progress of a negotiation, because information technology can perform complex analyses in real time; identified problems can be linked to appropriate advice. *Negotiator Assistant (NA)* for example incorporates the primary mediation activities of diagnosis of the current state of the negotiation, analysis of the sources of inflexibility and impasse, and advice to overcome impasses. Different disciplinary foundations are the basis for e-mediation and e-negotiations. This is also reflected by the goals of the systems. While economists aim to maximize efficiency in negotiation, social psychologists aspire to maximize the effectiveness of negotiations, by increasing the prospects of agreement.

A set of experiments was conducted to compare e-mediation with a variety of non-electronic mediation conditions [8]. The results showed that separate use of the e-mediation system *NA* (compared to no mediation/reflection and paper advice) produced more agreements but less satisfaction with the process. When used jointly by the negotiators, *NA* produced more agreements and more willingness to compromise but less satisfaction than a live mediator who performed the same functions. The e-mediation condition did not, however, produce more integrative statements (joint gains) during the bargaining process than the live mediator. Thus, e-mediation has been shown to facilitate agreements even though it is not viewed as being particularly helpful by the negotiators. These findings and other research conducted to date on e-mediation are a basis for the following hypotheses:

H4: More agreements will be reached by negotiators provided with BDS implemented in *vienNA* than by those who have no access to the system.

H5: Negotiators who use the BDS implemented in *vienNA* will not produce more integrative (joint gains) agreements than those who have no access to the system.

H6: Negotiators who use the BDS implemented in *vienNA* will be more willing to compromise than those who have no access to the system.

H7: Negotiators who are supported by the BDS implemented in *vienNA* will be more satisfied with outcomes than those who have no access to the system.

H8: Negotiators who are supported by BDS implemented in *vienNA* will be less satisfied with the negotiation process than those who have no access to the system.

Although previous research has not examined the impacts of combined system use, effects can be inferred from the results on single system use reviewed above. The synergies that may occur from combining EDS and BDS are captured in the following hypotheses:

H9: Negotiators who are supported by both the EDS implemented in the eNSS *Negoisst* and the BDS implemented in *vienNA* will produce more agreements than those who are supported by only one or neither of the systems.

H10: The combined use of both the EDS implemented in the eNSS *Negoisst* and the BDS implemented in *vienNA* will not result in more integrative (joint gains) outcomes compared to situations involving only one or neither of the systems.

While EDS guides negotiators' attention to negotiation outcomes and maximization of individual utility, it might increase competitive negotiation behavior and could cause impasses as captured by hypotheses 1-3 above. On the other hand, BDS focuses on the facilitation of negotiation processes. The emphasis on flexibility and resolving conflicts to settle the negotiation may lead to more, but less efficient (integrative) agreements as indicated in the hypotheses. In this study we combine and compare the two support approaches in order to evaluate the hypotheses stated above. Hypothesized effects are evaluated in terms of processes, outcomes, and perceptions. In addition, further analyses of the negotiation process are conducted to shed light on other possible impacts of the two support systems.

3 Method

To evaluate the set of hypotheses, we conducted a laboratory experiment. The experiment uses the 2 x 2 symmetric design summarized in Table 1. In November, 2010 a total of 224 undergraduate students of negotiation courses from four different European universities participated in 112 negotiations.

The treatments of the design were implemented by providing the participants with the respective support via the subsequently described support systems. In all four treatments participants were provided with communication support implemented in *Negoisst*. The treatments, however, differed in the decision support that was provided. In the first treatment participants were provided with EDS (implemented in *Negoisst*) and BDS (implemented in *vienNA*). In the second treatment participants had access to EDS only. In the third treatment users had access to BDS only. The control group of the fourth treatment did not have access to EDS or BDS, but they were provided with communication support of *Negoisst*. To ensure the usage of *vienNA* in the two respective treatments, each dyad had to go through the e-mediation at least once before finishing negotiations.

Table 1. Experimental design (number of dyads)[1]

Treatments		EDS	
		Yes	no
BDS	yes	33	25
	no	37	17

3.1 Systems

Negoisst. *Negoisst* is a web-based eNSS. It is based on a holistic approach offering various support components for all phases of an electronic negotiation. In detail, *Negoisst* provides decision support, communication support, and document management. However, here the focus is on the first two components since they were the ones utilized in this experiment.

Decision support is one of the most important features of EDS in negotiations. *Negoisst* uses a Multiattribute Utility Theory (MAUT) approach. The user specifies preferences using compositional preference elicitation methods (such as direct preference elicitation and paired direct comparison), indirect methods (such as adaptive conjoint methods and analytic hierarchy process) or hybrid models. Based on the elicitation procedure, the system will then create a linear-additive utility model which can be used for situation analysis during the ongoing negotiation. Several analytical support modules have been integrated in order to provide comprehensive assistance for the task at hand. These indicators can be divided into numerical indicators (i.e. part worth, ranges and total utility) and graphical representations (i.e. negotiation history graph). The negotiation history graph shows the total utility of all previous offers according to only the negotiator's own preferences which can, therefore, be seen as an asymmetrical analytical support module.

In *Negoisst*, users communicate via electronic messages formulated in natural language (see Figure 1). The *communication support* offers assistance on all semiotic levels. On a syntactic level, the users follow a negotiation protocol. On a semantic level, users can specify formal meanings for attributes using ontologies to make sure that all participants have the same understanding of the business case. On a pragmatic level, message types can be explicitly defined in order to distinguish between formal (offers, counteroffers, agreements, and rejections) and informal (questions and clarifications) communication and to show the sender's intention. The main objective is to reduce the disadvantages of the electronic medium and to assure effective and efficient communication. All of these elements of *Negoisst* (i.e. analytical tools and communication modules) support the negotiator and yield valuable information for decision making. All subject groups had access to the communication support components of *Negoisst*. The decision support components were available only to subjects receiving the EDS treatment.

[1] Varying treatment sizes are due to the need to match participants from different universities to avoid spill-over of private information.

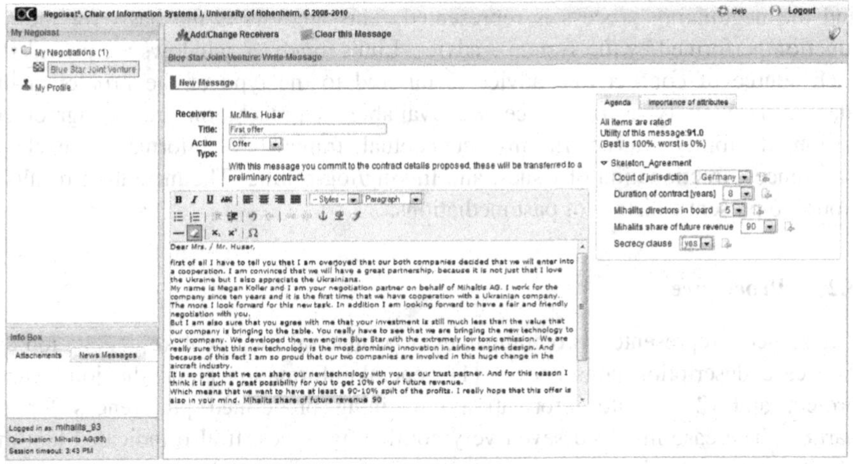

Fig. 1. Negoisst Interface

vienNA. *vienNA* is based on *NA* and assumes tasks usually performed by a human mediator in face-to-face negotiations: (i) diagnosis, by monitoring the progress of the negotiation towards or away from an agreement, (ii) analysis of the causes of impasse, and (iii) advice to overcome impasses based on diagnosis and analysis. These support functionalities strive to increase negotiators' flexibility, thereby elevating the possibility of reaching an agreement.

The system gathers information on the parties' flexibility with regard to the issues of dispute and the negotiation process by means of an electronic survey. The diagnosis is drawn from a knowledge base generated by a meta analysis of factors influencing negotiators' flexibility [7]. These results are the basis for determining the extent to which each question contributes to negotiating flexibility. The weighted flexibility scores for each party are visualized in the grid shown in Figure 2. A grid is generated, in which the flexibility score for the answers on the survey about the issues

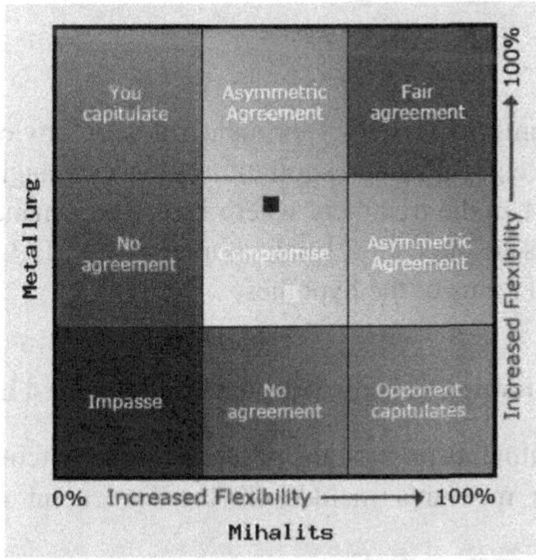

Fig. 2. vienNA Flexibility Grid

and the negotiating process is represented. This analysis is the basis for the third function performed by the system – advice. Links to advice windows are provided for each source of conflict; the advice is tailored to the type of the problem that is identified. Nine types of advice are available: approach, integrative agreements, options/flexibility, fairness/norms, conceptual framework, information exchange, differences, fractionation of issues, and linking/log-rolling. The mediation results are stored to present a history of past mediations.

3.2 Procedure

The subjects represented two companies in a bilateral joint venture negotiation case. The case description consisted of (1) general information about the joint venture project and (2) private information containing predefined preferences for both parties[2]. The case involved seven very conflicting issues. It also indicated that there are alternatives to the current negotiations, so that parties did not have to settle at all costs.

Instructors provided a briefing of the systems one week before the start of the negotiations. Furthermore, participants received test accounts to practice the use of the systems and explore their functionalities. The case was sent to all participants one day before the negotiations started. The first time that participants logged into the system they were administered a quiz about the case to ensure that they understood its most important aspects. A pre-negotiation questionnaire was given to gather information about demographics of the participants and to control for the influence of language skills and the familiarity with electronic negotiations and mediation. Participants were allowed a maximum of two weeks to reach an agreement, however, they could terminate negotiations with or without agreement at any time before the deadline. After completing the negotiations, participants answered a post-negotiation questionnaire. The negotiation transcripts, exchanged offers, and all responses on the pre- and post-negotiation questionnaire were recorded.

4 Results

Dyads that did not conform to the experiment rules or obviously did not take the negotiations seriously (e.g. finishing negotiations after exchanging only two messages or not using the *vienNA* in the treatment where its use was mandatory) were excluded from the data set. This resulted in a final sample size of 103 dyads. The following results are organized in terms of the hypotheses.

4.1 Impact of Economic Decision Support Implemented in *Negoisst*

The impacts of the treatments on various measures of the outcome are shown in Table 2. Objective outcome measures include (i) the agreement rate as a measure of

[2] Case descriptions and preference information can be obtained from the authors.

negotiators' effectiveness, (ii) the joint utility as a measure of efficiency and (iii) contract imbalance as a measure of fairness. Joint utility is defined as the sum of the utility values of both negotiators within one dyad. The contract imbalance shows the absolute difference between individual utilities of both negotiators within one dyad in the final agreement. Therefore, contract imbalance acts as a proxy for fairness in the final outcome, where smaller values indicate more fair agreements. Although most agreements were reached in the BDS condition, the BDS conditions did not result in significantly more agreements than the non-BDS conditions ($\chi^2(1)$=.000, p=.576, 1-tailed). Furthermore, the differences in joint utility (t(59)=.055, p=.479, 1-tailed) as well as in contract imbalance are not significant (t(59)=.650, p=.259, 1-tailed). Therefore, H1-H3 are not supported.

Table 2. Objective outcome measures

Treatments	BDS+EDS	EDS	BDS	Control
Agreements	17	21	12	11
Agreement rate	58.6%	56.8%	60.0%	64.7%
For dyads that reached an agreement:				
Joint Utility	1.05	1.06	1.05	1.06
Contract Imbalance	.103	.096	.123	.108

4.2 Impacts of Behavioral Decision Support Implemented in *vienNA*

With regard to hypothesis 4, negotiators in the BDS-conditions did not reach more agreements ($\chi^2(1)$=.000, p=.576, 1-tailed). Therefore, hypothesis 4 is rejected. As hypothesized in H5, subjects in these treatments did not achieve higher joint gains than those under the non-BDS conditions (t(59)=-.892, p=.376, 2-tailed). Furthermore, even though negotiators supported by BDS show a higher contract imbalance indicating less fair outcomes, this difference is not statistically significant (t(52)=-.433, p=.667, 2-tailed).

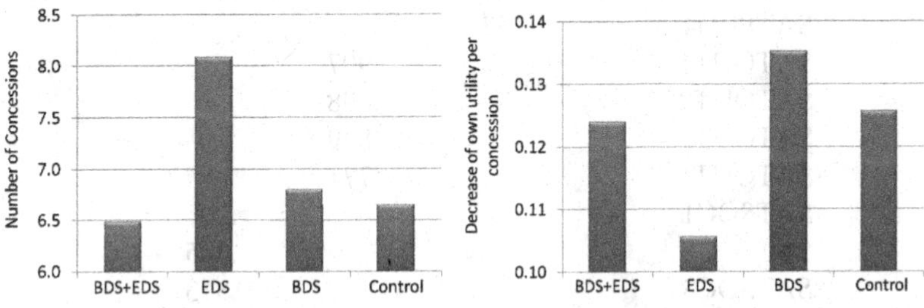

Fig. 3. Number of concessions and average utility change per concession

In addition to the results concerning communication, we also examined the concessions made during the negotiation process. Figure 3 shows that most concessions were made by negotiators only supported by EDS. In contrast to our expectations, negotiators in the BDS treatments made less concessions than negotiators in the non-BDS conditions (t(100)=-2.157, p=.033, 2-tailed). However, the average utility per concession shows a different picture. Negotiators supported by BDS made significantly larger concessions than users not supported by BDS (t(100)=2.018, p=.046, 2-tailed). Thus, negotiators provided with BDS engaged in fewer but larger concessions than those without BDS. This result provides support for H6 in terms of size but not number of concessions.

To holistically evaluate the negotiation outcomes along distinct dimensions, we also considered subjective outcome measures. Satisfaction with the process, outcome, and social aspects of the negotiation were measured via several items in the post-negotiation questionnaire. To test construct validity, we performed a principal factor analysis with oblimin rotation. All three constructs show satisfying convergent and discriminant validity as well as sufficient Cronbach alpha values (see Table 3 for the pattern matrix) and explain in combination 71.09% of the total variance. Analyses of the factor indices show that negotiators provided with BDS exhibit a slightly higher satisfaction with the negotiation outcome (t(68)=-1.390, p=.085, 1-tailed). In contrast, negotiators supported by EDS are somewhat more satisfied with the negotiation process compared to negotiators without this type of support (t(48)=-1.489, p=.078, 1-tailed). Moreover, negotiators in the control group, using neither support approach, show a tendency to have the highest satisfaction with the social aspects of the negotiation process (t(17)=1.908, p=.073, 2-tailed). Therefore, H7 and H8 are supported by our data, while negotiators with neither support exhibit the highest satisfaction with the social aspects of negotiations.

Table 3. Pattern matrix of satisfaction measures with the negotiation process, outcome, and the social aspects of the negotiation

Loadings (>.4)	SATPRO	SATOUT	SATSOC
SATPRO1	.659		
SATPRO2	.616		
SATPRO3	.568		
SATPRO4	.523		
SATOUT1		.907	
SATOUT2		.898	
SATOUT3		.849	
SATOUT4		.771	
SATSOC1			.901
SATSOC2			.895
SATSOC3			.813
SATSOC4			.806
Cronbach Alpha (std.)	.775	.945	.927

Note: KMO=.861, $X^2(66)=695.524$ (p<.001)

4.3 Interaction between Behavioral and Economic Support

The data reported above in Table 2 show a lack of support for hypothesis 9. Negotiators in the combined condition did not produce more agreements than those in the other treatments ($\chi^2(3)$=.314, p=.374, 1-tailed). Hypothesis 10 is confirmed by our data, because negotiators supported by EDS and BDS did not reach agreements with a higher joint utility than negotiators in the other treatments (F(3,57)=.304, p=.823).

As described above, *Negoisst* distinguishes between formal (binding) and informal (non-binding) messages. We used an ANOVA and Games-Howell post hoc tests to investigate differences for both formal and informal messages (variances were weakly significant in the groups F(3,98)=2.360, p<.1 and F(3, 98)=2.256, p<.1). Post hoc tests reveal a tendency for negotiators supported by both EDS and BDS to exchange less formal messages than negotiators supported by economic decision support only (t(64)=-2.406, p=.088). In contrast, we find several differences concerning the informal messages. ANOVA reveals that negotiators provided with both EDS and BDS exchanged more informal messages than negotiators provided with BDS only (t(47)=2.783, p=.019) and negotiators with neither support (t(44)=2.609, p=.032). Moreover, negotiators provided with EDS exchanged slightly more informal messages than negotiators provided with BDS (t(55)=2.424, p=.084). Looking at the groups with the highest mean values, it is obvious that in the conditions with EDS (treatment 1 and treatment 2) negotiators exchange the highest number of informal messages (t(101)=-3.726, p<.000).

Table 4. Number of messages exchanged in negotiations

Treatments	BDS+EDS	EDS	BDS	Control
Formal messages	10.28	12.43	11.40	10.94
Informal messages	1.90	1.68	0.75	0.71
Total	12.17	14.11	12.15	11.65
n (dyads)	29	37	20	17

Taking a closer look at the quality of agreements in terms of joint utility, we conduct a linear regression incorporating six predictors (see Table 5). The explanatory factors are experimental design variables and a respective interaction term as well as the number of formal and informal messages and a respective interaction term[3]. The general fit indices indicate satisfying results for the model. Regression analysis confirms that the use of EDS has no impact on the joint utility of the final agreements. However, the time when BDS was used - operationalized as the number of formal messages exchanged before the start of e-mediation - has a negative effect on the joint utility. This demonstrates that the longer negotiators waited to refer to BDS, the lower was the quality of the agreement. This negative effect is further enhanced when

[3] The use of interaction terms requires the use of centralized, conditional main effects influencing the interpretation of results.

negotiators had access to the EDS. The predictor for informal messages shows that the exchange of one or more informal messages results in a lower joint utility – keeping the number of formal messages constant at the respective mean value. In contrast, the number of binding messages shows a positive impact on the quality of the agreement. This holds true only when negotiators exchange one informal message. The last predictor, the interaction term between formal and informal messages, shows that the positive effects of formal messages on the joint utility is decreased by an increase in the number of informal messages.

Table 5. Regression analysis – Impact of process variables on the quality of outcome

Coefficients	B(SE)	B	p
Time BDS	-.006(.002)	-.487	.010
EDS	-.013(.015)	-.123	.404
Time BDS*EDS	.008(.003)	.435	.026
Informal Messages (IM)	-.013(.004)	-.414	.005
Formal Messages (FM)	.005(.002)	.316	.025
IM*FM	-.003(.001)	-.389	.010
(Intercept)	1.070(.012)		

Note: R^2=.27, F-ratio=3.332 (p<.001), Durbin-Watson=2.149

5 Discussion

The results of our empirical study present a complex picture of the effects of the different types of negotiation support we have studied. On one hand, we find several, sometimes unexpected, effects of support on the negotiation process. On the other hand, these differences in process characteristics are not reflected, at least not to a statistically significant extent, in the objective outcome dimensions.

Concerning the effect of support on process variables, we observe the surprising situation that both economic and behavioral support seem to affect exactly those process dimensions that one would a priori associate with the other type of support. The use of EDS significantly increases the amount of informal communication, and the use of BDS affects concession making and thus the substantive side of the negotiation process. This is reflected as well in negotiators' satisfaction. Negotiators supported by EDS were more satisfied with the process, while negotiators supported by BDS indicate a higher satisfaction with outcomes. Interestingly, neither type of negotiator was as satisfied with the social aspects as were those in the control group. Focusing attention primarily on the support tools, both types of electronic support may serve to distance negotiators from each other. These findings remain to be explored further.

The impact of decision support on communication behavior could be interpreted as a complementarity effect. EDS as it is implemented in *Negoisst*, namely the utility evaluation of offers, adds more "weight" to formal messages. The impact of each message on a negotiator's position becomes more salient. This increased level of consciousness for what is going on at the substantive level of the negotiation could trigger a need for a deeper understanding also at the informal, relationship-oriented level of the process, thereby inducing more exchange of informal messages. The increase in informal communication could also more directly be related to the decision support tool because of an increased need for clarification and explanation of the substantive content of messages. To clarify the actual use of the informal messages, their content needs to be analyzed. While content analysis is beyond the scope of this paper, it will be part of future analyses of the data obtained in the experiments.

Whereas EDS had a significant effect on communication behavior, BDS significantly affected concession patterns and caused a shift in concession structure towards fewer, but larger concessions. While an increase in the size of concessions could be expected given the focus of *vienNA* on supporting the successful conclusion of agreements, the effect on the number of concessions is unexpected and requires additional analysis.

Concessions are a central element for the successful conclusion of negotiations [19]. An increase in concession size counterbalanced by a decrease in the number of concessions could be one explanation for the fact that *vienNA* did not have a significant impact on either the number of successful negotiations or the quality of results in cases where an agreement was reached. Furthermore, it is not only the number or total extent of concessions that affect the efficiency or fairness of negotiation results. Efficiency, which we measured here in terms of joint utility, requires that bargainers make concessions, but also that they make the correct concessions. Such actions may not only decrease their own utility, but also increase the utility of their opponent. Even if EDS would affect the extent of concessions in terms of a party's own utility, there is no reason to expect that decision support is able to promote concessions that are particularly useful in terms of the opponent's utility. This occurs because decision support only takes into account a negotiator's own utility function. In contrast, BDS could have an indirect effect on such concessions. If BDS succeeds in increasing the exchange of preference information between parties, it would thus enable negotiators to make concessions that really benefit their counterparts. Given the empirical results, BDS did succeed in this respect, i.e. increasing the joint utility of the final agreements only in an early use. Concession patterns of negotiators could be better supported if BDS is attuned to provide preference information in a clear manner.

Likewise, fairness of agreements depends not only on the concessions made by one side, but on the interaction of concession patterns of both sides. Symmetric concessions will also lead to a symmetric agreement (or no agreement at all, if both sides make insufficient concessions). Asymmetric concessions will also result in an asymmetric agreement. Although a support intervention which treats both parties in the same way could still trigger asymmetric reactions (if parties simply react differently to the same stimulus), it will not do so in a systematic way. A significant improvement in fairness would require a support strategy that specifically targets the party making insufficient concessions.

Our results, in particular the lack of impact of support strategies on outcomes, convey an important message to the designers of negotiation support systems: An eNSS cannot be seen as a system that deals with each negotiating party just on an individual basis. The system has to take into account the larger picture including both sides of the negotiation. It might need to deal differently with each side in order to promote a fair and efficient agreement (or any agreement at all).

While our research provides some important insights, it is not without limitations. Our results are based on one, albeit quite large, experiment using a single case and a particular group of subjects. In order to create a need for mediation, the experiment involved a case with a high degree of conflict. The impact of both types of support could be different for lower levels of conflict. For example, if a negotiation problem has a large integrative potential with plenty of possibilities for joint improvement, decision support that indicates benefits for both sides could be helpful. Although we took great care to ensure that participants take the negotiation seriously, actual negotiations can be quite different from experiments with student subjects. This fact limits the generalization of our results.

Untangling the complex relationships between the variables involved requires a deeper analysis of both communication content and the detailed structure of the negotiation processes. Such an analysis could lead to a clearer picture of the impact of different forms of support on detailed characteristics of the negotiation process. This, in turn, could be the basis for more elaborate eNSS which specifically target particular aspects of the process in order to have a profound and positive impact on outcomes.

Acknowledgments. This research was partly funded by the Austrian Science Fund (FWF) – P21062-G14.

References

1. Bichler, M., Kersten, G., Strecker, S.: Towards a Structured Design of Electronic Negotiations. Group Decis. Negotiation 12, 311–335 (2003)
2. Schoop, M., Koehne, F., Ostertag, K.: Communication Quality in Business Negotiatons. Group Decis. Negotiation 19, 193–209 (2010)
3. Stroebel, M., Weinhardt, C.: The Montreal Taxonomy for Electronic Negotiations. Group Decis. Negotiation 12, 143–164 (2003)
4. Schoop, M.: Support of Complex Electronic Negotiation. In: Kilgour, D.M., Eden, C. (eds.) Handbook of Group Decision and Negotiation, pp. 409–423. Springer (2010)
5. Dannenmann, A., Schoop, M.: Conflict Resolution in Electronic Negotiations. In: 10th International Conference on Wirtschaftsinformatik (2011) (in German)
6. Schoop, M., Jertila, A., List, T.: Negoisst: A Negotiation Support System for Electronic Business-to-Business Negotiations in E-Commerce. Data Knowl. Eng. 47, 371–401 (2003)
7. Druckman, D.: Determinants of Compromising Behavior in Negotiation - a Meta Analysis. J. Conflict Resolution 38, 507–556 (1994)
8. Druckman, D., Druckman, J.N., Arai, T.: E-Mediation: Evaluating the Impacts of an Electronic Mediator on Negotiation Behavior. Group Decis. Negotiation 13, 481–511 (2004)

9. Druckman, D., Ramberg, B., Harris, R.: Computer-Assisted International Negotiation: A Tool for Research and Practice. Group Decis. Negotiation 11, 231–256 (2002)
10. Raiffa, H.: The Art and Science of Negotiation. Harvard University Press, Cambridge (1982)
11. Sebenius, J.K.: Negotiation Analysis: A Characterization and Review. Manage. Sci. 38, 18–38 (1992)
12. Kersten, G.E., Noronha, S.J.: WWW-Based Negotiation Support: Design, Implementation, and Use. Decis. Support Syst. 25, 135–154 (1999)
13. Thiessen, E.M., Loucks, D.P.: Icans: Interactive Computer Assisted Negotiation Support. In: Shell, R. (ed.) Computer Assisted Negotiation and Mediation: Prospects and Limits, Harvard Law School, Harvard (1994)
14. Lim, L.-H., Benbasat, I.: A Theoretical Perspective of Negotiation Support Systems. J. Manage. Info. Syst. 9, 27–44 (1992-1993)
15. Bellucci, E., Zeleznikow, J.: A Comparative Study of Negotiation Decision Support Systems. In: Proceedings of the Thirty-First Hawaii International Conference on System Sciences, pp. 254–262. IEEE Computer Society, Los Alamitos (1997)
16. Kemp, K.E., Smith, W.P.: Information Exchange, Roughness, and Integrative Bargaining: The Roles of Explicit Cues and Perspective-Taking. Int. J. Conflict Manage. 5, 5–21 (1994)
17. Galin, A., Gross, M., Gosalker, G.: E-Negotiation Versus Face-to-Face Negotiation. What Has Changed - If Anything? Computers Human Behav. 23, 787–797 (2007)
18. Koeszegi, S.T., Srnka, K.J., Pesendorfer, E.-M.: Electronic Negotiations - a Comparison of Different Support Systems. D. Betriebswirtschaft 66, 441–463 (2006)
19. Filzmoser, M., Vetschera, R.: A Classification of Bargaining Steps and Their Impact on Negotiation Outcomes. Group Decis. Negotiation 17, 421–443 (2008)

Author Index